Sickness or Sin?

Sickness or Sin?

Spiritual Discernment and Differential Diagnosis

Edited by

JOHN T. CHIRBAN

HOLY CROSS ORTHODOX PRESS
Brookline, Massachusetts

On the cover: Four images from Codex 5, Gospel Book (1387), Iveron Monastery, Mt. Athos. As found in "The Treasures of Mount Athos, Illuminated Manuscripts," Vol 2, by S. M. Pelekanidis, *et. al.,* Athens: Ekdotike Athenon, 1975. Used with permission.

LIBRARY OF CONGRESS CATALOGING–IN–PUBLICATION DATA
Sickness or Sin: spiritual discernment and differential diagnosis/ edited by John Chirban.
    p. cm.
Includes bibliographical refernces.
ISBN 1-885652-49-6 (pbk.)
1. Discernment of spirits. 2. Psychology and religion.
3. Medicine—Religious aspects—Orthodox Eastern Church.
4. Health—Religious aspects—Orthodox Eastern Church.
5. Diseases—Religious aspects—Orthodox Eastern Church.
6. Sin. 7. Orthodox Eastern Church—Doctrines. I. Chirban, John T.

BX323.S53 2001
261.5'61—dc21

00-054169

PRAYER TO THE HOLY SPIRIT

Heavenly King, Comforter, the Spirit of Truth,
who is everywhere present and fills all things.
The Treasury of all Blessings and the Giver of all
Life. Come and dwell within us, cleanse us from
every blemish, and save our souls, gracious Lord.

Βασιλεῦ Οὐράνιε,
Παράκλητε,
τὸ Πνεῦμα τῆς ἀληθείας,
ὁ πανταχοῦ παρὼν καὶ τὰ πάντα πληρῶν,
ὁ θησαυρὸς τῶν ἀγαθῶν καὶ ζωῆς χορηγός,
ἐλθὲ καὶ σκήνωσον ἐν ἡμῖν
καὶ καθάρισον ἡμᾶς ἀπό πάσης κηλῖδος
καὶ σῶσον, Ἀγαθέ τὰς ψυχὰς ἡμῶν.

Science without religion is lame,
religion without science is blind.

Albert Einstein,
Science, Philosophy and Religion, 1941

CONTENTS

FOREWORD

Each book is an invitation. Readers are invited to share in the experience of the author and/or editor, who shares his or her study, research, reflection and vision of particular issues, histories, disciplines, hopes and dreams. A very warm invitation is extended to the reader of this text by its editor, Dr. John T. Chirban, and by the numerous fellow authors who join him in extending an invitation to journey with them. This document is a well-versed and sensitively disciplined exploration of spiritual health: its identification, its loss, its rediscovery, its absence, its presence, its ultimate necessity.

Disciplined, organized thought developed on delicate themes can sometimes appear strict and stiff, clinical and sterile. Such is not the case with this text. The authors expose the vulnerability we all know and have experienced in our personal journeys: our periods of health and our times of illness, our days of strength and our hours of weakness, our expressions of virtue and our acts of sinfulness, our moments of holiness and our embraces of temptation.

Life indeed is a product of love. As being created by our loving God, we are called to loving patterns of wholesome altruistic love. As Saint John the Theologian so tenderly writes: "We love Him because He first loved us. (1 John 4:19)." Specifically, because God is love, because God shares His love, because God beckons us to live within His love, we can experience living patterns of wholesome love. Renewal, reconciliation, forgiveness, restoration and a continuum of healthy existence and co-existence can be existentially known by each pilgrim.

Clergy are pilgrims who embody at different times health and illnesses, holiness and sinfulness. Clergy, like all health care givers, are called upon to decide upon referrals to a plethora of professional health care disciplines. This much-needed and insightful collection, *Sickness and Sin: Spiritual Discernment and Differential Diagnosis*, presents a mosaic of responsible counsel. It offers comfort for the pastoral sensitivities that challenge clergymen as they exercise their privileged stewardship of the Gospel of Christ. As a clergyman with nearly four decades in diakonia, I find this volume to be successful in addressing its topic. It represents the highest degree of spiritual archery as each writer sails his or her bow to the very center of the envisioned target.

Our Christian Orthodox faithful and the people of our world are deserving of this engaging book. I am thankful to Dr. Chirban and his co-comforters for their invitation to journey with them. I encourage all readers (clergy and laity) to meditatively and prayerfully welcome their invitation and to share in their journeys.

Father Nicholas C. Triantafilou
President of Hellenic College –
Holy Cross Greek Orthodox School of Theology

PREFACE

Twenty-five years ago, Dr. Karl Menninger confronted society with an indictment of the times in his powerful book *Whatever Became of Sin?* He observed that the word "sin" had almost disappeared from our vocabulary. Because of the avoidance of attention to moral values, he perceived that guilt and spiritual matters were being reframed into scientific terms that failed both to explain our problems and to offer the needed spiritual resources for healing and health. In essence, one might judge that our abandonment of traditional wisdom was "modern" but not "advanced."

The topic of sickness and sin has been considered in several productive interdisciplinary dialogues since. Today there is a resurgence of interest in the spiritual, and it may be fair to suggest that the pendulum has swung to the other side. The complexity of this subject has led us to recognize both the strengths and the limitations of scientific and religious methodologies, languages, and approaches to grasp Christ's spiritual truths.

Attentive to the inherent biases in the discrete fields of modern study, this volume represents perspectives from several disciplines of modern natural and social science and Orthodox Christianity, regarding the assessment of sickness and sin, spiritual discernment, and differential diagnosis. The book identifies some methodological problematics of interdisciplinary studies while offering heuristic options for an integrative, holistic understanding of the human condition. The chapters of the book were originally presented at conferences and symposia of the Orthodox Christian Association of Medicine, Psychology and Religion, an organization dedicated to promoting dialogue among the disciplines.

The selections here acknowledge the value of medical, psychological, and spiritual perspectives to show how methodological and linguistic barriers may (or may not) be overcome. Ultimately, we find that employing a dialogical perspective, in contrast to singular or polarized perspectives, permits us to address theoretical concerns of sickness or sin – caring, curing, healing – and also specific real-life problems through particular topics that are herein presented.

We hope that this book will be of value to Orthodox Christian clergy, psychologists and health care professionals as well as to non-Orthodox who are interested in the dialogue among medicine, psychology and religion.

John T. Chirban
Carlisle, Massachusetts

INTRODUCTION – SICKNESS AND SIN

John T. Chirban

Do you not yet perceive or understand? (Mark 8:17)
Having eyes, do you not see, and having ears, do you not hear?
(Mark 8:18)

Jesus frequently struggled with the inability of his disciples and others to discern His message – to grasp His purpose. By contrast, His ministry provides the model and standard par excellence of spiritual discernment – a model of one who "sees" and "knows." At every turn, Christ demonstrates discernment of body, mind, and soul: as he *detects* the complexity of Legion, the Gerasene demoniac (Mark 5:1–20), as he *reveals* the wily maneuvers of the Pharisees (Mark 12), and as he *anticipates* the wavering of Peter in the Garden of Gethsemane, whose faith he knows will fail three times by the time the cock crows twice (Mark 14:26–31). Each move reflects Christ's clairvoyance and critical judgement, consonant with His attunement for perceiving, and for understanding the events at hand.

Spiritual discernment provides clarity about the will of God. Christ as discerner does not only tell stories of the past. He also demonstrates *astonishing* insight about what is going on, and He invites us to do the same. We are not only invited to tell stories, but to shape our environs through our perceptions and participation in the creation of new stories. The message of Christ is inherently *revolutionary,* calling us toward seeing God's Kingdom on earth. So we who heal body, mind, and soul are all the more directed to discernment.

Through the Gospel form, each of us is portrayed in the vari-

1

ous dramas as characters who are discerned and who, on another plane, are called also to see, to hear, to perceive, and to understand like Christ, by discerning in terms of ultimate purpose.

Spiritual discernment is both an art and a gift. As an art, it may be developed; as a gift, it is a charisma by the spirit of God for the good of others. Spiritual discernment identifies the locus where the divine and the human meet and work (1 Corinthians 12). Spiritual discernment is an outgrowth of a vital and viable Christian life.

Therefore, the quality of spiritual discernment in our Church serves as a barometer for the health of the Church. Who and where are the discerners today? Where are the lights up ahead? Throughout the history of the Church, enlightened souls, those with discernment, have directed the faithful toward God's path. But where are such visionaries today?

To a large extent, social planning and personal choices are driven by the contributions of certified professionals in our culture who are identified as specialists of body, mind, and soul. This book specifically addresses the place of spiritual discernment and differential diagnosis in the work of Orthodox caregivers in medicine, psychology, and religion.

Why Spiritual Discernment and Differential Diagnosis?

Both spiritual discernment (a tool of spiritual leaders) and differential diagnosis (a tool of leaders in the sciences) seek to understand human experience. Although their methods and goals differ, their interests may be significantly complementary.

"Spiritual discernment" is defined here as *a process for knowing what God wills for us to do in particular situations*. Spiritual discernment in this definition has three dimensions:

First, *vision*, knowing the goal toward which one is headed. Some Church Fathers refer to this as θεοπτία, God-vision, choosing and acting in awareness of one's relationship with God (Chirban, 1986).

Second, *perception*, seeking to understand truth according to one's abilities. Each of us is limited by his or her own development, experience, and aptitude to see and to understand.

Third, *intervention*, acting to implement Christ's wisdom in life. Spiritual discernment does not involve spiritualism or theoretical religion. Spiritual discernment transforms. Therefore, as truth seekers, we are not bound by traditionalism but are opened up to ways that work in the service of Christ's love.

"Differential diagnosis" has a more specific definition in the sciences. It means *to distinguish human problems through investigation on the basis of specific medical or psychological criteria* (Harvey, 1979). In an effort to "discern" human struggles, scientists analyze health problems according to the scientific method to diagnose illness and offer treatment.

Both of these approaches recognize a *process* by which change or transformation occurs, and that the *relationship* between the individual and the discerner or diagnostician is critical to the process of change. In life, we are affected by various forces that are natural, destructive, or directed to God. Discernment directs us. Differential diagnosis enables us to investigate the intricate and complex self and its relation to the world.

St. Anthony the Great states, "The intelligent are…[t]hose whose soul is intelligent, who can judge what is good and what is evil… and practice what is good and profits the soul…" (Kadloubovsky, 1963). By combining differential diagnosis and spiritual discernment, we draw upon the power of natural facts and spiritual direction. Spiritual discernment describes the healer's spiritual attunement which is dependent upon God's grace. Differential diagnosis identifies methods and approaches in the service of facilitating that end. These disciplines together require clear thinking and a posture of faith to render one whole.

By relating "spiritual discernment" and "differential diagnosis," we seek to bring together perspectives that together attend to holistic nature of the person and affirm the psychosomatic interaction of body, mind, and soul. Moreover, we integrate the encounter of life with a vision of faith. At the same time, by clarifying the importance of the interdependent relationship between body, mind, and soul, we differentiate these approaches and distinguish their distinct tasks.

The Challenge

In the Gospel (Mark 8:14), Jesus Christ appears exasperated that his disciples are upset about forgetting to bring bread; they do not remember that shortly before, Christ had blessed five loaves to feed the five thousand (Mark 8:19). Their lives, in spite of His physical presence, had become mundane; the disciples are anxious. The issue is not only that they do not *know* who He is, that they cannot remember that He can perform miracles, but that they do not demonstrate awareness – the spirit of προσοχή (attention) and νῆψις (wakefulness). Of course, the point is *not* that they should be impressed by His ability to perform miracles but rather that they should be attuned to His message and His person. They are in the midst of the God-man! The disciples fail to grasp the inherent power of what it means to walk in "faith, hope, and love." Jesus demonstrates that discerning who they are, who He is, and who they are in relationship to Him is a process. And He asks of them, and so of us, "Do you not *yet* understand?" (Mark 8:21).

The Gospels are filled with examples of discernment where Christ serves as the healer of all manner of sickness, disease, and confusion. He knows what's wrong. He reveals that the body and mind cry out because the soul suffers. His acts of healing center the whole person. He not only removes cataracts and provides antidotes but also draws upon the resources within the person and aligns the person, restoring him or her to wholeness.

The act of healing provides a "critical moment" for those who are entrusted to care for the body, mind, and soul so as to transform lives, as did Christ Himself. Knowing *what to do* and *how and when to do it,* characterizes the essence of spiritual discernment and differential diagnosis. This critical moment of understanding provides an opportune time for initiating the restoration toward wholeness. At this juncture, as a discerner and diagnostician we may participate in the transformation process – so long as we are spiritually attuned.

Therefore, the task for the Orthodox Christian health professional in medicine, psychology, and religion is to go beyond our formal requirements, to walk in Christ, to be transformed, and to be transforming, through living our faith. By growing in the life of the Spirit, we develop the marks of authentic life in Christ, "the fruits of the Spirit," "love, joy, peace, patience, kindness, goodness, trustfulness, gentleness, and self-content" (Galatians 5:23). This provides our context to participate in the healing processes, as we are commissioned to enable the blind to see, the deaf to hear, the lame to walk – not merely on a natural plane but for our ultimate purpose in life.

By actively integrating spiritual discernment and differential diagnosis through the disciplines of medicine, psychology, and religion, we do more than provide particular services in these fields. By invoking a God-consciousness in our work, we experience Christ through an existential encounter that affects our service. In this way, we find that our works, our lives, and the people whom we serve are changed.

Problems of Spiritual Discernment and Differential Diagnosis

Although this challenge sounds engaging, discernment is not conferred with baptism, nor does it result from a professional degree, whether acquired in seminary or in medical school. For several reasons, many regard spiritual discernment as elusive and complex.

First, "the spirit" is God-based, transcendent, and invisible. The Holy Spirit is not subject to human ways of construing.

Second, the individual discerner or self is likely to rationalize from a biased perspective and to interpret in ways that suit his or her own personal interest or understanding, rather than being or serving as a vessel of revelation.

Third, many issues to be "discerned" or assessed are themselves complex and not easily resolved (Wicks, 1988).

Fourth, for spiritual discernment and differential diagnosis to work in conjunction with each other, there is an underlying assumption that the discerner or practitioner is open to the methods of both approaches. Although this perspective is encouraged by some and is acceptable on patristic grounds (Chirban, 1993), few are adequately trained and sufficiently skilled in interdisciplinary studies to apply both spiritual discernment and differential diagnosis in specific situations.

Nonetheless, we must do what is possible according to our abilities, as Christ challenges us to discern. He asks us, as He asked Peter who was with Him: "Are you still without understanding?" (Matthew 15:15–16). It is our call, particularly as healing professionals of the body, mind, and soul, to understand and to assist others in their path.

Some caregivers are so awed by the task of spiritual discernment that they do not even approach the subject, much less struggle with its complexity. Today, in doing this work, we often avoid or balk at such questions as "What are the spirits to be discerned? What choice or choices are involved in the discerning process? How are we to determine and verify the nature of a discerner's choice? How can we go about learning the discernment process?" (Cunningham, p. 204).

Process of Discernment and Differential Diagnosis

How can Orthodox healing professionals develop the perception, vision, and capabilities to determine appropriate intervention that are consistent with both the science of our disciplines and our faith?

First, spiritual counseling, like psychotherapy, often addresses "unseen warfare" within the individual where spiritual acuity is imperative. To do this work, we must cleanse ourselves. Understanding spiritual matters presumes experience and growth that is both intellectual and personal. The healer needs to be in the

Spirit, God-based. Through the experience of practicing humility, holiness, action, love, and prophecy, and especially through prayer, we may grow as healers. Discernment is born out of one's effort to αναγνωρίζω (realize) one's true identity. We attain true self-realization in communion with God. Our values affect our work and the people with whom we interact, even when not explicitly stated.

Second, the temptation to call holy and true that which is merely one's own perceptions is an outgrowth of self-deception and inadequate professional training. Protection from such confusion is available through spiritual direction and through interaction with a community of peers. Discernment occurs within the context of Christian community and is not merely individual illuminism (Mueller, 1991). Joan Mueller's (1996) discussion of case studies identifies a systematic approach for understanding discernment that draws on objective criteria.

Third, the human person is complex. The commonly held vision of personhood which compartmentalizes human beings into body, mind and soul establishes an inadquate construct for understanding the breadth of human experience. Therefore, an open holistic, interdependent understanding of personhood is Orthodox in concept and requires a continuous, unified, and cooperative approach from people of faith for deepening the connections between body, mind, and soul and the disciplines that study these areas.

It is the business of Orthodox healers in medicine, psychology, and religion to generate a model of personhood that integrates faith and science in a way that realizes the full potential of the person. Today, we are objectively demonstrating the results of spirituality which affirm the power of spirit and life. We find that the sciences in non–religiously affiliated institutions often investigate and present the benefits of spiritual dimensions of human life more effectively than religious institutions do (Plante and Sherman, 2001). Toward this end, we must develop further programs of research and referral between spiri-

tual, medical, and psychological healers, to assist us in developing a discipline of Orthodox Christian discernment and diagnosis.

Fourth, the development of a radically open understanding
of human nature, based upon an Orthodox anthropology
(Chirban, 1986) and leading toward *theosis* – union with God –
represents a concrete response in modern times to what the
church historian Father Georges Florovsky calls for in his "neo–
patristic synthesis" which integrates our developing understanding of life with the message of Christ (1986). We are challenged
here to develop a community of faith-based healers of body,
mind, and, soul who integrate the care of the whole person.
Demetrios Constantelos (Constantelos, 1977) described this
engagement of science and faith occurring in the relationship
between physician and priest in Byzantium.

The doctors of the Church led the way for a synthesis in
theological work that drew upon the sciences of the day. In this
spirit, the integration of spiritual discernment and differential
diagnosis constitutes a rich soil from which may grow the fruits
of a genuine Orthodox psychology that is integrated with the
goals of Orthodox anthropology.

Throughout Church history, διάκρησις, charismatic discernment, has been valued as critical for spiritual growth. Beginning with Jesus and continuing through the Desert Fathers, the
monasteries, and mystical theology up to this day, discernment
is fundamental for spiritual life. All that brings clarity to the
human life is relevant to theological understanding, purpose,
and goal. So, differential diagnosis provides not only a method
that seeks a refinement of understanding human problems, but
essential information about human functioning (Wicks, 1988).
The sciences, given their specific and unique methods, may be
critical to clarify what is interrupting or blocking one's spiritual
path.

REFERENCES

Chirban, John T. "Healing in the Orthodox Church," *The Ecumenical Review*. July 1993.

Chirban, John T. "Developmental Stages in Eastern Orthodoxy," in Ken Wilber, ed., *Transformations of Consciousness* (Boston: Shambhala, 1986), pp. 285-314.

Harvey, A. McGehee. *Differential Diagnosis: The Interpretation of Clinical Evidence*. Philadelphia: W. B. Saunders, 1979.

Kadloubovsky, E., and G.K.H. Palmer, ed. "St. Anthony the Great: 170 Texts on Saintly Life." *Early Church Fathers from the Philokalia*. London: Faber and Faber, 1963.

Constantelos, Demetrios. *Byzantine Philanthropia and Social Welfare*. Princeton: Rutgers University Press, 1977.

Cunningham, Agnes. "Irenaeus of Lyons." *Studies in Formative Spirituality*. May 1990.

Florovsky, George. *Collected Works: Bible, Church Tradition – An Eastern Orthodox View*. Belmont, Massachusetts, Publisher at School 1972.

Plante, Thomas and Sherman, Allen, Eds. *Faith and Health*. New York: Guilford Press, 2001.

Muller, Joan. *Faithful Listening: Discernment in Everyday Life*. Kansas City: Sheed and Ward, 1996.

Muller, Joan. "The Theology of Discernment: A New Historical Overview." *Studies in Formative Spirituality*, February, 1991.

Wicks, Robert J. "Clarity and Obscurity: Critical Thinking and Cognitive Therapeutic Principles in the Service of Spiritual Discernment." *Thought*, March 1988, pp. 76-85.

PART ONE

SPIRITUAL DISCERNMENT AND DIFFERENTIAL DIAGNOSIS

The Path of Growth and Development In Eastern Orthodoxy[*]

John T. Chirban

Concern for growth is basic and essential to Eastern Orthodoxy Christianity. Spiritual growth begins as an innate, natural quality of every person, who is created in the "image of God," and progresses through experiences of prayer, contemplation, and action to a state of "likeness of/union with God," which Christian writers describe in various terms as a state of "potential," "unfolding," and "knowing" beyond cognitive and intellectual faculties. This article examines accounts of the process of spiritual development in the writings of two early Christian writers and ten saints: Origen, Evagrios, St. Macarios, St. Basil the Great, St. Gregory of Nyssa, St. Dionysios the Areopagite, St. Maximos, St. Isaac the Syrian, St. John Climacos, St. Symeon the New Theologian, St. Gregory Palamas, and St. Seraphim of Sarov. In their individual searches and paths for knowledge, parallels are identified in five basic stages of spiritual development common to spiritual growth and development in Eastern Orthodox tradition. The five steps of spiritual development are (1) image, εἶναι: potential, the human capacity to develop, to create, to live morally, to exercise free will, to rise above one's impulses, to reason, and to love; (2) conversion, μετάνοια: transformation, the conscious commitment to direct one's life toward God; (3) purification, ἀπάθεια: cleansing, bringing one's emotions in line with one's goals so that one is no longer distracted by worldly passion; (4) illumination, φώτησεις: light, direct experience with God; and (5) union, θέωσις:

[*] This chapter has been edited from "Development Stages in Eastern Orthodox Christianity," *Transformations of Consciousness*. Ed., Ken Wilber (Boston: Shambahla, 1986), pp. 285-314.

13

deification, a state of being in participation with the Holy Spirit in life. In the Eastern Orthodox approach, knowing is both experiential and participatory in a way that goes beyond human intellect. It involves a way of life in which body, mind, and soul engage in harmony with Christ's message and thus with God.

In addition to summarizing how each of the spiritual writers describe the process of spiritual growth, a chart shows parallels among their stages of development. This schema presents a guide to compare the unique and similar experience of those seeking to attain wholeness by following the Orthodox Christian path. The Orthodox tradition holds that healers "who seek to respond to the needs of the whole person" must balance both the rational and experiential aspects.

The Christian doctrine concerning the nature of the human being has been traditionally based upon the interpretation of the expression κατ᾽ εἰκόνα καὶ καθ᾽ ὁμοίωσιν, wherein God is said to have created humans in God's image and according to God's likeness. Christian writers are indebted to St. Basil for the distinction between the two words "image" and "likeness." The word "image" refers to the innate, natural quality of the person; the word "likeness," to that dimension of the person which yearns to become Godlike. Therefore, the human being is created with the potential to become Godlike.

What is the *process* of spiritual growth from "image" to "likeness?" Although there exists no single, systematic discussion or prescriptive plan by the Church concerning development or stages in Eastern Orthodox spirituality, concern for growth is basic and essential to the faith. This chapter identifies first the elements that inform one of the attitudes concerning growth and development in Eastern Orthodoxy and second the stages that emerge as consistent, whole, and hierarchical experiences in the tradition of saints in Orthodoxy. Heretofore, there has not been an effort to make parallel the stages of spiritual growth in individual lives and to identify discrete patterns that emerge from individual experiences.

Anthropology

The meanings of the terms "image" and "likeness" influenced the thought of many Christian Fathers. They have served the purpose of expressing the basic Orthodox teaching that men and women were not initially created as perfect but they were endowed with all the gifts necessary for communion with their Creator (St. Basil, N.D., St. Gregory of Nyssa, N.D., Cyril of Jerusalem, N.D.).[1]

Therefore, the human being is endowed with *intrinsic gifts*. According to Irenaeus, "man was created as a child," νήπιον, who emerged from a state of *innocence*, destined and *empowered to grow* to maturity (Irenaeus, N.D.).

In the writings of the Church Fathers, the term "image" includes the qualities of one's *rational faculties* (Clement of Alexandria, N.D., Origen, N.D., St. Athanasios, N.D., St. Basil, N.D., St. Gregory of Nyssa, N.D., St. John Chrysostom, N.D.). The Church Fathers emphasized reason because they believed that by its proper use one is able to learn of his or her Creator and to enjoy communion with the Creator. By stressing the rational nature of the human being, the Fathers tried to emphasize the faculty that gives humanity superiority over other creatures.

Many Church Fathers relate the image of God of the person to humanity's original state of sinlessness and innocence, as well as to the individual's capacity for *moral perfection*. This capacity was given to humans potentially (δυνάμει), and it was required of them to develop from the stage of innocence and childhood to mature holiness, and to approximate the holiness of God in accordance with the divine commandment: "῎Εσεσθε οὖν ὑμεῖς τέλειοι ὡς ὁ Πατὴρ ὑμῶν ἐν οὐρανοῖς τέλειος ἔστιν" (Matthew 5:48).

St. John of Damascus points out that men and women, although having this gift, are in need of the sustaining power of

God's grace in order to be able to achieve any degree of similarity to the Holiness of God (John of Damascus, N.D.). In this way it is suggested that there is in human beings a natural *relational "dependency"* upon love shared with God and neighbor.

Further, the human person is presented by the patristic sources as a *"creative being"* (δημιουργικόν ζῷον) (John Chrysostom, N.D., Theodoret of Cyrus, N.D., St. John of Damascus, N.D.). A person can create civilizations and cultures and realize the ideas that he or she conceives, reflecting the example of the First Creator: "And God said, 'Let us make man in our image, after our likeness; and let them have dominion over the fish of the sea, and over every creeping thing that creepeth upon earth'" (Genesis 1:26). Theodoret of Cyrus explains the manner of this power *to create* (Theodoret of Cyrus, N.D.). He notes that God alone is able to create (*ex nihilo*) without effort and pain. But the human being needs preexisting matter in order to build, and his or her creativity requires time and effort.

One of the most important characteristics of the human person, according to the Church Fathers, is his or her choice to act, or *free will* (αὐτεξούσιον). Inextricably related to God's unconditional love, the individual has the freedom to choose between good and evil. According to the way in which that free will is exercised, he or she is able to know self and God (Basil, N.D., Cyril of Jerusalem, N.D., St. Gregory of Nyssa, N.D., St. John Chrysostom, N.D., St. John of Damascus).

Another important element in the image, which sheds light upon the human being as a *spiritual* being, is the fact that one is able to *rise above his or her impulses* (Basil, N.D.) and to direct his or her spiritual powers toward realities other than those that are naturalistic (Tatian, N.D.). This human power to transcend the material being is called "innate" by the Fathers (Basil, N.D., Caesarios, N.D., Cyril of Alexandria, N.D.).

Also, we note that the image of God in men and women is discussed by the Church Fathers in terms of one's *capacity to love*, a capacity that St. Basil also thinks is innate in humanity

(Basil, N.D.). St. Gregory of Nyssa is emphatic concerning the importance of love as a quality of the image. He is of the opinion that if this love is lacking, then the whole character of the image is altered (Gregory of Nyssa, N.D.).

Theology and Life

The spirituality of Eastern Orthodoxy is characterized by a quality of sobriety and contemplation. This is not by chance but is a direct result of how theology affects life and, specifically, how the Eastern Orthodox search for likeness to God necessarily requires inner peacefulnes and attentiveness to the "movement of the soul." In order for one to experience the meaning of "image" as it has been presented here, contemplation is essential. Through such contemplation, I would suggest, we may speak of Orthodoxy's "theology of silence." The fundamental purpose of "silence" is to provide a setting, an opportunity for the reidentification of one's person with his or her true, genuine, original identity – the image of God.

> If you gaze upon yourself attentively, that will adequately lead you to the knowledge of God. If you reflect upon yourself, you will not have heed of the structure of the universe to look for the Demiurge, but in yourself, as in a microcosm, you will clearly see the great wisdom of your Creator (Basil, pp. 213D–316A).

And St. Isaac the Syrian admonishes:

> Enter eagerly into the treasure-house that lies within you, and so you will see the treasure-house of heaven, for the two are the same, and there is but one single entry to them both. The ladder that leads to the Kingdom is hidden within you, and is found in your own soul. Dive into yourself, and in your soul you will discover the rungs by which to ascend (Chariton, 164).

It is precisely this type of self-evaluation and internalization that cultivates one's intrinsic faith and movement toward "likeness." This is not to suggest that this quality of silence in Eastern Orthodox spirituality is characterized solely by a physical posture. To the contrary, although there is a tone of sobriety in Orthodox spiritual growth and development, the work in this process is quite righteous and active.

In the New Testament there are numerous references to methods that clarify this silent desire for cultivating one's "image": γρηγορεῖτε (keep awake; Romans 7:5–25), ἀγρυπνεῖτε (keep sleepless; Matthew 26:38–43, Mark 14:34–40); ἔγειρε (awake; Mark 13:33–37, Luke 21:24–36), βλέπετε (look; Ephesians 5:14–15). These directives take on even greater definition by the Desert Fathers, who expand upon the notion of active contemplation from their experiences. They advise προσοχή (attention), νήψις (wakefulness), ἀντίρρησις (opposition), ἔρευνα (observation), φύλαξις νοός (guarding of the mind), and νοερά ἡσυχία (mental quietness) (Φιλοκαλία, 1893).[2]

In summary, the nature of the human person in the Christian tradition emphasizes that there is a godliness in the human being "the image," and a potential for growth to self-protection, "the likeness." Often, however, religious literature speaks of the goal, perfection, in a vacuum in such a way that one is left with the impression that there are missing links or a lack of clarity concerning the process between the present and future (perfected) states. A better understanding of spiritual development is provided through focusing on the development of Orthodox saints as well as on their goals. The autobiographies of saints and their other writings reveal their human struggles and document their valuable processes for change that biographies often mistakenly omit. When the saints speak of themselves, one can easily relate to their humanity and thereby understand their growth and development. It is precisely their activity of being in touch with the self and engaging in movement toward a spiritual goal that makes them what they are.

St. Gregory of Nazianzus writes after the death of St. Basil:

You ask how I am...Well, I am very bad. Basil I have no longer;

Caesarios I have no longer; the intellectual and the physical brothers are both dead. "My father and mother have left me," I can say with David. Physically I am ill; age is descending on my head. Cares are choking me; affairs oppress me; there is no reliance on friends, and the church is without shepherds. The good is vanishing; evil shows itself in all its nakedness. We are travelling in the dark; there is no lighthouse, and Christ is asleep. What can one do? I know only one salvation from these troubles, and that is death. But even the world to come seems terrible to judge by the present world (Campenhausen, 1955, 101–102).

In spite of this full-fledged depression, St. Gregory has not given up. For the goal of his life, *theosis*, glimmers ahead, and he pursues his spiritual path. The dynamic between individual struggle and spiritual forces is quite essential for understanding Eastern Christian development. The saints are not static and perfect; rather, they work to develop themselves, and ultimately they grow.

Theosis, deification, or the acquisition of the Holy Spirit, constitutes the aim of the Orthodox Christian life. The life of Jesus Christ serves as the model for *theosis*. St. Athanasios writes, like St. Irenaeus before him, "God became man so that man might become God." It is said that Christ inaugurates the Kingdom of God on earth, which is yet to be fulfilled and fully realized. *Theosis*, however, is not an eschatalogical potentiality or a mere promise but rather the intense ascent of one who struggles to find the Kingdom *in this present life*. *Theosis* is an example *par excellence* of theological and spiritual doctrine that is demonstrated in the alert, arduous spiritual *askesis* (exercise) or development of the Christian as he or she yearns to achieve union with God.

From the very earliest Christian times, Orthodox spirituality has been characterized by the goal of *theosis*. One may observe that Western Christianity often treats mysticism as a subjective and emotional religious state. In the final analysis, this understanding evokes a feeling that mysticism is both unstable and undemonstrable. As Orthodoxy interprets mysticism, or the development of *theosis,* it is not a static ideal, an abstraction, or an idealistic potential for the human being. Rather, Orthodox mysticism is an objective, historical reality achieved first and fully by Jesus Christ, who redeemed humanity by His incarnation, death, and resurrection. Likewise, the Orthodox understanding of "mystical" participation in the Body of Christ does not suggest a symbolic or metaphysical meaning but an "invisible participation in Christ's nature" (Monk, 1968). The spiritual process toward *theosis* is demonstrated in the lifelong struggle and lifestyle of numerous church saints, some of whom will be discussed in this chapter. The saints' lives, therefore, serve as testimonies to the objective reality that they describe, and which this author regards as Orthodox spiritual development.

Knowledge and Experience

Those who have defined knowledge and faith in the Orthodox tradition have done so on the basis of their lives. Although they express consensus in their doctrinal beliefs, their experiences in "knowing" and "faithing" (the activity resulting from their beliefs), so to speak, bear unique descriptions. The thrust of the Orthodox approach to knowing (since understanding God's essence is impossible) is not by way of concept or formula but through union, which transcends human intellectual category and expression. By underscoring the necessity of life in a "holistic" (body, mind, soul) harmony with Christ's transfiguring message, one sets upon an eternally continuous path of knowing. This path of knowing, which is more fully participatory, leads one to discover that there is always more to be comprehended (Turner, 1975).

In the 14th century, St. Gregory Palamas developed an experiential concept of knowledge, emphasizing that by being in communion with God, one may enjoy a direct knowledge of God, which is differentiated from a purely intellectual process.

This knowledge is based upon the theology of the image of God in the human person, which emphasizes that one naturally possesses the ability to transcend oneself and reach the Divine (Meyendorff, 1975).[3]

In patristic thought, the understanding of "knowledge" follows, in part, the tradition of Greek philosophy, which emphasizes that knowledge is a spiritual activity of the fruit of inner illumination. Theology therefore denotes the *pure science* of in-depth knowledge (ἐπιστήμη) as used in Greek philosophy. It is the employment of knowledge that points out that there is no dichotomy between reason and spiritual reality. (For example, St. Gregory of Nyssa, in spite of the "mystery" surrounding Trinitarian theology, states without any hesitancy that the Trinitarian dogma is in accord with "the exact standard of rational knowledge.") At the same time, Orthodox epistemology is diametrically opposed to both idealism and empiricism because they suffer from the limitations of locking one into the realms of ideas and matter. In the final analysis, Orthodox epistemology affirms that reason (in full operation) is the guide to truth according to the degree to which it maintains communion with the Holy Spirit (Stephanou, 1976). This approach to knowing explains why Orthodoxy cannot limit itself to scholarly research and writing alone but *requires* the experiences of faith, i.e., a place for solitude, prayer, and quiet.

St. Basil very clearly explains that one may have both *eo ipso* and *a priori* knowledge. He points out that this knowing is influenced by evil and good powers and by a third force, indifference, (ἀπαθῆ or ἀδιάφορα), wherein one discerns things within oneself (leading to confusion). He notes, however, that the purpose of the mind is the apprehension of truth, and that God is truth. Therefore, the Cappadocians emphasize the positive value of reason, stating that it may lead one to "true knowing." St. Gregory Palamas says that true reason leads one to follow the commandments of God (understood to include not only formal but also substantive experiences of prayer, fasting, sacraments, almsgiving, and actions as a result of knowing, and further leading to the two love commandments) and to approach knowledge that is accessible to God (Krivoshine, 1955).

Natural knowing can be understood within a framework that strives to accentuate "true knowing." When it is seen as an end in itself, however, it is considered to be self-deluding and empty:

> ...those who possess not only powers of sensation and intellection but have also attained spiritual and supernatural grace are not limited by being in their knowledge but know also spiritually about sense and intelligence, that God is Spirit. For their entirety they become God and know God in God (Myendorff, 1964, p. 127).

Therefore, natural knowing has always been valued in Orthodoxy, but it has been considered to be only a partial and sometimes digressive approach to true knowing. Clearly, knowledge includes both *intellectual* and *existential* dimensions: the former provides some insight and (if one is sensitive) leads toward the latter, or toward salvation and communion with God. It is the spiritual dimension, however, that is considered to be the higher type of knowing.

The knowledge about which the Fathers speak is more than intellectual; it is moral, affective, experiential, ontological, and in agreement with connaturality. Intellectual knowledge alone is viewed as placing limitations upon the subject and object. So, even a superior degree of knowledge (as conceptual and intellectual) remains partial without the moral, affective, and experiential. True understanding comes from the dynamics of all these dimensions.

St. Basil delineates basically two aspects of knowing: sensorial-intellectual knowledge, which is philosophical, and extra-sensorial knowledge, which is ethical and experiential. He believes that the former leads directly to the latter – or to knowledge of faith (Basil, 1955; Letter 235).

Basil observes that intellectual knowledge is not able to pass beyond its bordered conditions. True knowing, therefore, surpasses the cognitive abilities of the mind. Hence, faith-knowing requires that one go through the second category of knowing, beyond intelligence. Basil explains that intellectual knowledge leads to knowledge by faith. Faith is not simply belief; emotional and moral elements are present. It is that "whole experience" which is faithfulness (Basil, 1955, Letter 234).

According to St. Gregory Palamas, knowledge comes through prayer. He states that there are those who know nothing about knowledge except through experimental sciences. Again, it would be inaccurate to infer that Palamas, or other Orthodox writers in general, ignore the uses of natural science or scholarship,[4] but they insist that when one permits this more basic approach to knowledge to dominate his or her work, "neglecting the knowledge of true reason," according to St. Gregory, "They recognize nothing on account of the ignorance of their science."

St. Gregory further emphasizes that natural knowing will not help one apprehend God because "God knowing" cannot be described. It is rather knowing out of *participation* in God that gives one clarity in the true vision of the world.

In his treatise "On the Three Degrees of Knowledge," St. Isaac the Syrian clarifies the point further:

> 1. The first form of knowledge is parallel to the body. This knowledge gathers provisions in riches, vainglory, honors and elegant things, bodily comfort, means to guard the body...zeal for rational wisdom...and to be the originator in wisdom for crafts and learning...Dependent upon human knowledge, this works in darkness.

> 2. The second form of knowledge turns toward meditation and psychic love. Although this knowledge is still a bodily nature it is occupied with excellence of person. As an outward stage, it accomplishes its activity by deeds perceptible to the senses of the body.

> 3. Called God-presence (θεωρία), this stage is raised above the cares of the world. When knowledge elevates itself above

earthly things...faith swallows knowledge, gives a new birth
to it. It is now able to examine spiritual mysteries which are
attained by simple and subtle intellect. This light is perceived
by spiritual eyes (concealed by eyes of fleshly men) according
to Christ's words: "I shall send you the Spirit, the Comforter,
whom the world cannot receive and He will guide you in all
truth" (John 16:13).

St. Isaac explains that the first stage of knowledge "cools the
soul" and actually forbids the work of God; the second stage
"warms the soul and leads to faith," and the third stage "brings
rest and faith." One should note that this direction of knowledge does not aim at being dead to the world (actually it is quite
the contrary), but it is being dead to the motivations of the
"worldly" (Isaac, N.D.).

Finally, what becomes apparent is that the Eastern Orthodox
attitude and approach to knowledge and experience are directly
related to growth of the image of God in the person. St. Basil
states that in the image "a particle" of God's grace orients one to
God. For St. Basil, the image is the starting point in the journey
to knowledge; thus, the mind is naturally directed to knowing
God.

> The mind is a wonderful thing (καλόν μέν ὁ νοῦς) and
> therein we possess that which is after the image of the Cre-
> ator (...καί ἐν τούτῳ ἔχωμεν τό κατ' εἰκόνα τοῦ
> κτίσματος...) and the operation of the mind is wonderful;
> in that in its perceptual motion it is frequently carried to the
> truth (Basil, Letter 233).

STAGES

Although many individuals seek to grow in their faith, they
are not always clear about how this is to occur, i.e., the process
by which one achieves his or her goal. For Orthodox Christians, the process is not so opaque, since the saints of theChurch
"light the way."

In Orthodox Christian literature, distinctions are made by

the saints that reflect their sensitivities to the different needs people may have as they develop in faith. The saints may even differentiate between "stages of growth" from their own experiences. St. Paul, for example, distinguishes that some are (spiritually) to be fed milk and others meat. In this way, St. Paul is attentive to individual abilities or capacities. St. Maximos the Confessor writes about three levels in development: (1) εἶναι (being), (2) εὖ εἶναι (well-being), and (3) ἀεί εἶναι (eternal being). In this way, St. Maximos is attentive to actual stages in spiritual development (Lossky, 1963).[5]

Although one frequently comes across references to spiritual "development" in Church literature, no statement or systematic explanation is to be found regarding *the process* of spiritual development in the Orthodox Christian Church. In attempting to answer the question "What is the model for Orthodox Christian development?" it seems that we could learn the answer through approaching the question and the search for an answer with an appreciation of "true knowledge" (as it has been discussed in this chapter), i.e., with an appreciation of both the intellectual and the existential dimensions of growth in the lives of saints.

After reading the lives of Church saints, we find that no single pattern outlines *the* path in the spiritual development of all. Rather, it is indicated that there is a similar foundation in the experiences of the saints, which emphasizes that one is to be grounded in "the right faith," the Holy Scripture, Holy Tradition, all of which St. Irenaeus includes as "the arsenal of faith," and to encounter a first-hand experience of the Holy.

In reading the lives of ten saints and two Early Church theologians with particular attention to their spiritual growth patterns, we find that although each saint or theologian uses different language to discuss the spiritual development, they do, nevertheless, encounter similar experiences or stages of growth. This "different language" for the saints and theologians may be accounted for by the fact that their discussion of growth is a product of *personal* experiences in development, rather than of formula. What is particularly interesting, however, is that although each saint describes his own experience (often in his unique way), basic parallels emerge as one compares the stages of the saints with one another. This sameness confirms the catholicity of their experience, affirming their "right faith." It appears that five stages can be identified, which are basically consistent among the ten saints and two theologians.[6]

On the basis of this study I have defined the five stages in Orthodox spiritual development: (1) image, *einai*, potential; (2) conversion, *metanoia*, transformation; (3) purification, *apatheia*, cleansing; (4) illumination, *photesis*, light; and (5) union, *theosis*, deification.

Stage One: Image (Einai) or Potential

"Image" refers to the natural state of the person, what has already been discussed in this chapter as the "nature of humans" – that is, the potential of the individual to develop (to love, to reason, to create). By beginning the model of development in this way, all human beings are, by birth, in the process of spiritual growth.

Stage Two: Conversion (Metanoia) or Transformation

Metanoia is a stage of conversion, wherein the individual makes a conscious commitment, a choice, to direct his or her life in "Christ."

Stage Three: Purification (Apatheia) or Cleansing

Apatheia (purification or transformation) occurs when one is distanced from worldly passions and is free in his or her spirit from things that distract from a goal. The saints say that in this stage one is "purified." Often this term is translated as "passionlessness," suggesting that a person at this level is without emotion. This is an inaccurate rendering of the meaning of the term, as the stage of *apatheia* does not exclude emotion but reflects the state in which emotions are consonant with goals.

Stage Four: Light (Photeseis) or Illumination

Light is the stage of illumination, an experience of God's light. The Church Fathers use the metaphor of fire and iron to describe how a person as a product of creation (iron) is illumined as he or she approaches the light of God (fire).

Stage Five: Union (Theosis) or Deification

Theosis (union) is not an end state but a goal into which one enters, as St. Gregory of Nyssa says, "from glory to glory." It is a state of being "in communion, participation" with the Holy Spirit in life. The figure at the end of this chapter illustrates the findings of this inquiry concerning spiritual development with a five-stage model. Brief summaries of development in the saints' and theologians' lives are given in the following section.

EXAMPLES

The following excerpts from the writings of saints and theologians focus upon the stages in spiritual development as they discuss them. It may be helpful to compare the content of these sections with the schematic drawings of spiritual development in the figure at the of the chapter.[7]

Both Origen and Evagrios are presented for background rather than as examples of Eastern Orthodox Fathers. They typify the intellectual, *cataphatic* approaches.

Origen: Systematized Spirituality (Origen, d. ca. 254, theologian and scholar in Alexandria)

The theme of prayer recurs continuously in the Fathers; the priority of prayer, time and again, for the Fathers indicates that these learned men were first pastors. Although he is not considered a Father, a discussion of spiritual development would be incomplete without noting the contributions of Origen – "A mystical writer in the hightest sense of the word" (Cayre, 1969). Origen outlined the contemplative life by "observing" that Christians are divided into camps, the active and the contemplative. The former he said, "stand in the outer courtyard of the temple" (like Martha), whereas the latter "enter into the house of God" (like Mary). He explains that Christians must climb to three levels: πρακτική, struggle for *apatheia* and love; φυσική θεωρία, knowledge of the mysteries of God; and θεολογία, the knowledge of the mysteries of creation. Origen emphasizes that perfection consists in being assimilated to God, noting St. Paul, who says if the human mind is made "one mind with God" it is because in the totality of consciousness the mind comprehends God. Contemplation, according to these steps, enables one to be deified. In his 27th homily on Numbers, Origen explains that the Israelite "stations" in the desert are stages on the road to the vision of God. Calling the journey "the exodus of the soul," Origen articulates the growth in terms of progressive detachment from corporeal things.

Lossky explains Origen's notion about spiritual growth in this way:

> The Word comforts the soul by visions or visitations which undoubtedly correspond to the perception of the divine by the spiritual senses – the first contacts of the soul with God. But at more elevated levels the visions cease, making room for gnosis, for illumination of the purely intellectual order which tends to become and is already a contemplation – θεωρία. However, the intellectual elements in gnosis appear only at first; they are obliterated more and more, to the extent that the soul is united with Christ and the spiritual marriage (πνευματικός γάμος) with the Logos is accomplished (Lossky, 1963, pp. 48-52).

Origen comments that in the Logos the soul is an image (εἰκών) and that by vision of God it recovers likeness (ὁμοίωσις), being deified.

Evagrios: Pure Prayer (Evagrios/Ponticus, d. 399, Libyan monk and mystical writer)

Although in the company of the great Cappadocian Fathers, Evagrios of Pontos tried to realize the ideal of contemplation outlined through the intellectual system of Origen. Evagrios' stages follow Origen's pattern; however, he tried to adopt the life of the Egyptian desert anchorites in his system of spiritual ascent. Evagrios distinguishes between πρᾶξις or πρακτική μέθοδος, and θεωρία or γνῶσις; the former being a fight against the passions and essentially a prerequisite to entering the latter, "intellectual" or perpetual prayer and the crown of ascetic practice – St. Paul's "pray without ceasing" (1 Thesalonians 5:17). Προσευχή, true prayer, is Evagrios' comparison to Origen's last stage, θεολογία. Only after passing *apatheia* (which he defines as overcoming gluttony, lewdness, avarice, sadness, anger, vainglory, pride, etc.) can one enter this "supreme love," which carries one off to the "summit of intellect." Here, the light of the "Trinity shines in the spirit of purified man." This state of "intellect" is the summit through which prayer is compared to vision, being more divine than all virtues (Myendorff, 1969).

Evagrios' doctrine of θεωρία is used in the spirituality of St. Gregory of Nyssa (who will be presented shortly). Evagrios understands the vision of the light of God in the deified νοῦς as the summit, "the end which admits no transcendence." Evagrios vigorously rejects all visible theophanies. He claims that this doctrine belongs to the stoics, who imagined that God, having no physical nature, assumes appearance according to His will in order to appear to men. He considers this a demonic illusion (Lossky, 1963).

St. Macarios: Mysticism of the Heart (St. Macarios, d. 1400, spiritual master in the Egyptian desert of Scete)

St. Macarios represents a major shift between Eastern Orthodox spirituality and the intellectual systems of mysticism from such thinkers as Origen and Evagrios. "Experience" is the proof of truth rather than formulae. St. Macarios writes, "ἐγεύσαμεν καί πεῖραν ἔσχομεν" ("We have tasted of God, we have experienced Him.")

He emphasizes that one develops spiritually through all the

senses rather than the "limited intellect." He does not see life as active prayer of the intellect but as actively generated toward a deeper fulfillment of baptism by way of the Holy Spirit (*Ibid.*). So, as Christ was clothed in human flesh, our response is to be clothed in the Holy Spirit: being

> "kindled by the Holy Spirit…making them burn like candles before the Son of God. This divine fire flows the fluctuations in the human will; now it is shining brilliantly as it embraces the entire being; now it diminishes and no longer sheds its radiance in hearts that are darkened by passions…" (Myendorff, 1974, pp. 26–29).

For St. Macarios the unceasing prayer of the monk does not yearn to free the spirit from the flesh but rather allows one to enter the eschatalogical reality of the Kingdom of God. He emphasizes, "The whole man, body and soul, was created in the image of God and the whole man is called to divine glory." He explains, "Christians live in a different world: they have a table that belongs to them alone, a delight, a communion, a way of thinking uniquely theirs." And elsewhere, "The sons of light, ministers of the New Covenant in the Holy Spirit, have nothing to learn from men; they are taught by God. Grace itself engraves the laws of the spirit on their hearts…for it is in the heart that intelligence dwells." St. Macarius explains that God is the food and drink, the sweetness (γλυκήτις) of grace we taste within. He says, "He who enjoys illumination (φωτισμός) is greater than he who only tastes, for he has within himself the assurance of vision (τίνα ὁράσεων)." But beyond even this, he explains, is revelation (ἀποκάλυψις); here the mysteries of distinction are revealed to the soul (Lossky, 1963).

St. Basil the Great: Journey of Knowledge (St. Basil, d. 379, Bishop of Caesarea)

St. Basil discusses a person's spiritual development as a "spiritual journey" from the image of God, which is in all persons, to the "archetype." It is a journey that enables one to "know" God.

St. Basil explains that as individuals "advance" in knowledge, they realize their own weaknesses; such is the case with Abraham and Moses: "When they had seen God as much as it is possible for a man to see Him, each humiliated himself; the former called himself 'clay and dust,' the latter described himself as 'being of few words and stammering.'" About the state of knowledge in this journey, St. Basil says,

> The word wise (σοφός) applies equally to whoever desires wisdom, and to whoever already finds himself in progress in the contemplation of wisdom, and to whoever is already perfected (ὁ τετελειωμένος) in this contemplation by habituation (ἕξις). Now, all of them, the lover (ἐραστής) of wisdom, or the one who has already advanced in wisdom, will become wiser always progressing in the knowledge of "divine dogmas" (Θείων δογμάτων) (ibid.).

St. Basil notes that the knowledge of God through observing the commandments of God, for example, is "intellectual" knowledge in the restricted sense, which is to know God "half-way" (εξ ἡμισείας). He insists that "knowing" God occurs by participation in "the true life...returning to the original goods." In this participation God offers "intimacy" as a result of our "affective" and "moral" knowledge of God. Further, St. Basil elaborates that advancement in the journey comes by "casting off the old man who goes corrupting himself in the thread of delusive desire and clothing (oneself) in the new man who plods toward true knowledge." The continuous renewal and progress that are recommended presuppose purification and ascesis, spiritual training. St. Basil notes, "The words of God are not written for all but for those who have ears according to the interior man." This is developed by preparation through two steps: first, "destruction of sophisms and all haughty power (ὕψωμα) which rise up against the knowledge of God (κατά τῆς γνώσεως)," and second, "making all thought captive to lead it to obey Christ." Later he presents "elements" that constitute the "advancement." In terms of the negative step, one must leave "the anxiety of life" (τήν βιωτικήν) and slavery to the senses and to the passions (πάθη) of the body.

In the positive step, one must be concerned with "purification of the heart" (καθαρότης καρδίας) so that the Spirit is permitted to illumine. St. Basil's Trinitarian formulations are thereby possible. "The indwelling (ἐνοίκησις) of the Spirit entails that the Son (παρενοικήσαντες... δια... 'τόν Χριστόν) leads us to the Father (ἐπάνοδος εἰς οἰκείωσιν Θεοῦ)." St. Basil explains the last stage as the "journey from the conscience of God." This, he says, comes to those who are worthy (according to the outlined preparation) of God. Finally, it is noted that one does not meritoriously achieve, but rather "the Lord grants it by Himself to those who have believed in Him (Aghiorgoussis, 1964).

St. Gregory of Nyssa: Developing from Glory to Glory (St. Gregory, d. ca., 395, Bishop of Nyssa)

St. Gregory points out three levels of spiritual development. These, however, advance beyond Origen's understanding. What is the apex of most spiritual systems, the way of light, is only the beginning for St. Gregory. He says, "Moses' vision of God began with light; afterwards God spoke to him in a cloud. But when Moses rose higher and became more perfect, he saw God in the darkness" (Gregory of Nyssa, 1969). This "darkness" is not anything like the "darkness of sin," for, quite obviously, "the darkness of sin" precedes the first stage, where one struggles against the passions. Now at one level of *apatheia*, St. Gregory explains, *parrhesia* (παρρησία), or a child-like confidence in God, develops; it comes when "fear and shame" are banished. Then the second stage, which St. Gregory compares to a cloud, comes into view. St. Gregory raises the rhetorical question and then responds:

> What is the significance of Moses into the cloud and his vision of God?...Leaving behind all appearances...it turns always more to the interior world, until by the effort of mind

it penetrates even to the Invisible and the Unknowable and then it sees God. For in fact true knowledge and true vision of the One it seeks consists in seeing that He is invisible, wrapped all around by His Unknowability as by a cloud (Myendorff, pp. 42–43).

It is the knowledge of God "within the mirror of the soul," that overshadows all appearances and slowly guides "the soul to look towards what is hidden." This rather obscure-sounding stage is the "awareness of grace," an experience of God's presence.

The more the soul discovers that God infinitely transcends all that it can know of Him, the nearer it comes to the third stage – knowledge of God, which St. Gregory explains in his life of Moses:

> ...as the soul makes progress, and by a greater and more perfect concentration comes to appreciate what knowledge of truth is, the more it approaches the vision, and so much the more does it see that the divine nature is invisible. It thus leaves all surface appearances, not only those that can be grasped by the senses but also those which the mind itself seems to see, and it keeps on going deeper until by the operation of the spirit, it penetrates the invisible and incomprehensible, and it is there that it sees God. The true vision and the true knowledge of what we seek consists precisely in not seeing...thus that profound evangelist John, who penetrated into the luminous darkness, tells us that no man hath seen God at any time, teaching us by this rejection that no man – indeed, no created intellect – can attain a knowledge of God (Gregory of Nyssa, 1969, p. 29).

The darkness is not negative but a "luminous darkness"; as our awareness of God always falls short, it is still enticed to a more perfect knowledge, though with ignorance. St. Gregory thus emphasized a doctrine of continuous progress, perpetual growth, what he called ἐπέκτασις (tension, expansion). This word captures the double aspect of the soul's progress: ἐπί, at or toward, in a sense of being in participation, divinization. At the

same time God is constantly beyond, ἔκ, out of, as one must
continuously move out to go beyond the stage one has reached.
In the last analysis, St. Gregory explains that all the stages are
good, and for the one who participates in the growth, each stage
is always being obscured by the new "glory" that constantly exists beyond (Boyer, 1961).

St. Dionysios the Areopagite: Apophatism and the Ladder of Prayer
(Dionysios, Psuedo-, the Areopagite, ca. 500, mystical theologian)

St. Dionysios, in turn, distinguishes three levels of spiritual
development: first, a purification stage; second, an illumination
stage; and third, a unification stage. St. Dionysios, like St. Gregory of Nyssa, speaks of mystical theology through divine darkness. He uses "apophatic" (negative) theology. With ἀγνωσία
(unknowing, darkness), the realization that no finite knowledge
of God can reveal Him, one may know Him better. St. Dionysios
explains that as excess of light yields darkness invisible, likewise
excess of knowledge destroys ignorance, which leads to God. St.
Dionysios delineates five ascending stages of degrees in prayer
and contemplation that constitute a ladder, which leads the as-
piring soul from finitude into infinitude: (1) the prayer of simplicity (vocal), (2) the prayer of mind (voiceless), (3) the prayer
of recollection (the perfume or answer prayer), (4) the prayer of
quiet (beyond thoughts), and (5) the prayer of union, degrees
of rapture, ecstasy, "glorious nothingness" (Dionysios, 1965).

St. Maximos: Wills of Man and God (St. Maximos, d. 662, "the
Confessor," Greek Theologian)

St. Maximos the Confessor discusses deification by offering a
striking application of Christological dogma to spiritual life.
This he does by identifying human will with divine will. He
explains that our experiences of Christ's incarnation, death, and
resurrection "contain the meaning of all the symbols and enig-
mas of scripture, as well as the meaning concealed in the whole

of sensible and intelligible creation." By employing the tripartite schema again, Maximos discusses three successive levels of perfection: εἶναι, attainment of being through the Incarnation; εὖ εἶναι, attainment of well-being through conforming to divine will leading to the Cross; and ἀεί εἶναι, attainment of eternal being through the Resurrection. In this system, St. Maximos recreates the Evagrian program with the Dionysian "darkness" in the last stage. Rather than seeing intellectual participation in terms of perfection as focal (Evagrios), Maximos emphasizes "total participation" in Jesus Christ:

> The admirable Paul denied his own existence and did not know whether he possessed a life of his own: "I live no more, for Christ lives in me…" (Galatians 2:20)…[Man], the image of God becomes God by deification; he rejoices to the full in abandoning all that is his nature…because the grace of the Spirit triumphs in Him and because manifestly God alone is acting in him…(Myendorff, 1974, pp. 44–45).

Importantly, St. Maximos observes that ἀγάπη, love, is the instrument of growth:

> …knowledge of God is not the goal of charity in the sense that would make charity purely a means to an end. We would speak more accurately if we said that knowledge is the effect, the sign of the union which God brought about by love, but an effect which reacts in turn from the cause, intensifying the love. (Lossky, 1963, pp. 105–109).

St. Isaac the Syrian: Spirituality of Balance (St. Isaac, d. ca. 1260, great hesychast master)

As a product of a tradition that placed value on the intellectual approach to spirituality, reflected in works by Origen and Evagrios, and of an approach that was highly experiential, as reflected in works by St. Maximos the Confessor and St. Dionysios the Areopagite, St. Isaac's spiritual development is a fusion of both these streams of spirituality. His writings are written by a "solitary" to "solitaries," focusing on the person of Jesus

Christ. The process of growth unfolds through one's continous experience of *metanoia*, a radical "change of behavior" and attitude. He recommends that this awareness of change must be kept alive "at every moment of the 24 hours of the day." It is a continuous awareness of God's presence, a "remembrance of God."

In the process of this *metanoia*, St. Isaac emphasizes that one must be totally trusting in God and know that there are "no fortuitous events"; nothing occurs by mere chance, but rather as an opportunity for growth. The posture for spiritual growth necessitates that one "approach God with a childlike mind." In this spiritual experience, St. Isaac discusses a state of ecstasy or "spiritual drunkenness." The spiritual journey, St. Isaac notes, however, is one that most do not follow. He points out that "only one in 10,000 is found worthy" of it (Brock, 1975). St. Isaac's spirituality breathes a personal spirit. And through the personal, mystical, spiritual ascent he notes that one moves from repentance to purification to perfection (Wensink, 1969).

St. John Climacos: Steps to Paradise (St. John, d. ca. 650, great Sinitic doctor of St. Catherine's Monastery)

St. John Climacos prepared one of the most remarkable manuals of spiritual attainment, entitled *The Ladder of Divine Ascent*. St. John describes the way of spiritual attainment through 30 steps. Each step addresses spiritual virtues or sins, and, as illustrated in the icon of the ladder, angels and demons work upon the faithful to assist them and thwart them, respectively. The ladder, having thirty rungs whose base is fixed on earth and whose top reaches heaven, indicates (when illustrated) the first steps at an angle (enabling one to climb more easily) and the later steps going up vertically (indicating the greater difficulty involved in attaining the higher spiritual levels). The 30 steps must be mastered if spiritual progress is to be attained. In general, the steps are not ordered or developmental but are often thematic; for example, steps 17 through 30 address virtues of positive achievement such as solitude, prayer, love.

The choice of the word "ladder" in the title (probably inspired by the vision of Jacob's ladder) symbolizes the author's conception of the whole purpose and progress of spiritual life. Therefore, it does not offer a systematic program for growth and does not purport that step 14 necessarily *precedes* step 20. The process is dynamic and holistic. St. John approaches each step analytically, using anecdotes by way of illustration, e.g., step 1, obedience, is one of the longest on the ladder. The method presupposes and insists on direction by a spiritual father. In summary of his work, the author writes:

> ...Let us hasten until we attain to the unity of faith and of the knowledge of God, to mature manhood, to the measure of the stature of the fullness of Christ, who, when he was baptized in the thirtieth year of his visible age [note the correlation in St. John's ladder], attained the thirtieth step in the spiritual ladder (concerning the linking together of the supreme trinity among the virtues); since God is indeed love, to whom be praise, dominion, power in whom is and was and will be the cause of all goodness throughout infinite ages. Amen (John Climacos, 1959, p. 226).

St. Symeon the New Theologian: Spiritual Experience and Realism
(St. Symeon, d. 1022, monk and mystical theologian)

More so than any of the "guides" of Orthodox spiritual development cited, St. Symeon emphasizes the freshness and authority of experience of the Divine, and the importance of the intense realism in Christocentric mysticism. St. Symeon prayerfully writes:

> ...by Your Grace, I was granted to contemplate a still more awesome mystery. I saw You take me with Yourself, and rise to heaven; I know not whether I was still in my body or not – You alone know, You who alone created me...For the first time You allowed me, a vile sinner, to hear the sweetness of Your voice. You spoke so tenderly that I had tumbled and was amazed, wondering how and why I had been granted

Your gifts. You said to me: "I am the God who became man for love of you. You have desired me and sought me with your whole soul, therefore, henceforth you shall by my brother, my friend, the co-heir of my glory…" (Meyendorff, 1974, pp. 49–51).

Understandably, St. Symeon's approach and emphasis on genuine form created ecclesiastical provocation and raised the conflicts of prophet versus priest and experience versus institution. Although he opposes any suggestion of mechanization in worship, prayer, or sacraments, these methods were an integral part of his "spiritual universe." (Because St. Symeon does not offer a developmental approach, he is not presented on the schematic drawing).

St. Gregory Palamas: Experience of Theoptia (St. Gregory Palamas, d. 1359, monk and mystical theologian)

Often associated with it, St. Gregory Palamas was the inheritor of the rich spiritual tradition of hesychasm,[8] which actually has its roots in the early Desert Fathers. St. Gregory, however, defended hesychasm as a viable method for attaining the vision of God, Θεοπτία, thereby *theosis*. Questions had been posed about the hesychasts that accused them of an illogical system of prayer. Barlaam the Calabrian condemned them on two points, particularly: the Aristotelian postulate that all knowledge, including knowledge of God, is derived through perception of experience; and a Neoplatonic postulate that explains God as being beyond sense experience and therefore unknowable. St. Gregory Palamas responded by saying, "God is indeed unknowable but he does he not reveal himself?"

For one to attain contemplation, he or she must pass through the negative stage of intellectual perfection. Gregory writes:

Illumination appears to be pure intelligence to the extent that it is liberated from all concepts and becomes formless…
All visions having a form to the intelligence, that is to say to the act on the passionate part which is the imagination…come from a ruse of the enemy (Meyndorff, 1964, p. 141).

Then, St. Gregory explains, by "monological prayer" (προσευχή μονολόγιστος ἀδιάλειπτος) one enters the positive realm of spirituality. This is St. Paul's "pray[er] without ceasing." He says, "We supplicate with this continuous supplication, not to convince God...but to lift ourselves to him." This prayer cannot be mechanical but is conscious and active. Palamas explains that fulfillment in spiritual life comes through progression inward (συνεξέλιξις). The neophyte hesychast achieves this stage by specific techniques, but the mature hesychast realizes it through his strong will and the unceasing Jesus Prayer.[9] The total individual (body, mind, and soul) participates and experiences the eternal warmth, the fire that Elias mentions as he sees God, a part of the experience of Divine Light. Hesychasm places great emphasis on the immediate vision of God, but this is not to be confused with pantheism.

St. Gregory says, "We partake of the divine nature, and yet at the same time we do not partake of it all." He argues that the assertion regarding the existence of God cannot be proved by answering that the proof of God's existence (the genuineness of the vision of God) is founded upon other than Aristotelian logic. Gregory maintains that the spiritual purposes of the ascetic are fulfilled through συνεξέλιξις of the mind – that is, through continuous self-concentration and looking or turning within (ἐσωτρεφόμενον). In reaching this state, one encounters the Divine Light, achieving mystical union with God (Christou, 1966). He clarifies that the difference between the vision of light the Apostles witnessed on Mount Tabor and that of the hesychasts is that Peter, James, and John saw the light "exteriorly," while Christians contemplate the light "interiorly." But further, the hesychasts can develop potentialities with God's grace, to the point that they find God, thereby experiencing "uncreated" light.

Knowledge, according to St. Gregory, comes through prayer. He states there are those who know nothing else about knowledge except through the experimental sciences. He sees those

persons as adoring and protecting Hellenistic studies and neglecting the Gospel. In the end, he points out, they recognize
nothing on account of the ignorance of their sciences:

> If we ask how the mind is attached to the body, where is the
> seat of imagination and opinion, where is memory fixed, what
> part of the body is most vulnerable and so to say directs the
> others, what is the origin of the blood...it is the same...with
> all questions of this sort about which the spirit has given us
> no plain Revelation; for the spirit only teaches us to know
> the truth which penetrates everything (Myendorff, 1964).

St. Seraphim of Sarov: Acquisition of the Holy Spirit (St. Seraphim, d. 1833, monk in Russia)

Less than two centuries ago, the ascetic St. Seraphim of Sarov
responded to the question of the "purpose of Christian life" in
his famous "Conversation Concerning the Aim of Christian
Life." Although his response of "acquiring the Holy Spirit" may
sound vague and nebulous at first, a close examination of his
response and its background and implications adequately captures the plethora of teaching about Orthodox spiritual growth.
He explains that while such means – "prayer, fasting, watching,
almsgiving, and all Christian acts" – are not the ends, they are
the only means of acquiring the "Spirit of God." St. Seraphim
notes that "prayer is always possible for everyone" but that the
"method," which must be grounded, is a "right faith in our Lord":
"Thus, if prayer and watching give you more of God's grace,
pray and watch; if fasting gives much of God's Spirit, fast; if
almsgiving gives more, give alms."

Here, he expresses the doctrine and diversity: Christians,
though unified in the same truth, diversify as they express it. In
response to the questions "Is the Holy Spirit then to be seen?
How am I going to know whether He is with me or not?" Seraphim answers that there is nothing incomprehensible about true
visual encounters with God. He explains, "This fortune to understand comes about when we have wandered from the spa-

cious vision of the early Christians. Under the pretext of education we have reached such a darkness of ignorance that now to us seems inconceivable what the ancients saw clearly." He continues by explaining that because of our inattentiveness to the work of salvation "we do not seek the grace of God, because in the pride of our minds we do not allow it to enter our souls…we have not true enlightenment." Seraphim's life was a testimony to his words, rather than the inverse. It is out of experience that he concludes, "For the Kingdom of God is the human heart…the Kingdom of God is not meat and drink, but righteousness and peace in the Holy Spirit. Our faith consists not in persuasive words of human wisdom, but in the demonstration of the Spirit and of power" (Seraphim, 1973).

CONCLUSION

This presentation seeks to clarify the concept of, and approach to, growth in Eastern Orthodoxy. What we learn from this study is that although the spiritual journeys of the saints are very personal and experientially based, they nonetheless reveal discrete patterns of development. Somewhat paradoxically, although the stages of growth may be discussed *rationally*, they are necessarily encountered *experientially*. Balancing the rational and experiential aspects of life is necessary for those who seek to respond to the needs of the whole person. Attention to the lives of those who described the experiences of growth may illumine us as we seek effectively to attain the important goal of being whole.

REFERENCES

Aghiorgoussis, Maximos. *La Dialetique de l'image de Dieu chez Saint Basil le Grand.* Unpublished Doctoral Dissertation. University of Louvain, France: School of Theology, June, 1964.

Basil, Saint. "Letters 232 to 236." Translated by Phillip Shaff and Henry Wace. *The Nicene & Post Nicene Fathers.* (Volume 8, Grand Rapids, Michigan, 1955).

Bouyer, Louis. Translated by Mark Perkins Ryan. *Introduction to Spirituality.* Collegeville, Minnesota: Liturgical Press, 1961.

Campenhausen, Hans von. *The Fathers of the Greek Church.* New York, New York: Pantheon Books, 1955.

Cayre, F. Translated by W. Webster Wilson. *Spiritual Writers of the Early Church.* New York, New York: Hawthorne Books, 1969.

Chariton of Valamo, Igumen. *The Art of Prayer.* Translated by E. Kadloubovsky and G.E.H. Palmer. London, England: Faber and Faber, 1967.

Chirban, John T. *Human Growth and Faith: Intrinsic and Extrinsic Motivation in Human Development.* Washington, DC: University Press of America, 1981.

_____ . "Developmental Stages in Eastern Orthodox Christianity," Wilber, Ken (ed.), *Transformations of Consciousness,* Boston, Massachusetts: Shambala, New Science Library, Random House, 1986.

Climacus, John. Translated by Archimandrite Lazarus Moore. *The Ladder of Divine Ascent.* Willets, California: Eastern Orthodox Press, 1959.

Christou, Panagiotis. "Γρηγόριος ὁ Παλαμάς." Θρησκευτική καὶ Ἠθική Ἐγκυκλοπαίδεια: Athens, Greece, Martios, 1966.

Dionysius of Areopagite. Translated by the Editors of the Shrine of Wisdom. *The Mystical Theology and Celestial Hierarchy.* Surrey, England: The Shrine of Wisdom, 1965.

Gregory of Nyssa. *From Glory to Glory.* Edited by Jean Danielou and Herbert Musurillo. New York, New York: Charles Scribner's Sons, 1969.

Hausherr, S.I. "A Propos de la Spirituality Hesychaste." *Orientalia Christiana Periodica.* Volume 3. Rome, Italy, Pontificum Institum Studiorium, 1939.

Krivoshine, Basil. "The Ascetic and Theological Teachings of Gregory Palamas." *Eastern Churches Quarterly,* 1955.

Lossky, Vladimir. *The Mystical Theology of the Eastern Church.* London, England: James Clarke & Company, Ltd., 1968.

Lossky, Vladimir. Translated by Asheleigh Moorhouse. *The Vision of God.* Clayton, Wisconsin: The Faith Press, 1963.

Meyendorff, John. *Byzantine Theology.* New York, New York: Fordham University Press, 1975.

_____ . *Christ in Eastern Christian Thought.* Washington, DC and Cleveland, OH: Corpus Christ Books, 1969.

_____. *St. Gregory Palamas and Orthodox Spirituality*. Crestwood, New York: St. Vladimir's Press, 1974.

_____. *A Study of Gregory Palamas*. London, England: The Faith Press, 1964.

Monk of the Eastern Church. *Orthodox Spirituality – An Outline of the Orthodox Ascetical and Mystical Tradition*. London, England: SPCK, 1968.

Papademetriou, George. "The Teaching of Gregory Palamas on God." *The Byzantine Fellowship Lectures*. Number Two. Brookline, Massachusetts: Holy Cross Orthodox Press, 1975.

Pelikan, Jaroslav. *The Christian Tradition: A History of Development and Doctrin II-600-1700*. Chicago, Illinois: The University of Chicago Press, 1977.

Φιλοκαλία τῶν Πατέρων. Volume Two. Athens, Greece: 1983.

Sarov, Seraphim of. *Saint Seraphim of Sarov*. Edited by Franklin Jones. Los Angeles, California: The Duon House Press, 1973.

Stephanou, Eusebius A. *Charisma and Gnosis in Orthodox Thought*. Fort Wayne, Indiana: The Logos Ministry for Orthodox Renewal, 1976.

Syrian, Isaac the. Οἱ Ἀσκητικοί Λόγοι τοῦ Ἰσαάκ. Athens, Greece.

Xintaras, Zachery. "Man – The Image of God According to the Greek Fathers." *Greek Orthodox Theological Review*. Volume 1, Number 1, August, 1954, pp. 48-62.

NOTES

[1] See Zachary C. Xintaras, "Man – The Image of God According to the Greek Fathers," *The Greek Orthodox Theological Review* (Volume 1, Number 1), August, 1954, pp. 48-62. This well researched guide renders foundational references in Orthodox anthropology. Note that some references that Xintaras reports in his article are not accurately interpreted, e.g., Xintaras credits St. Irenaeus rather than St. Basil for the theological distinction of "image" and "likeness."

[2] The precept to watch, not allowing oneself to be weighed down by sleep, is strongly emphasized by the Eastern Fathers. It demands the full consciousness of the human person in all degrees of its ascent towards perfect union. See Vladimir Lossky, *The Mystical Theology of the Eastern Church* (London, England: James Clarke & Co., Ltd., 1968), p. 202.

[3] Meyendorff explains that St. Gregory's position differs from Western

Christianity, since Western scholasticism has assumed that knowledge is based upon revealed premises – Scripture or church magisterium – which serve as a foundation for development by the human mind, in conformity with Aristotelian logic.

⁴ St. Gregory does not deny that scientific research is important, but he warns that its conclusions are relative and incomplete and need to be completed by true knowledge, a participation in the Divine Light.

⁵ The first stage, εἶναι, refers to the natural state of every human being, who is created in the image of God – i.e., blessed with the potential to love, to create, to reason, to choose. St. Maximos correlates this stage with human participation in the stage of Christ's incarnation. The second stage, εὖ εἶναι, is the point of decision, where one makes a conscious commitment to follow Christ. It is the human response to change one's ways and to embrace the life in Christ's kingdom: μετάνοια, a radical change of mind. St. Maximos relates this stage to one's "picking up his cross and following Christ" or to the stage of Christ's crucifixion. Finally, ἀεί εἶναι is the eternally ongoing experience of illumination or θεοπτία, a stage at which one enjoys God-presence. This goal parallels the stage of Christ's resurrection.

⁶ Origen and Evagrios are early Church theologians whose spiritual "formulations" corresponded to the lives of the saints. The two theologians are representative of the cataphatic approach to theology (frequently the form of Western Christian spirituality), in distinction from the saints, who are representative of the apophatic approach to theology (which typifies Eastern Orthodox spiritual development). For a discussion of the two different approaches in spiritual development, see John T. Chirban, *Human Growth and Faith: Intrinsic and Extrinsic Motivation in Human Development* (Washington, DC: University Press of America, 1981).

⁷ The schematic diagram is read from right to left. The last two theologians are representative of cataphatic theological approaches; the saints are representative of apophatic theological approaches. The five stages that are described begin from the bottom of the page (left column) and progress upward. Note that terms shared by the Church leaders who are presented in the schematic are not repeated in the diagram.

⁸ Hesychasm, ἡσυχασμός, "the way of stillness and repose," is a psychophysical method of prayer that leads to "vision of God" (see S.I. Hausherr, "A Propos de la Spiritualite Hesychaste," *Orientala Christiana Periodica*, Volume 3 (Rome: Pontificum Institum Orientalium Studiorum, 1939), p. 261.

⁹ "Lord Jesus Christ, Son of God, have mercy upon me, a sinner."

Schematic Drawing of Spiritual Development

APOPHATIC APPROACHES

STAGES	St. Isaac the Syrian	St. Seraphim of Sarov	St. Gregory Palamas	St. John Climacos	St. Maximos	St. Dionysios
V. UNION	(3) Perfection	Acquisition of the Holy Spirit	(3) Theosis	Step 30 – Likening	(3) Ἀεί εἶναι (eternal being)	(3) Unification, prayer of union
		Kingdom, rightousness, peace				(Prayer of quiet)
IV. ILLUMINATION		Illumination	(2) Divine light, pure hesychasm	Steps 29, 28, 27 Hesychasm		(2) Illumination
						(Prayer of recollection)
III. PURIFICATION	(2) Purification					(1) Purification
						(Prayer of mind)
II. CONVERSION	(1) Repentance		(1) Prayer, labor	(1) Steps 1–26 Stages of Spiritual development	(2) Εὖ εἶναι (well-being)	
		Prayer, fasting, almsgiving				(Prayer of simplicity)
I. IMAGE					(1) Εἶναι (Being)	

	St. Gregory of Nyssa	St. Basil	St. Macarios	Evagrios	Origen
STAGES	(3) Knowledge of God	(2) θέωσις	(2) Ἀπονάλουψις		Ὁμοίωσις
V	(2) Cloud (darkness)	Luminous		(2) Προσευχή	(3) Πνευματικός Γάμος Θεολογία
	(Light)	(Illumination)	φωτισμός	(2) θεωρία (Γνῶσις)	
IV	Ἀπάθεια Παρρησία (God confidence)	(2) Καθαρότης καρδίας		(1) Πρᾶξις (Πνευματική)	Πρακτικός
III.	Ἐπίκτασιος (Tension)	(1) Σοφία	(Baptism)		
	(Darkness of sin)	(Intellectual knowledge)			
II.		Journey of knowledge)	Γλυκήτις		
I.		(Image of God)			(Εἰκών)

INTELLECTUAL STATES

Discernment and Diagnosis in Human Development: An Orthodox Theological Perspective

Theodore G. Stylianopoulos

A striking example of discernment and diagnosis in religious life is found in the Gospel account of the woman caught in adultery who was brought to Christ for judgment (John 8:3–11). "Teacher," Jesus was challenged by some religious leaders, "the law of Moses commanded that such should be stoned. What do you say about her?" Jesus, put on the spot in the presence of a crowd, remained silent, scribbling on the ground. When the question persisted, he stood up and said to the accusers, "Let him who is sinless among you be the first to cast a stone." Again he bent down to scribble. Hearing his words, the accusers went away, one by one, beginning with the oldest. Then Jesus said to the woman, "No one has condemned you? Neither do I condemn you. Go, and do not sin again."

Although scant in historical detail, this dramatic account leads us to perceive divergent kinds of religious discernment and diagnostic action. On one hand, the religious leaders discerned that a serious breach of God's law had to be applied, lest God's will be subverted and the authority of the tradition be compromised. On the other hand, Christ's teaching about God's love and mercy toward sinners dictated a chance at a new start for the woman, forgiveness, and a call to responsible future behavior. The religious leaders were concerned about upholding the authority of the law and tradition. Jesus was concerned about God's ultimate purpose behind the law and God's will for this woman, namely, to be saved and not to be condemned. Moreover, there was a trap in the question. Christ's adversaries intended to expose him before the crowd either as advocating subversion of God's law or as contradicting his own principle of mercy toward sinners. Religious values and warrants were being used in an attempt to destroy the woman as well as Jesus, who undoubtedly appeared to be the greater threat to the religious tradition. In a masterful way, Jesus not only escaped the trap but also succeeded in his salutary purposes. He granted a new start to the woman. He also provided a way of escape for his adversaries, who withdrew, hopefully with much food for thought about religious values. And the crowd witnessed a concrete, dramatic expression of God's love and forgiveness toward a sinner through Christ.

What is discernment and what is diagnosis in the religious realm? More important, what is true discernment, and what is correct diagnosis that is spiritually and theologically grounded? And how are such discernment and diagnosis, related to other fields of knowledge, applied to human development? These questions involve complex issues. Formally speaking, discernment and diagnosis are parallel terms having to do with knowing and knowledge. Both derive from verbs meaning to "recognize," "distinguish," and "come to know" something in a penetrating way. Discernment is the power and skill to see, analyze, compare, assess, and arrive at a deep insight about any given matter. Diagnosis is the conclusion or result of the exercise of discernment. Often inseparable and indistinguishable from each other, discernment and diagnosis may well be largely intuitive and inspirational. Yet, they are also a part of a process of observation, thought, and aptitudes developed through accumulated wisdom and trained skill.

At the heart of the issue is the question of truth, both theoretical and functional: truth as the basis of fullness of life. But truth is as comprehensive as it is complex, embracing all reality. There are, consequently, different kinds and various levels of discernment and diagnosis pertaining to the diverse yet related dimensions of human existence and fields of knowledge such as religion, philosophy, politics, sociology, economics, and physics, as well as medicine and psychology. An engineer who discerns cracks in the structure of a bridge will make the necessary diagnosis for repairs, lest it collapse and cause harm. A marriage counselor who discerns cracks in a marriage will provide a diagnosis for healing, lest the marriage break apart. A pastor who discerns cracks in a Christian's life of prayer will provide the diagnosis for spiritual growth, lest the Christian lose all sense of relatedness to God. The obvious challenge is how the tasks of discernment and diagnosis in various fields can become cooperative and mutually supportive in the pursuit of truth and the enhancement of all life in its ecological totality.

From the perspective of classic Christian tradition that Eastern Orthodoxy represents, an assessment of the nature of theological discernment and diagnosis must take into account at least two fundamental presuppositions. The first is the ecclesial character of theology and theological truth as sources of discernment by diagnosis. By "ecclesial" is meant not something abstract but the Church in all its concreteness, its experience of God, worship, core teachings and values, disciplines of piety, and spiritual ethos. Of course, all fields of knowledge are in various degrees sociologically conditioned because the language and symbols used for communication are part of the given cultural heritage. Yet, in most fields of human affairs, such culturally conditioned elements can be modified, corrected, and even rejected or replaced by new elements in the course of the interaction of cultures and the progressive accumulation of human knowledge. In the case of classical theology, however, there are a number of deep and abiding truths and values that are not open to revision because they are grounded in revelation, that is, the self-disclosure of God Himself as a gift to be received by the community of faith but not controlled by human will, reason, or skill. Although such truth must be received, understood, and interpreted by human beings, they nevertheless pertain to core experiences, principles, and values constitutive of the deep nature and self-understanding of the religious community born in integral connection with the great moments of revelation, such as the resurrection of Christ and Pentecost, as events of the new creation.

Moreover, the ecclesial experience of God is a reality located not only in the past but also in the present, namely, in the worship, prayer, study, work, recreation, and Christian living of believers. In other words, the Church as a community is a concentrated locus of God's gracious action and the healing context within which Christian discernment and diagnosis, as well as their application, occur. Unless engagement of the divine presence is taken with utter seriousness, talk about spiritual or theological discernment and diagnosis remains hollow and is easily coopted by psychological models and considerations. The integrity, power, and efficacy of Christian discernment and diagnosis derive not simply from theoretical considerations, as accurate as they may be, but also from the actual cooperative dynamics between God's saving presence and the grateful response of human beings who pray, worship, and live together in spirit and truth. The prayers and supportive love of a simple Christian may be more healing for a hurting soul than the counsel of a professionally trained pastor empty of the divine presence. The integrity of the pastor himself *qua* pastor is always rooted in one's God-given call to, and empowerment in, that ministry.

The second fundamental presupposition that determines the nature of theological discernment and diagnosis is the universal vision of Christian theology. Classical theology stands on the claim that it seeks to understand and interpret all of reality from the standpoint of God. The adjective "theological" and the noun "theology" signify not the knowledge of God as metaphysical speculation but the revealed knowledge of God appropriately applied to all spheres of life. Therefore, theological discernment and diagnosis do not pertain only to specifically religious behavior or to a narrowly defined religious realm, but rather to all human endeavors valued and interpreted from the standpoint of the revealed Creator, His truths, His purposes, and His will for humanity and creation. Thus, a true Christian going out into the world – whether as a doctor, psychologist, engineer, economist, lawyer, politician, businessman, or consumer in a shopping mall – cannot leave his or her Christian convictions at home. The dynamic process of discernment and diagnosis, like the struggle for truth and life, is always at hand. If this reality of revealed truth in its universal scope is not taken seriously, any theological judgment is rendered impotent. Theology itself becomes either sectarian or a coopted vehicle of culture's latest wisdom and favored values. However, when theology holds to its true position and function as a reflection on, and interpretation of, God's self-disclosure for the whole world, it retains its authenticity and power and remains the queen of the sciences – a service it should perform in humility.

We have emphasized the ecclesial or communal character of theological truth grounded in the experience of God in the life of the Church. We have also insisted on both the personal and the universal scope of theological truth applicable to all walks and areas of life. We have also suggested what now may be stated directly, namely, that theological discernment and diagnosis constitute responsibilities not only of the Christian pastor, teacher, counselor, or other professional but also of every Christian. Each Christian is a free and synergistic agent in the process of spiritual growth and ultimate salvation. Each Christian, with the help of others, especially pastors, must always seek to discern deeper and wider aspects of God's presence and God's truth, make the appropriate diagnosis regarding personal and social considerations, and live by this truth with faithful integrity. Even in a close pastor/parishioner relationship, the Christian's personal responsibility of discernment is never eclipsed by obedience to a spiritual father, for example, in the case of temptation to violate a clear commandment. The same goal is set before all

Christians, lay and clergy, in the words of the Epistle to the Ephesians: to grow "to mature personhood, to the measure of the stature of the fullness of Christ (Ephesians 4:13). As St. John of the Ladder much later put it, the essence of true Christian life is "to imitate Christ in thought, word, and deed as far as this is humanly possible."

In Orthodox theology and spirituality, masters and students of the subject have proposed several patterns or stages, variously named, for measuring spiritual growth. A basic one consists of a paradigm of three stages: (1) purification (*katharsis*), (2) illumination (*photesis*), and (3) perfection (*teleiosis*). One might use this three-stage pattern as a heuristic model to discuss three levels of theological discernment and diagnosis in Christian life. We should not think that these levels or stages are sharply separated. On the contrary, they are dynamically connected, interpenetrating each other especially at the points of the differentiation, and each level includes gradations of considerable magnitude. To give them titles for discussion, these three levels of discernment may be called (1) practical, (2) spiritual, and (3) mystical. Some remarks on each are in order.

The practical level of discernment pertains to the entire range of Christian practices, such as worship, study, ethical obedience, fasting, service to others, and unceasing struggle against evil. Practical discernment has to do with such matters as learning to pray, finding time to pray, perceiving and cultivating patterns of Christian behavior at home and work, distinguishing and choosing priorities according to Christian behavior at home and work, distinguishing and choosing priorities according to Christian teaching, finding ways of seeking forgiveness and reconciling with others, anticipating and avoiding occasions of sin, and many other similar nuts and bolts of Christian life. Such insights deserve to be called theological because they involve elementary knowledge of God's truths and God's will about what is good and evil, right and wrong, appropriate and inappropriate, pursuable and avoidable, based on received tradition. This practical theological discernment is strongly guided by the community of faith and its leaders. To be sure, the personal is intricately involved and is not without profound and complex struggles, beginning with true repentance: a deep conversion of the mind and heart to Christ. Yet, one's own discernment is elementary, based on the teaching, guidance, and way of life of the Christian community.

The goal of this first stage is purity of heart from evil passions, that is, the liberation of personhood from the bonds of fallen humanity: the whole corporate and personal pattern of selfishness, manipulation, greed, exploitation, corruption, anger, hatred, cynicism, and despair. The saints teach that sin and evil are foreign to human nature, a distortion of the image and likeness of God, a beclouding of reason and moral sense, a sickness of the soul, a corruption of humanity and creation. By "sin" is not meant some moralistic transgression, as sin is often trivialized by some, but the power of sin expressed in human life through wrong choices, wrong goals, wrong relationships, wrong attitudes, wrong values, wrong acts, wrong use of things— all those things that define the forces of alienation and disintegration in humanity, community, and the environment. The way to health and wholeness is through the grace of God and the stable practice of the evangelical virtues: faithfulness, humility, self-control, service, holiness, and love as well as the renouncement of self-will, egomania, and indulgence of evil passions. Because unruly human nature easily follows its own ways and falls prey to many temptations, the ascetic disciplines of regular prayer, fasting, and meditative reading help in centering the mind on the living God, freeing persons from ingrained habits of sin, purifying the heart, restoring human rationality and moral capacity, and opening the way to ongoing inner transformation. Among the fruits and criteria of progress in this way of life are growing stability of Christian behavior, an inner sense of purpose and well-being, moments of true peace and joy in the Lord, and a desire to learn more about, and grow closer to, the mystery of the living Christ.

The Holy Spirit is active in all the stages of Christian growth, but its gracious action in the Christian becomes conscious in the second stage of illumination. Spiritual discernment, a critical mark of illumination, begins in the higher levels of the previous stage and is signified by the occasional warm and joyful stirrings of the Holy Spirit in the depths of one's being. As these stirrings become more frequent, the Christian experiences illumination. At this second stage, the Spirit becomes a more abiding presence, a growing flame, a lantern of the soul, and a source of living waters, as Christ said. At this level, discernment may be called truly spiritual, primarily because it is a gift of the Holy Spirit and secondarily because through illumination the Christian acquires a deeper understanding of the meaning of what he or she practices as a Christian. We need not quibble about terminology. In the Patristic tradition, this second stage is called *theoria*, often translated as "contemplation." However, it is not contemplation in the sense of meditative or cogitation on a verse of Scripture, a Christian truth, or an aspect of creation, which in themselves are of course commendable. Rather, *theoria* is a dynamic state of being in which the Christian can testify to an inner, conscious awareness of grace working in the heart, a profound sense of being surrounded and penetrated by the divine presence, and a radiant sense of awe, wonder, and gratitude about everything. *Theoria* may be translated "consciousness of grace," "awareness of God's presence," or "spiritual vision," that is, "vision of God," as the etymology of the term *theoria* indicates. However, it is not an actual mystical vision of the uncreated glory of God, and certainly not a psychological vision in terms of created images, but an abiding, lively awareness of God's presence: precisely a spiritual vision of all things in the light of the Divine Presence.

At this level spiritual discernment is neither directly connected to, nor necessarily dependent on, acquired theological knowledge. One may possess a theological doctorate and be known as a famous scholar in theology but be entirely devoid of spiritual discernment (and, alas, sometimes even of practical discernment). However, it coherently builds on and transcends practical discernment just as *theoria* builds on and transcends the first stage of *praxis* without ever leaving the *praxis* behind. To give some examples, practical discernment perceives the Christian obligation to speak the truth; spiritual discernment perceives the freedom that truth works. Practical discernment distinguishes the importance of love; spiritual discernment is guided by the power of love. Practical discernment knows that prayer brings one before God's presence; spiritual discernment delights in prayerful communion with God. In the first case, discernment is based on theological knowledge, whether elementary or expert, acquired from the ongoing tradition of the community and based on God-given abilities of reason and moral sense. In the later case, discernment is a gift of the Holy Spirit that has cleansed the powers of the soul and crowned the received knowledge with a spiritual light. In the full stage of *theoria*, knowledge of God is no longer simply pedagogical or abstract; it is personal communion with God. Theology becomes spirituality, and spirituality is true theology. The Orthodox definition of theologian is not a person who holds a theological degree but a person who knows God through a life of deep prayer.

Many examples of spiritual discernment can be given from the saints. There is a story in the Desert Fathers similar to the account of the adulterous woman brought before Christ. A certain brother in a monastery fell into disgrace. He came before the Elder Anthony, and with him came many brothers who, wishing to restore him to proper monastic discipline, overwhelmed him with reproaches. The Elder Paphnoutios was also present, and he told the brothers a parable they had never heard before. "I saw," said Abba Paphnoutios, "on the bank of the river a man sunk to his knees in the mud, and some came up with outstretched arms to pull him out, and they sunk him to the neck." Then Abba Anthony said, "Behold a man who can

truly heal the soul." Hearing these words, the brothers were cut
to the heart, repented of their overzealous tactic, and restored
the erring brother to the community. In a similar spirit, Abba
Makarios used to say, "A proud and ill word would turn good
men to evil, but a good and humble word would turn evil men
to better." And another Father said, "The devil cannot cast out
devils."

One has, of course, much to learn from such stories and all
the treasures of the wisdom of the saints. One should also seek,
with humility and prudence, to practice such teachings and principles even while striving at the first stage of purification. However, at the stage of *theoria*, spiritual discernment is *ad hoc*: spontaneous, intuitive, truly inspired by the Holy Spirit. Spiritual
discernment not only perceives spiritual insights but also expresses and applies them with spiritual power and freedom appropriate to the needs and circumstances of the moment, often
transcending and even seemingly going against Christian con-
vention. The Jewish religious leaders who came before Jesus,
just like the accusing brothers who came before Anthony and
Paphnoutios, had a legitimate claim to uphold their respective
traditions. Yet, Jesus and the two elders of the desert perceived a
far greater truth, a truth of love, that did not necessarily reject
the demand of the law but affirmed the more profound purpose of the law: to give life.

The third stage of Christian growth, the stage of perfection,
cannot occupy our attention for long because only the perfect
can speak about perfection. The lives and writings of St. Isaac
the Syrian, St. Symeon the New Theologian, and others give
evidence of a truly mystical level of union with God in His
uncreated glory. These saints speak of actual visions of the risen
Christ as uncreated light, which penetrates the beholder and
transforms him or her into light as fire radiates through glow-
ing iron. Such saints – including Moses, the great prophets, the
Apostles, St. Paul and many others known and unknown in the
tradition – are primary witnesses to the revelation and pillars of

the life of the Church. At this level, one might speak of a truly mystical cognition, mystical discernment, grounded in the actual experience of *theosis*, often prophetic, radical, and disturbing in its bold call for repentance and a life worthy of God. "It is not [your] theological knowledge which is the light," cried out St. Symeon to Byzantine theologians of his time, "but the [uncreated] light which is the knowledge." He called emperors, patriarchs, bishops, priests, and laypeople to deep repentance and to apostolic life through an adult baptism of the Holy Spirit. He was cast out of Constantinople and died in exile. Within one or two generations, the Church proclaimed him a saint and gave him the distinct title New Theologian.

Now for a few words pertaining to Christian professionals, especially those who occupy leadership positions in the Church, such as priests, teachers, administrators, missionaries – all those who share in the guidance ministry of the Church, and others who work outside the Church but who take the adjective "Christian" seriously. What benefits can we derive from the above paradigm of Christian life and growth so integrally representative of the essence of the Orthodox way of life? First, we must be vitally concerned with our own continued spiritual growth to the attainment of spiritual discernment. We may remember the exhortations of St. Gregory the Theologian and of St. John Chrysostom that those who seek to guide others to purification must themselves be purified. The chief qualification of Church leadership is spiritual life. From this viewpoint, for example, it is a question whether one should be ordained unless one has reached at least the beginnings of the stage of illumination, or *theoria*. How can God's people be guided with spiritual discernment otherwise? The spiritual vigor of the Church and the efficacy of its witness as Church to society are directly related to the depth of spiritual life of its leaders.

Second, Christian professionals can work together to develop patterns of diagnosis based on Orthodox spirituality to be used in teaching, counseling, and pastoral care. Such work would

not guarantee higher degrees of spiritual discernment to anyone on the basis of professional credentials but would surely
support the process of spiritual growth. The Church Fathers
have conducted extensive analysis of personhood and life and
have written detailed instructions on basic virtues and vices,
offering diagnoses for healing and growth. St. Nikodemos of
the Holy Mountain composed a handbook on confession that
discusses the person of the confessor, the nature and dynamics
of various sins, and the application of spiritual therapy. A number of these handbooks on confession have been written in the
twentieth century. All of these resources need to be studied,
interpreted, and presented in a form useful to the ministry of
the Church today. If the professionals in psychiatry and psychology have devoted such ongoing, systematic attention to the
dynamics of the human personality, should not theologians do
the same on the basis of the riches of the Christian tradition?
One of our great sins of omission as Orthodox leaders and theologians in modern times is our virtual surrender and abandonment of the Church's ministry of counseling to secular psychiatry and psychology, which have eagerly filled the vacuum.

Various models of patterns of discernment and diagnosis could
be proposed. One is the paradigm of these three stages. Another
might be a paradigm constructed on the basis of fundamental
relationships that define the meaning and quality of human life.
There are four such fundamental relationships: to God, to self,
to others (including the Church), and to things. These can serve
as structural categories for the development of flexible and dynamic diagnoses toward spiritual growth. For example, under
the category of the relationship to God, the pastor could appropriately assess a Christian's or even a congregation's depth of
relationship with God in terms of specific criteria such as formal or living faith, personal trust or doubt, love or fear, and
sense of distance from or communion with God. He then could
apply therapy with genuine openness to the Holy Spirit through
renewed emphasis on worship, prayer, and relevant topics in

preaching and teaching. Under the category of relationship to self, the pastor could explore with a Christian the degree of honesty, self-acceptance, willingness to take responsibility, participation in the sacraments, and evidence of the fruit of the Spirit in a Christian's life. Under the category of relationship to others, the defining criteria of diagnosis might be openness or capacity to enter into relationship with others, respect for the personhood of others, service to others, responsibility for and enjoyment of community, and the like. Under the category of relationships to things, the critical referents might be degree of attachment or detachment, use or abuse, whether self-worth is derived from things, whether things have become more important than people, and degree of appreciation of things as God's gifts to be enjoyed, shared, and protected. All of these elements could be flexibly organized and prayerfully offered to Christian professionals as they seek to fulfill their ministries with constant openness to the Holy Spirit.

In this essay, we have not touched on issues pertaining to psychopathology, demonology, or addiction to substances such as alcohol. To take an example, there is a strange case reported by Dorotheos of Gaza in his *Discourses*. A brother came to him and confessed that he constantly stole food to eat. Dorotheos asked the steward to give the man all the food he wanted, so he would not steal. But the brother kept stealing and hiding scraps of bread, dates, figs, and onions under his bed or in other places, or giving the food to the monastery's donkey. "My dear brother," Dorotheos asked, "did I not give you everything you wanted? Why do you steal?" The brother replied, "Forgive me, I don't know why. I simply feel the urge to steal." Dorotheos used this case as an example of the plight to which indulgence of passions can lead, but he did not provide a therapeutic diagnosis. The poor man obviously suffered from kleptomania. Such cases deserve special attention and close cooperative work with professionals in medicine and psychology.

References

Catanzaro, C.J. de trans. *Symeon the New Theologian Discourses*, New York: Paulist Press, 1980.

Chamberas, Peter A., transl. *Nicodemus of the Holy Mountain: A Handbook of Spiritual Counsel.* New York: Paulist Press, 1989.

Hausherr, Irenee. *Spiritual Direction in the Early Christian East.* Trans. A.P. Gythiel. Kalamazoo, MI: Cistercian Publications, 1990.

Luibheid, C. and N. Russell. *The Ladder of Divine Ascent.* Trans J. Climacus. New York: Paulist Press, 1982.

Miles, M. *Fullness of Life: Historical Foundations for a New Asceticism.* Philadelphia: Westminster Press, 1981.

Palmer, G.E.H., P. Sherrard, and K. Ware, eds. *The Philokalia* Vols 1-3. London: Faber and Fater, 1979-1984.

Patton, John. *Pastoral Care in Context: An Introduction fo Pastoral Care Problems in Pastoral Care.* Philadelphia: Westminster Press, 1976.

Pruyser, P.W. *The Minister as Diagnostician: Problems in Pastoral Care.* Philadelphia: Westminster Press, 1976.

Thumberg, Lars. "The Human Person as Image of God in Eastern Christianity." In *Christian Spirituality: Origins to the Twelfth Century.* Ed. B. McGinn, J. Meyendorff and J. Leclerq. New York: Crossroads, 1987.

Waddell, Helen. *The Desert Fathers.* Ann Arbor: University of Michigan Press, 1960.

Ware, Kallistos, "Ways of Prayer and Contemplation: Eastern." In *Christian Spirituality: Origins to the Twelfth Century.* Ed. B. McGinn, J. Meyendorff and J. Leclerq. New York: Crossroads, 1987.

Wheeler, E.P. *Dorotheos of Gaza: Discourses and Sayings.* Kalamazoo, MI: Cistercian Publications, 1977.

PART TWO

ASSESSING SPIRITUAL DISCERNMENT
AND DIFFERENTIAL DIAGNOSIS

Understanding Healthy and Unhealthy Adaptions of Religion: The Case of Odessa*

Client Demographic Characteristics

The client, age 50, was a black woman, originally from a southern state. She was a Seventh-Day Adventist of more than moderate orthodoxy and devoutness. A convert to the Seventh-Day Adventist faith, she has been raised as a Roman Catholic. At least of high normal intelligence, she had begun the first year of junior college but had been unable to continue because of family finances. Odessa was born into a lower middle-class family; her father was a plumber's helper and her mother was a homemaker. She was the next to youngest child in a family of two sisters and two brothers. Odessa was married and had five daughters.

Client History

Odessa had two brothers who were older than she was. One of her brothers was mentally retarded. Her father and both brothers had forced her older and younger sisters to have sexual intercourse with them. When they attempted to force themselves on Odessa, she fought back in such a fierce way that she dissuaded them from any attempts to sexually assault her. However, they occasionally physically abused her from age 13 to age 18. At 18, she left home to get a job and to share an apartment with another younger woman. While living with her parents, she had thoughts of seriously harming the male family members, and she harbored ambivalent feelings toward her mother for being

* From Richards and Bergin (1997) *A Spiritual Strategy for Counseling and Psychotherapy,* Chapter 11, Case Reports of Spiritual Issues and Interventions – Case 5 Odessa (pp. 81–83).

so unprotective of her and toward her sisters for being so passive with her father and brothers and for being ineffectual in general.

Her father beat her mother, too, and the mother turned her head away when he and her sons attacked Odessa and her sisters because she was trying to escape his cruelty herself. Odessa, feeling vulnerable to and angry at the persecutors and victims in her family, as well as her mother for not rescuing her from that horrible predicament, nonetheless wanted both to protect and physically attack her mother. She also was furious that she had no adequate female role model and a terrible male figure in her childhood experiences. Furthermore, she resented that her parents never encouraged her to further her education. She differentiated between her parents actually having money for this (which she realized they did not) and at least motivating her to achieve.

PRESENTING PROBLEMS AND CONCERNS

When she came to therapy, Odessa was feeling deep shame, guilt, and depression. Her guilt and shame concerned her familial captive position in physically being abused and witnessing her mother and sisters being abused; her inability to protect the other female family members from their abusers; and her hatred toward her parents, siblings, and herself. Her religious and spiritual background espoused love and respect for her parents and siblings, to "not let the sun go down on her anger," but she did not think that she could obey such commands without becoming seriously emotionally disturbed.

She regretted that she had married and had children. She was concerned that she would physically abuse her children when they failed to unconditionally respect and obey her. She also was angry at her husband for being passive in family matters and for not taking the major part, or at least sharing equally, in the disciplining of the children. Her self-hate and self-blame were apparent, too. Her intense anger, guilt, shame, and ambivalence toward all her family members also contributed to several physical problems, such as hypertension, high blood pressure, and diabetes, for which she was under regular medical treatment.

When Odessa began her individual psychotherapy treatment, she had a low-level (GS-2) government job, primarily because of her hesitation in asserting herself and in learning new material on her job. She also was not willing to assert herself as head deaconess at her church. She felt plagued with too much responsibility in this role, although concurrently she felt compelled to volunteer for that level of involvement. She resented the fact that other women in the church were not doing their share. Her husband, the head elder in their church and a Sabbath school teacher, had a second job to help support their family. She was angry at him for not having enough time for her and the children.

Furthermore, she blamed her husband for not discouraging female admirers in the Sabbath school class. She wondered how much she had to accept in "Christian humility and silence" or "suffering" and how much deference she had to give to the patriarchal concept of the male head of the household. Besides the need for both of them to have at least one job to give their children a religious education, they interpreted church teachings as requiring that they be busy performing Christian works most of the time. Thus, Odessa was tired much of the time at church and at work, Odessa saw herself as a religious Cinderella whose accommodating nature and deep desire to please others in order to gain approval were taken advantage of by a bad parent, boss, or religious leader and by bad sisters, coworkers, or congregants.

THE CASE OF ODESSA: A PSYCHIATRIC PERSPECTIVE

Jeff Rediger

In discussing the case of Odessa, it is important to remember that Odessa's challenges are less uncommon than is traditionally thought. Many of the people one meets in school, at church, or at the grocery store have experienced or are experiencing hidden, secret losses and traumas that are not evident to the untrained eye. One in three to five girls and one in five to seven boys experiences sexual or physical abuse before the age of 18. Many more are emotionally abused, abandoned, or neglected.

The implication of this is that the issues raised by Odessa's struggles are similar in nature and content to those of many parishioners. In what follows, Odessa's case will be examined by a focus on two aspects of healthy and unhealthy adaptations of religion: fatherhood, and the canonical distinction between personhood and nature. Throughout, effort will be applied toward thinking about some of the differences between an Orthodox understanding of faith, psychology, and medicine and that of their traditionally Western counterparts.

FATHERHOOD: WHAT KIND OF FATHER IS GOD?

In traditional Orthodox theology, God is the good Father. He creates each person with love and care, and seeks to be with and enjoy his creation. He takes an infinite, undying delight in the particularities of each individual person. He heals our wounds and is the source of all life and vitality.

Odessa was raised as a Roman Catholic and then converted to Seventh-Day Adventism. It's clear that her faith was very important to her. One of the questions raised by Odessa's childhood experience with an abusive father has to do with how this affected her assumptions about who God is as a Father to her. How did her experience with her own father limit or change her capacity to know and confidently trust that God the Father delights in all of who she is, and that He bestows infinite respect and freedom on her needs and desires?

Most faith communities, particularly in the West, appropriate their faith in a way that is more or less patriarchal in nature. Although God actually is beyond our typical conceptions of male and female – He contains both male and female characteristics and supersedes such categorizations – He typically is viewed exclusively as Father rather than also as Mother. Only male pronouns are used in reference to Him, and the characteristics attributed to Him are traditionally masculine in substance. Although Roman Catholicism's patriarchialism may be somewhat offset by the presence of the Virgin Mary (which is in itself quite different from the Eastern Orthodox appropriation of Mary as the Theotokos), Seventh Day Adventism is typically completely patriarchal in tone and ethos. And, as the Creator and Sustainer of all that exists, as the Ground of Being, He is not just a Father. He is *The Father*. He is *The Man* – incomparable, omnipotent, omniscient, omnipresent. He has all conceivable power, and He can find her wherever she is; there is no place she can go where He is not also there.

Unfortunately, perpetrators of physical and/or sexual abuse, like Odessa's father, typically also act in relatively omnipotent, omniscient, and omnipresent ways, keeping most of the power for themselves and sharing little with their victims. Power and knowledge are often used largely for their own appetites and impulses, and the needs or desires of the victim matter little, if they are noticed at all. They tend to behave in controlling ways. Not only do they often threaten the child (or adult) with severe retaliation, or even death; if the person reports the abuse or fights back, they often attempt to regulate the person's life in minute detail, demanding too much control of the person's privacy, bodily functions, etc. They demand absolute obedience and respect for themselves but typically do not have the same regard for others. God the Father is, in important respects, created in the image of Odessa's own father. It is her father who taught her what it means to be powerful and at least to some degree inescapable. God has some of those same characteristics but, as God *The* Father, the Source and Sustainer of all that is, the volume is turned up to its highest possible setting. Given the imperfection of fathers in general, this is a complex, usually unconscious problem for all people. For victims of childhood or other abuse, however, the problem, though unrecognized, may color and darken every minute and decision of their lives. If God is all-knowing, present everywhere, and out to get her, for instance, or at least can not be trusted, then the very ground of her being is shaken. Like a fish who does not know what wet is because it has never known anything else, she probably will not recognize the source of her constant anxiety and worry because she too has not known anything else.

This means that Odessa's history of abuse places her at risk of being further exploited by the church. Her religious background led her to believe that having respect for parents and church authorities should be at the top of her list of priorities. She felt intense guilt, and as if she were not a Christian whenever she felt put upon and when she didn't put other's wishes and desires above her own. Instead of volunteering as head deaconess because she wanted to do so, and out of a belief that she had the requisite talent, time, and energy, she did so out of a feeling of compulsion. She did not want all that responsibility, did not have the necessary time and energy for the task, and shrank from asserting herself in that position. But she believed that she should be doing something to minister to others. In other words, consistent with the self-respect and self-care difficulties faced by other victims of abuse, she typically denigrated her own needs and desires in favor of some standard or level of performance that she felt should be attainable by her. She felt that she should be performing Christian works much of the time, on top of a job and raising her children almost alone, since her husband worked two jobs.

It is no small wonder that she then she resented other women who she felt were not doing their share. One of the spiritual and emotional issues for Odessa to work through would be to come to realize how different God the Father is from her own father, and to come to some awareness of how her experience with her father has unconsciously shaped and curtailed her assumptions about how God the Father wants to be with and know her. Part of her healing would involve coming to know God as the One who delights in her as she is, and who wants to know and be with her rather than change her. She would come to experience God as wanting more than anything else to know her needs and desires, and would then know that any church activity she assumes would be a grateful, heartfelt response that wells up inside her for the love that she feels from her God. She would learn to take on only activities that would not cause resentment within her, and would use the potential or actual feeling of resentment as one clue as to which activities she had energy and desire for, and which activities and commitments she might do better to avoid at the present time.

Another complex problem created not only by having her father, but also by her placement in a patriarchal society and her membership in an almost exclusively patriarchal faith community, where men historically have relegated relatively more power and privilege to themselves, had to do with her feelings about her husband's actions. It was difficult for Odessa to watch her husband enjoy the attentions of other women in the Sabbath school class. Many churches talk about Christian humility and silence for women, and about men being the head of the household. There's scriptural support for these positions. The concern is that this could be appropriated in a way that affirms what her mother taught her: that women don't have a voice, and that their place is only on the periphery. An important question has to do with how the church is to guide her in integrating its teachings about womanhood and women's place in a way that dignifies and celebrates womanhood rather demeaning or delegitimating it.

When I was an undergraduate, I did an internship in a Mennonite psychiatric hospital. I took a 12-year-old girl named Margaret down to the quiet room one day and was shocked at the depth of her rage and hatred as she repeatedly slammed phone books against the wall. I didn't know anything about her. I asked her why she hated so much, and what place love had in her life. Her response? "My daddy told me he loved me and wanted to make love to me." Though Odessa successfully fought off her father, he did attempt to use her in the same manner as Margaret was used and, given the conflicts she carried with her, no doubt was successful in less tangible ways. When Odessa heard God described as her Father and that He loves her as a father loves his child, how did she take this in? What would it take for her to experience God as loving her, rather than using her for his own needs? Odessa was vulnerable to believing that God is less interested in her than He is in using her to accomplish his Grand Plan. This vulnerability could be easily exploited by a busy and active church. An important question for the church has to do with how many people are routinely caught up in this kind of dynamic, and in doing so, lose the capacity for a genuine and vital experience of the God who pursues us and desires to know and delight in all of who we are.

PERSONHOOD: POWER, LOVE, AND SELF-CONTROL

According to traditional Orthodoxy theology, our understanding of the human person is rooted in the belief that men and women are created in the image and likeness of God. What is known of human persons is believed to reflect the kenotic reciprocity and mutuality that exists between the Divine Persons of the Father, Son, and Holy Spirit.

Starting with the fourth ecumenical council, Orthodox canonical theology has traditionally made a critical distinction between person and nature in its elucidation of God. This same distinction has also been important for understanding human persons as God's image-bearers. Briefly, nature has to do with the roles one plays, with the face that one presents to the world. As part of their nature, some people have blond hair; others have dark hair and blue eyes. Some people are doctors or professors, whereas others are grocery store clerks or homeless alcoholics. One is an elderly grandfather; another is a young child, dependent on her parents and in competition with her siblings for love and affection.

Aspects of nature can also be quantitatively analyzed and scientifically manipulated. At the level of nature, people's characteristics can be compared and contrasted. Medicine analyzes chemical components of the blood and uncovers disease by comparing the characteristics of persons with certain symptoms with those of others who have similar or dissimilar symptoms. Psychology frequently deals with less tangible aspects of mind and consciousness but is similar in that it frequently compares and contrasts indices of cognition or emotion that are observable or inferable based on what is believed about the nature of the mind. The emphasis, with special credit to our Cartesian heritage, is on what is objective, measurable, and replicable, with the term "objective" understood as related to what is tangible and capable of being understood from the "outside," as it were, i.e., as being susceptible to a common understanding or interpretation by anyone who views the same phenomena.

Personhood, on the other hand, has to do with the primacy of being human, i.e., with the fact that, created in the image of God, every person is a unique and unrepeatable gift of God, given to us for our delight and sustenance. Nothing – not anything the person does or does not do with his or her life – can change that unalterable reality. The created image of God is a much deeper and more important datum within each person than one's fallenness, or failure to become all that God has created that person to become.

Personhood cannot be analyzed or known in any way from the outside, or through methods that are typically characterized as "objective" and demonstrable. A person can only be experienced. As Antoine de Exupery's little prince said to the roses in *The Little Prince* (credited by Zizioulas as an excellent description of the ontology of love):[1]

> "You are beautiful, but empty," he went on. "One could not die for you. To be sure, an ordinary passerby would think that my rose looked just like you – the rose that belongs to me. But in herself alone she is more important than all the hundreds of you other roses: because it is she that I have watered; because it is she that I have put under the glass globe; because it is she that I have sheltered behind the screen; because it is for her that I have killed the caterpillars (except the two or three that we saved to become butterflies); because it is she that I have listened to, when she grumbled, or boasted, or even sometimes when she said nothing. Because she is my rose."[2]

The red fox, as the teacher of the little prince, went on to say: "And now here is my secret, a very simple secret: It is only with the heart that one can see rightly; what is essential is invisible to the eye."[3] In other words, what is fundamental and sacred about a person is invisible to conventional vision and available only to the eye of the heart. Only one who takes an infinite delight in the particularities of this one person can truly know the other, who is necessarily also the beloved. The person has intrinsic value because he or she is a person created by God, not because of his or her gifts or attractiveness.

Orthodox theology emphasizes in a radical way the primacy of personhood over nature. Grasping the full implications of this is difficult, particularly in American culture, which emphasizes the importance of nature over personhood. In American culture, roles and the faces that one presents to the world are often viewed as definitive valuations of the person's worth. In other words, senators and lawyers are often more valued than homeless drug addicts or janitors, and talented, wealthy, or young people are often granted more esteem than disabled, poor, elderly, or otherwise less "useful" people. From an Orthodox perspective, personal value and dignity is at least as present in the disenfranchised and disabled as it is in the popular and attractive. Their presence in our lives, and the words they bring, may be even more important than the presence of those whose attention is more frequently sought and desired. "The last will be first and the first will be last."

In studying the Divine Person, we come to understand what personal dignity, freedom, and value really mean. We come to understand that who we are is more important than what we do, or how we compare to others. One implication of this is that personhood always precedes law. In other words, people don't exist for the law; rather, the law exists for the support and nurturance of human life and being.

As a child, Odessa was never been granted the status of being a person. An important question is how well her church was able to speak with her as a black, formerly degraded woman about dignity, uniqueness, emancipation, and liberation. This is what the Good News is. Salvation is an inner event. As a real inner event, it also changes one's experience and expectations about how one deserves to be treated.

As a symptom of the violation of personhood she had experienced, Odessa was ashamed of her feelings, felt they were bad, and couldn't express them easily. She couldn't accept that her feelings, whether she liked them or not, were a gift given to her by God, meant to be used as a clue to expressing her God-given uniqueness and unrepeatability. She had never been guided in knowing how to be true to the person God was creating her to be, in setting her own priorities and saying no if that was appropriate. To do so, she thought, would be un-Christian and selfish.

Several questions raised by Odessa's situation go beyond the confines of this article but should be mentioned briefly. For example, what is selfishness? What is an Orthodox understanding of anger? The Bible says: love your brother more than yourself; die to yourself; turn the other cheek. Conventional psychology says: find yourself; be yourself; do what you want; protect yourself; set boundaries. Is the Bible correct and psychology wrong? How is the following statement from the case to be considered: "Her religious and spiritual background espoused love and respect for her parents and siblings, to 'not let the sun go down on her anger,' but she did not think that she could obey such commands without becoming seriously emotionally disturbed"?

Some brief comments should probably also be made about anger, rage, and false shame. Anger is a protective mechanism given to us by God. It warns us that something is wrong, that a boundary has been crossed. It is meant to be felt, acknowledged, and then let go. It becomes self-destructive if it is retained. Rage, on the other hand, grows out of the flat, repeated violation of personhood. It is a reaction to not being seen as a unique and absolutely unrepeatable child of God that one knows oneself to be at a tacit and inexpressible level of being. Rage takes root when one has been repeatedly or severely treated as less than human. The only treatment for rage is to reinstate the inalienable right to be treated with absolute respect and dignity. Speaking as a psychiatrist who spends hours in the emergency and consulting rooms, I can state with assurance that mental illness and social problems are sometimes created and often significantly exacerbated by the failure to appropriate this right adequately in a lived way.

False shame and rage are members of the same family. False shame is the opposite of the innate goodness and sacredness of the person presupposed by the doctrine of personhood. If there is something fundamentally faulty with who you are, then you can try and try and try, but you'll never be good enough. This disease can easily penetrate churches and congregant's lives.

To speak in a different set of clinical terms, the only alternative to personhood is sadomasochism. Personhood can exist only in the context of mutuality with others. Personhood is about "power with" rather than "power over." Odessa was raised in a world where the only paradigms were sadism or masochism: either the violent "power over" of her father and brothers, or the mousy learned helplessness of her mother. In masochism, pain is preferred to isolation. You can be connected without being a self, without being responsible for who you are and what you bring into relationship. In sadism, control over the other allows one to be in a type of relationship that feels powerful and relatively invulnerable.

The distinction between person and nature and the priority of the former has implications for an Orthodox model of medicine. While attending a Protestant seminary, I listened rather uncomfortably to characterizations of the relations between mind, body and spirit, or psychology, medicine, and spirituality, as if each resembled pieces of a pie: if one has a spiritual problem, a priest or pastor is sought; if the problem seems more emotional in nature, a referral to a psychologist is in order; if the manifestation fits more along the lines of the physical, one visits the doctor. Some illnesses are characterized as strictly emotional and others as strictly physical. This presupposes a mind-body dualism that has more to do with the way in which our culture has developed than it does with the actual way in which illnesses fester and take root in people's lives.

Such a typically Western approach partitions off the parts of the person without intellectual attention to the reciprocity between the parts and the containment and participation of these aspects in a whole person, who stands behind and between and integrates the parts into a meaningful whole. Since converting to Eastern Orthodoxy, I have come to conceptualize spirituality as actually being the pie shell (or, alternatively, the rind of the orange) that contains the pieces, or aspects, of the person. In other words, the theological understanding of personhood, as characterized above, permeates and informs all levels of the human person.

A consideration of Odessa's hypertension and diabetes illustrates some of the implications that, though important to an Orthodox model of medicine, are typically ignored in modern Western medicine. Trauma causes changes in the body's fight-or-flight system, i.e., sympathetic and parasympathetic nervous systems. When a person lives under chronic stress and terror, the body adapts itself to the chronic secretion of stress hormones. The body wires itself into a chronic state of arousal and guardedness. This has concrete physiological implications for both Odessa's dysthymia and hypertension. Although some people are born with a genetic loading that presupposes them to the development of hypertension, others can be expected to develop hypertension if they harbor strong conscious or unconscious fears, aggression, feelings of helplessness, or threats to their security. The forces that take us toward life, vitality, creativity, and connection tend to reduce blood pressure, while the forces that take us towards destruction and death tend towards manifestations of illness.

The historical demoralization and racism perpetrated against blacks in the United States has direct physiological effects that are consistent with the current discussion. It is well known in medical circles that blacks have more hypertension than Caucasians if they live in the United States, but not if they live in their native countries. Presumably there is something about the lack of full personhood experienced by minorities, especially blacks, in the United States that has direct physiological effects that are deleterious to health.

An accumulating body of evidence substantiates this general argument. Michael Marmot, in 1976, measured heart attack rates among workers in different civil service ranks.[4] Those in the lowest employment grades were four times more likely to die of a heart attack than those at the top of the hierarchy. They were also much more likely to come down with strokes, cancers, and stomach diseases. The conclusions of the study were that wherever you are on the social ladder, your risk of early death is higher than it is for your social betters. In other words, there is a sense in which you can read social class from people's bodies. Even a small increment in social status was reflected in statistics on life and death. And class differences in health remained even after correction for differences in blood pressure, exercise, cholesterol, etc. Administrators who designed policies and set the strategies for executing them were half as likely to have a fatal heart attack as the executives who ran the various departments and carried out the policies dictated to them by the administrators. The clerks who worked for the executives had three times as many heart attacks as the administrators. Assistant clerks and data processors had four times the risk. These were all middle class people, but among them was a clear gradient.

This seems to indicate that the kind of stress a busy CEO or physician feels is very different from the stress experienced by a clerk whose life is under another's authority and scrutiny. According to an Orthodox model of the person, one would be inclined to examine how indices of respect and one's perceived value are related to these figures. Economist Richard Wilkinson wrote that if there were a virus as bad as the professional hierarchy, the offices would be evacuated and closed down as a health hazard.

There are other examples. In Roseto, Pennsylvania, during the 1950s, doctors discovered that the residents died of heart attacks at half the national rate. Yet, they smoked heavily and consumed vast amounts of lard. The difference seemed to be that they had a quality of social life wherein people felt known and respected. Several generations often lived together, and social life was centered on the church. The local priest knew everyone by name. "You go down the street and everyone says 'Hello, Hello!' You feel like you're the mayor," said one of the women. Where people are valued and known, morbidity and mortality improve.

CONCLUSION

The case of Odessa raises several issues relevant to a consideration of healthy versus pathological faith. In this essay, the implications of what is considered to be congruent with a distinctively Orthodox understanding of fatherhood and personhood have been briefly discussed. In contrast to Western theological concepts, which tend to emphasize nature over personhood and, as a result, sometimes inadvertently create a false dichotomy between holiness and what is perceived as intrinsically human, a traditionally Orthodox appropriation tends to view the attainment of holiness as that which takes one toward attainment of the universally human. This principle would seem to be a reasonable beginning criterion for healthy spirituality.

NOTES

[1] Zizioulas, John D., *Being as Communion: Studies in Personhood and the Church*, Crestwood, NY: St. Vladimir's Seminary Press, 1993, p. 49.

[2] Antoine de Saint-Exupery, *The Little Prince*, Fiftieth Anniversary Edition, New York: Harcourt Brace & Company, 1993, p. 73.

[3] *Ibid.*

[4] The following discussion is indebted to Epstein, Helen, "Life and Death on the Social Ladder," *The New York Review of Books*, July 16, 1988.

THE CASE OF ODESSA: A PSYCHOSPIRITUAL PERSPECTIVE

John T. Chirban

Odessa presents with torment and despair. Life has taught her that men retain power and abuse it in their world. They keep women as their victims.

Odessa resisted and fought back to save her soul. All the strength she was able to muster had served to secure her survival; true emotional and spiritual fulfillment remained ideals rather than her experiences from family or career, even when she was freed from the clutches of her tormentors.

How Do We Approach Religion and Spiritual Concerns in Treatment?

Before commenting on specific applications of psychospiritual concerns in the case of Odessa, I would like to identify five goals for clinicians concerned with the psychospiritual dimension in treatment:

First, express openness to religious, spiritual, and existential concerns. During the initial consultation, regardless of the presenting problem, I typically inquire about the patient's religious identification and involvement. This question signals my openness to discussing such material, so that the patient may follow up as he or she determines. I often continue with another question concerning whether or not he or she participates in a spiritual life practice. The goal here is to clarify the role of spirituality in one's life. It is not unusual for a patient to respond, "Oh, you're asking about *that*. That's actually very important to me, but I never thought we'd discuss it here." Our patients have learned to present themselves as fragmented in treatment before treatment fragments them. The purpose is to convey that the spirit affects one's whole life and one's whole life is our concern.

Second, appreciate the spiritual, and do not reduce it with psychological interpretations. The anticipated lack of support for spiritual matters on the part of mental health professionals often dissuades patients from revealing their spiritual concerns and disallows the opportunity to consider how it may provide a treatment resource. Assessing the patient's spirituality may enable the clinician to both learn about the patient's traditions and relate his or her faith and culture to the psychological concerns at hand.

Third, understand the value that the spirit holds, respecting the impact of spirituality in the person's life. Inviting a patient to discuss his or her spiritual interests provides a wellspring of information that informs the clinician of deep, personal experiences, influences, and ambitions. Here the task is to address the resources and impact offered by the patient's religious tradition as he or she functions in society in order to integrate the individual's spiritual and psychological dimensions.

Fourth, explore the spirit, recognizing how it affects the patient's life. As the patient is ready to examine the direction (as well as the costs and benefits) of his or her spiritual choices, the clinician may help the individual translate his or her spiritual tradition into life decisions and changes. By engaging this discussion, the clinician may explore positive and negative issues for understanding and integrating the patient's culture, history, and goals.

Fifth, attend to the impact of spirituality on the therapeutic relationship. Treatments that engage religious and spiritual concerns may accentuate our connection with patients and reduce the notion of the patient as pathological, affirming the individual in relationship. By recognizing how spiritual values enhance the patient's relationships with others, we can enhance our connection to our patients.

APPLICATIONS IN THE CASE OF ODESSA

Numerous religious and spiritual themes surface prominently in the case of Odessa. We are told she was of "more than moderate orthodoxy and devoutness" as a convert from Roman Catholicism to the Seventh Day Adventist faith. She "saw herself as a religious Cinderella" whose busyness, accommodating nature, and desire to please in order to gain approval "were taken advantage of by a bad parent, boss, or religious leader and bad sisters, coworkers, or congregants." Her religious traditions emphasized male dominance. She maintained an *image* of a "sincere loving Christian" who, while responding positively, gave beyond her resources. "Humility and silence" and "suffering" were mottoes of her faith that provoked dissonance within her. Feelings of deep shame, guilt, depression, anger, self-hate, and ambivalence, generated in her family relationships, characterized her emotional disposition. Is this a favorable scenario for one who devotedly espouses the spirit? How does a clinician with sensitivities to religious or spiritual concerns intervene?

First, we need to clarify our orientation in addressing spiritual and religious issues. Most mental health practitioners are not spiritual guides. In fact, we can observe that various postures exist for addressing psychology and religion. Some dominant personality theorists, who traditionally characterized the mental health stance, like Freud (1927) and Skinner (1953), maintained negative and suspicious interpretations of the spirit. Others, like psychoanalysts Rizzuto (1979) and Meissner (1984), offered a descriptive approach for how individuals process religion, on one hand pointing out the psychological usefulness of religious experience and, on the other, approaching the spirit as not unlike other phenomena. Still others, like Jung (1948) and Frankl (1985), embraced the spirit as a positive, essential aspect of the treatment process. Richard and Bergin (1997), in their recent volume *A Spiritual Strategy for Counseling and Psychotherapy*, published by the American Psychological Association, combine a clear theistic position for the therapist with respect for the scientific method. Are we clear about how our psychological perspective affects our approach to religion and spirituality? Do we have a consistent orientation?

Second, we need to have a basic knowledge of the patient's traditions, rituals, and symbols in order to interpret and understand the role of spirituality and religion in his or her life. Both of Odessa's faith traditions, Roman Catholicism and Seventh Day Adventism, emphasize conservative doctrine and traditions. Odessa converted to Seventh Day Adventism. Such information raises important questions for us: Did the rigorous Adventist world offer a safe, cohesive setting in contrast to her chaotic home life? Did she convert to distinguish or distance herself from her Roman Catholic family? Was the community of her new faith nurturing, supporting, and caring – thereby filling needs not met by her parents? Or was her conversion a function essentially of personal conviction?

In the context of Odessa's faith, we would like to understand the various conscious and unconscious needs that her spirituality and religion serve. We are not told why she converted, but we are advised of her intensity and dedication. Both of these faiths offer expression of intense religious fervor. In particular, Seventh Day Adventists require a more integrated consciousness to faith in daily life as a fervent Protestant group that emphasizes lifestyle changes for its members, belief in the imminent return and reign of Jesus Christ, the primacy of the Saturday Sabbath, and an emphasis on a healthy lifestyle and health care (Kelly, 1995). Odessa's religion may have responded to both her psychological and spiritual needs for a strong, protective, enveloping structure, which is compatible with her rather dependent psychological organization. The fact of conversion, however, may also point to her character strength (one of the few independent streaks noted in the synopsis of her life), demonstrated by her ability to fight of the incestuous attacks in her family and by her resistance to identify with her submissive mother, who epitomized passivity. Any or all of these conjectures are worthy of exploration. They may reveal her religious experience as a medium of emotional survival in addition to providing spiritual solace.

Given Odessa's devotion, it is important to remain especially sensitive to her religious investment in treatment. The significant value she places on her faith could make her unresponsive to psychological approaches that reduce or interpret her faith experiences or that use nonreligious language. Therefore, the religious symbols and biblical images of her tradition could be incorporated valuably into treatment. In view of Odessa's struggles, metaphors of her religious tradition could serve as a source of hope in her world of vulnerability, and freedom from her emotional bondage. While faith offers several images that parallel and preserve her psychological pathos, a religion may also provide models that enhance a positive self – for example, applying axioms and parables to her life such as "Love your neighbor as yourself." To love another, she needs first to know what it is to love herself. Examples from Jesus' life could serve this pupose, e.g., when Jesus expresses anger in the temple because of abuse, or when he confronts contemptible or unjust people. These provide metaphors and "inspiration" that may enable Odessa to experience more readily the range of her feelings – including the love and care that she seeks and needs. Another tool would be to explore Odessa's experience with prayer. We find that Odessa's punitive superego is internalized. By attending to how she perceives God, supporting her relationship with God as an available and caring parent figure rather than an all-powerful, potentially judgmental, and unaccepting authority figure, we can help Odessa begin to accept herself and understand the object relations that play out in her relationships.

Third, we need to differentiate between legitimate and illegitimate uses of religion. It is important to affirm Odessa's search for the spirit and for truth. Her faith offered her a viable community in which she could establish an identity. We recognize that

Odessa's rigorous adherence to her faith provided her with control in her unbounded life. Once a therapeutic alliance is established, the task is to understand Odessa's idealizations and choices. As she develops her self-concept, it would be valuable to understand the identification and the motivation that led to her spiritual and religious choices. Following her lead, we could reexperience the positive aspects as well as the negative process in her pilgrimage. The task may be seen as helping her to understand the function of her ideal self and to accept her real self, as Horney (1955) describes it. This permits us to confront the negative self-image that her adaptation in religion fosters. While her rigid, literal focus of Scriptures supports – as she interprets it – psychological dependence in abusive relationships, we observe that she is selective about the biblical passages to which she clings. Both home and religion locked her in situations of suffering. In the treatment process, we can identify the structures of Odessa's religion that recapitulate the contingencies and dynamics of her home, where, in spite of abuse, she felt obligated to love her enemies. Like her home, her religion similarly maintains a system of undefined boundaries that relegates her to second-class citizenship without rights or privileges, especially with regard to men. Significantly, both settings required deference to male authorities, and both settings left her without adequate approval.

When working with someone's religious beliefs, we must be cautious not to destroy inadvertently what is deeply valued. At the same time, it is important not to support conflictual adaptations under the guise of faith. Odessa's interpretations of such statements as "Do not let the sun go down on your anger" with regard to parents who abused her reflects distortions that may be confronted in therapy by considering interpretations of her faith and its impact on her self-concept. By empathically attending to and understanding her personal struggle, building on her personal strengths, and affirming *her* spirit by recognizing the elements of her tradition that serve her growth, we can help Odessa release herself from the guilt and harmful expectations implicit in her idealized self-image of a "sincere and loving Christian" so that she can begin to find, accept, and live her true self as Odessa.

Fourth, we need to attend to countertransference. Inevitably, spiritual material intensifies transference, resistance, and countertransference, and may complicate the therapeutic process. Just as with other complex themes, such as sexuality or politics, one must weigh the costs of sharing one's reactions and proceed with vigilance. Spiritual issues provide manifold opportunities to confuse boundaries and roles. Whatever posture the clinician decides to adopt, when conducting psychotherapy that addresses spiritual concerns, we must avoid collusions that may come from validating a patient's assumptions, but, rather, explore and examine them. As a rule of thumb, advice giving on spiritual matters and moralizing are outside the bounds of treatment.

From a psychological perspective, it appears that in spite of her torment and suffering, Odessa experiences guilt, shame, and ambivalence about her separation and individuation. The guilt is rooted in feelings that there has been gain at the expense of others.

Martha Stark (1999) observes the connection between guilt with shame, pointing out how beneathe one's perceived powerlessness and deep feelings of guilt and shame. She explained how the presence of highly charged victimizers-victim introjects gives rise to angry, *guilt-ridden depression* and how superior-inferior introjects give rise to empty, *shame-ridden depression*.

In a traumatic life such as Odessa, the child protects herself from the grief, deciding that it must be she who is bad, lest she confront the insecure, hopeless possibility that her parent is bad. Also, the conflict remains internal, where Odessa's problematic ego ideal is contemptuous of her inferior ego, so she acts smugly superior and denigrating. This results in empty shame-ridden depression.

In angry depression, representing the victimization-victim introject, characterized by anger, guilt, and a sense of self as bad, we find one's wish to confess and expose oneself as bad, and a wish to be punished. The empty depression, representing a superior-inferior introject, characterized by emptiness, despair, shame, and a sense of self as defective, inferior, or worthless, results in a wish to conceal and keep hidden, and not to be found out.

In therapy, the process of restoration begins when the therapist provides the opportunity for the patient to experience aspects of himself or herself through a relationship that is characterized by cohesion and trust. By pursuing spirit-related issues in therapy, Odessa may gain enough confidence to deepen her spiritual quest. Her faith may have "saved" her in more ways than one. Moreover, when a religious patient experiences the therapist's assurance through respect for the values of faith, hope, and love in God, not only is the therapeutic process experienced as less threatening, but the patient feels integrated more deeply into it.

By attending to the spirit in psychotherapy, we can support the patient's self-discovery of his or her inner motives, digging beneath the forms of religion to the heart. In this process we help people confront questions of truth about their life – their intentions, meanings, and actions. By engaging the spirit in those who are willing, and tapping it in those for whom it has been silenced, personal freedom – a shared goal of psychotherapy and of faith – is within our grasp.

REFERENCES

Erikson, E. *Identity: Youth and Crisis.* New York: Norton, 1968.

Frankl, V. *The Unheard Cry for Meaning: Psychotherapy and Humanism.* New York: Simon and Schuster, 1985.

Freud, S. *Future of an Illusion.* In *Complete Works of Sigmund Freud,* standard edition (Vol. 21, pp. 1-57). London: Hogarth Press, 1927.

Jung, C.G. *Modern Man in Search of a Soul.* New York: Harcourt, Brace and World, 1985.

Kelly, E.W., Jr.. *Spirituality and Religion in Counseling and Psychotherapy: Diversity in Theory and Practice*. Alexandria, VA: American Counseling Association, 1995.

Horney, K. *Neurosis and Human Growth*. New York: Norton, 1955.

Meissner, W.W. *Psychoanalysis and Religious Experience*. New Haven, CT: Yale University Press,1984.

Richards, P.S., Bergin, A. E. *A Spiritual Strategy for Counseling and Psychotherapy*. Washington, DC: American Psychological Association, 1987.

Rizzuto, A.M. *The Birth of the Living God: A Psychoanalytic Study*. Chicago: University of Chicago Press, 1979.

Skinner, B.F. *Science and Human Behavior*. New York: MacMillan, 1953.

Stark, M. *Treating Mind and Body and Soul*. "The Mind." Unpublished lecture presented at the 22nd Annual Lindemann Lecture. (Boston, MA), 1999.

Your Faith Is Making You Well:
Psychotherapy in an Orthodox Christian context

Stephen Muse

> For a Christian there are no answers to be found in looking
> for who is responsible for evil: it lives in every human heart.
> There will always be evil on the earth. Christ said, *In the*
> *world ye shall have tribulation, but be of good cheer, I have*
> *overcome the world* (John 16:33). The question to ask our-
> selves in times of peril or sorrow is whether in the suffering
> that comes upon us we draw closer to God, strengthened in
> faith.[1]

Good psychotherapy, like good religion, helps people suffer
for the right reasons and stop suffering for the wrong reasons.
When psychotherapy occurs in the context of shared Christian
faith between client and therapist, all other things being equal,
I believe the conditions are ripe for the highest-quality therapeutic alliance. Nevertheless, whatever the therapist may say or
do, it is essentially the grace of God working through the client's
growing faith that is at work, so that one may echo the words of
our Lord Jesus Christ to the woman with the 12-year hemorrhage who touched his garment and was made well: "Go in
peace, your faith has made you well."

To put it another way, we can say that the therapeutic alliance is a temporary relationship designed to clear away obstacles
to a person's permanent therapeutic journey in faith. Good pastoral psychotherapy occurs to the extent that we are least intru-
sive in people's lives while at the same time are most interested,
caring, and careful as we help them recognize the conscious and
unconscious obstacles to the grace of God working in them

through the presence of our Lord Jesus Christ and the power of the Holy Spirit.

Good psychotherapy requires a kind of informed, intentional naiveté and a continuing openness on the therapist's part to being surprised by the dissonance between his or her expectations and perceptions of the client and the actual reality of the other person's unfolding inner life and world. Navigating the bumps and twists and turns that occur from this requires a solid and trustworthy therapeutic alliance built up over time. At the end of his life, the late psychoanalyst Dr. C. G. Jung is said to have remarked that he had started over with each of his patients "as if I knew nothing." This is the attitude and wisdom of one who has come to understand how daunting a task it is to really appreciate the uniqueness of another person, to be able to call them by name while at the same time refraining from tampering with their freedom or abusing the power and privilege of having access to their most intimate parts and treasure house of their souls. This means that the therapist must always avoid shrinking persons to fit psychological diagnoses or developmental ideals that are far more narrow and less life-affirming than those which are part of being created in the divine image and likeness of God, a member of the Body of Christ, and destined for theosis! For this reason, pastoral psychotherapy is also a spiritual discipline. It occurs on holy ground. The encounter changes both therapist and client.

In presenting a portion of the therapeutic journey that Bonnie and I have taken together, I invite the reader to keep in mind that you are seeing only a kind of skeleton or X-ray of a living human document. The person and the relationship are being reduced to a set of actions and words removed from the here-and-now context of voice tones, gestures, and the quality of human presence that gives them their life. This is inevitable and reminds me of the distinction that Eric Fromm made in his classic little book *The Art of Loving*,[2] in which he compares the knowing that comes from examining a dead butterfly pinned to a page with watching the butterfly flitter and flutter among the flowers as a means of getting to know what the essence of the butterfly is.

First, the trustworthy quality of the therapeutic alliance, my interest in Bonnie, and my respect for her freedom are essential elements of the relationship upon which everything else is built. Beyond simply stating this as a proviso, owing to the limitations of space I have not made any literary attempts to try and convey this to the reader. That it exists can, I believe, be surmised on the basis of what follows. I simply remind the reader that the quality of the therapeutic alliance, existing as it does in the larger context of shared Christian faith, is the "cookie dough" in which the "chocolate chips" of any so-called psychological and/or religious interventions adhere.

Second, whatever we may say about diagnosis and the use of psychological labels to describe persons and events – and I will be using these because they are the lingua franca of the profession – it must be remembered that the larger context and most applicable diagnosis is that of being created in the very Image and growing likeness of our common Creator. This fundamental starting point guides what I do in psychotherapy and how I utilize psychological understanding and techniques in my attempts to assist persons in identifying and, when possible, dissolving the obstacles that block their appreciation of their full human life in Christ.

Furthermore, regardless of what I may think is happening or why, *causation* in the field of human relations remains a very nebulous idea – more difficult to pin down than the butterfly. There are simply too many interactive variables. When we add the element of prayer and God's grace, it is almost impossible to know what really has made the difference in alleviating symptoms. I may identify interventions that I think were helpful, but I may be off the mark. Even Bonnie herself may not realize how all the variables stack up. Nevertheless, with these caveats in mind, let me offer my few loaves and fishes, knowing that by

God's grace and blessing they may prove valuable for the readers in stimulating further conversation about the integration of psychotherapy and Orthodox Christian faith.

Three Greek words are used in the gospels to describe our Lord Jesus Christ's healing encounters with others: ἰῶμαι, θεραπεύω, and σώζω. Ἰῶμαι is used when Jesus heals someone's body part in a similar way as might a physician. Θεραπεύω describes healing of the whole body, and σώζω is used when the healing is in a salvational context.[3] These three words, with their respective contexts, remind me that God is present wherever any sort of healing occurs. However, healing has many aspects involving body, soul, and spirit, and these are all distinct though interwoven, just as the persons of the Holy Trinity are distinct yet one.

The domain of pastoral psychotherapy, as a matter of definition involves overlapping but somewhat discrete dimensions of the healing ministry to persons. Sometimes there is healing that does not directly involve salvational elements pertaining to the spirit. Frequently the client is not an Orthodox Christian, as is the case with Bonnie; yet, I hope and believe that the client still benefits from the fact that I am, even though I may not mention Christ at all in what I say. This is true for the field of medicine as well as psychotherapy; however, I believe that it is less problematic for the neurosurgeon who works on my brain if he or she is not an Orthodox Christian than if my pastoral psychotherapist is not a Christian. For neurosurgery, I want a knowledgeable and skilled practitioner. I am not particularly concerned about his or her faith stance. For pastoral psychotherapy, I want a knowledgeable and skilled practitioner who also shares my deepest religious belief and understanding, wherever possible, because we are talking about my *soul*. The following diagram is offered as a heuristic tool to orient the reader to the endeavor of pastoral psychotherapy as I have come to view it.

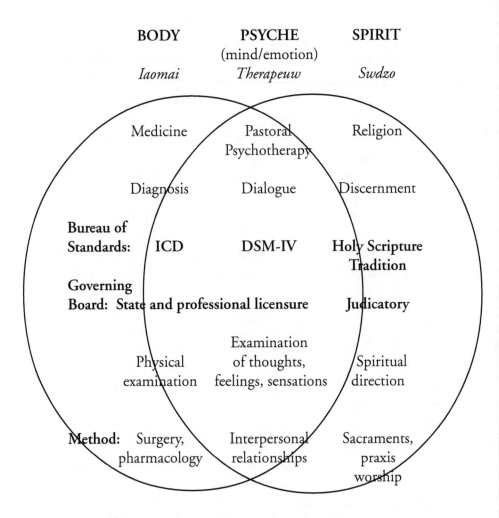

BODY	PSYCHE (mind/emotion)	SPIRIT
Iaomai	*Therapeuw*	*Swdzo*

Medicine — Pastoral Psychotherapy — Religion

Diagnosis — Dialogue — Discernment

Bureau of Standards: ICD   DSM-IV   Holy Scripture Tradition

Governing Board: State and professional licensure   Judicatory

Physical examination — Examination of thoughts, feelings, sensations — Spiritual direction

Method: Surgery, pharmacology — Interpersonal relationships — Sacraments, praxis worship

The lines of the diagram are of necessity elastic, so that the inner circle of overlap that constitutes the field of pastoral psychotherapy can be wider or more narrow at times, depending on the skill and training of the therapist as well as the circumstances, needs, and particular problems of the person(s) seeking help.

Also, the activity of healers working in the domains of body, psyche, and spirit identified in the diagram as separate and distinct are not nearly so distinct in practice as they appear. Human beings are essentially a psychosomatic and spiritual unity, except to the degree that we are divided by sin and unnecessary suffering. For example, a good physician will establish a caring relationship with a patient through appropriate dialogue, just as much as a good pastor will utilize referral of a person to a physician to address physical problems while at the same time utilizing the Sacraments, anointing the person with holy oil, and praying for healing. Likewise, the priest may hear a confession or suggest a particular penance or rule of prayer, and, depending on the factors involved, suggest that a person spend some time in pastoral psychotherapy in order to address related emotional issues that he is not trained to address and/or does not have the time to go into.

All three fields – medicine, psychology, and religion – work together. Another way of representing this is with the symbol of three interlocking circles, as the OCAMPR (Orthodox Christian Association of Medicine, Psychology, and Religion) logo signifies. The dialogue between these three domains is one that neither the Church nor medicine nor psychotherapy can afford to neglect if we are to minister to persons in the most effective ways in the twenty-first century.

Each domain has developed and continues to develop a body of knowledge and understanding of the forces of life that constitute the human being. Each of these bodies of knowledge has something unique to share. We gain most when all three perspectives are considered in partnership and when the aims and methods of medicine and psychotherapy are applied within the larger context of Orthodox faith and life. In any case, human beings are a psychosomatic and spiritual unity, and the treasury of blessings and giver of life in all three domains is the same God from Whom all good gifts come.

For the reader's information, the modern field of pastoral psychotherapy developed under the auspices of the American Association of Pastoral Counseling in the early 1960s. Practitioners were all, at that time, ordained clergy who had advanced degrees in counseling and/or psychology along with having received extensive personal therapy and supervision in order to lessen the chances of intrusion of their own problems and prejudices into the lives of those they work so intimately with. The focus was very clearly and intentionally on the *integration* of psychotherapeutic principles in the context of religious faith and in the personal and professional identity of the pastoral psychotherapist. Thus, the line that divides spiritual direction and counseling, per se, may be seen as even more elastic for pastoral counselors so trained than for secular clinicians without a pastoral identity, background, and/or experience in theological reflection and pastoral care.

This is certainly true for me, having served as an ordained Protestant parish minister for 11 years before my conversion to Orthodoxy. I am comfortable with both my roles as pastor and as psychotherapist. For me they are seamlessly wed. Thus, the more psychologically oriented reader may view my description of the therapy process as me relating to Bonnie as a pastor, while the clergy may notice I am using many psychotherapeutic tools. Medicines also are part of the healing picture, but they are not the focus of this article other than to note which ones have been used and have contributed to her well-being. (It should also be noted that Bonnie had been using medicines for many years without any real change occurring for her in the area of her grief, dissociation, and self-destructive patterns.)

Needless to say, given the constraints of a piece of paper to render a living relationship, and depending on the reader's own theoretical orientation and understanding, numerous questions will arise about why something was or was not done. This is part of the reason for offering the material to the public in order to stimulate dialogue. Bonnie herself has agreed to this and has read all the material before its publication. If she had had any objections to making it public, it would not have been published. I only ask the reader to keep in mind that the following description of almost three years of therapy, condensed as it must be for purposes of brevity, is open to a great deal of distortion. The reader will simply have to take "on faith" that the relationship is a solid one in which Bonnie has been in charge of her process, and any interventions on my part have been suggestions that she was free to reject or receive and that I would respect and modify accordingly.

Also, as the narrative flows, it appears much more orderly and linear than such a relationship actually is. Of necessity, most of the give-and-take that evidences the growth and development of the therapeutic alliance is omitted for brevity's sake. What remains is the skeleton of events that occurred, which point to various aspects of psychological and religious integration that are the subject of our inquiry. For the reader's benefit, I have placed in bold type the interventions that were more explicitly "religious" while offering brief details of the course of content and progress of the therapy so as to give some sense of the context in which they occurred. The reader is instructed not to forget that the interventions noted, in and of themselves, must be assumed to be occurring as suggestions at the appropriate moment in the relationship; otherwise, they might not have been received in the same way. They are specific for Bonnie and are not to be seen as applying in "cookie-cutter style" to others in apparently similar situations. Bonnie's faith is the key ingredient. It makes much possible in this arena that otherwise would not be, and I believe it is in fact her faith that is making her well.

Finally, some counselors are such excellent writers that they can convey a better feel for this than I, but even so, as some of the best material shows,[4] the actual encounter between persons in the presence of God is far more a mystery than we generally appreciate. I hope the reader will not lose sight of this while perusing the X-ray photographs of the following relationship frozen in time. It is offered as a means of furthering the dialogue about the relationship between Orthodox Christian faith and the practice of pastoral psychotherapy in the modern context.

BONNIE

Introduction of the Person

Bonnie is a 38-year-old Caucasian woman, married for 15 years. She and her husband have two children, aged 7 and 5. The older child is adopted. She has a masters degree and is currently assisting in a multistaff pastorate while getting further graduate education. She and her husband explicitly seek out counseling at the Pastoral Institute because of their desire to have a Christian faith-based counselor.

When I first saw her and her husband for the marital consult, Bonnie was feeling overwhelmed by her responsibilities, working in the social services field in a supervisory capacity. She reported increasing depressive mood swings, panic attacks, and binging and purging in the midst of interpersonal tensions with her husband.

Bonnie's face is very expressive of changes in her state of mind. She ranges from relaxed, warm, and open – at least outwardly – to frozen, sullen, frightened, and like the cat that swallowed the mouse. She yearns for love, affection, and affirmation and is tormented by a very controlling, task-oriented, critical, guilt-ridden internal aggressor.

Bonnie reported at the time of our first meeting that for 19 straight years she had suffered binging and purging episodes, beginning since she was raped in her first year of college by an older man who had been something of a father figure for her.

Though controlling the extent of binging and vomiting for short periods of time – weeks and months at best - she had never been able to stop. In addition, she tends to be hospitalized on a regular basis for respiratory illnesses, which recur in association with the stressors. Later it came out "that this is how I get some attention from my husband."

Bonnie's experience of life in her family of origin she describes as part of a family system that drew her close and then shunned her whenever she "didn't behave as the status quo." Her mother is a compulsive eater, weighing over 300 pounds who married her father at age 15; he frequently used to say that he had raised her along with the children. She described her father as harsh, critical, and controlling. He shamed Bonnie into not feeling, and she "grew numb in order not to be abandoned by him." At age 11 she heard him say he "had not wanted any girls." She felt not good enough and sometimes would turn the water in the shower to scalding hot in order to punish herself for being seen as "bad" by her daddy, or for not being trusted by him, or "just to feel something."

Bonnie reports that just as she was starting to get to know her father later, as an adult, he died following severe burns received in a fire. "All the family got to say goodbye to him except for me. By the time I was standing by his bedside, he would not (could not?) respond."

At the time of our first meeting, Bonnie had gained 50 pounds in the previous year and had been binging and purging several times a day for the past four months. She said, "The more weight I gain the more I despise myself."

Bonnie has a history of panic attacks, which she has controlled to some extent by Xanax. At the time of our initial consult, these had been occurring almost daily for the past 18 months.

Because of the multiple problems accumulating for Bonnie, after a few conjoint sessions, we agreed to work individually and save marital work until she was more stable. Her husband, by the way, was more than willing, as he denies his own extensive problems in the area of compulsivity, preferring to keep her the identified patient.

Initial Diagnostic Impressions
Axis I: 307.51 Bulemia Nervosa; 300.01 Panic Disorder w/o

agoraphobia; 296.22 Major Depression, moderate, recurrent, (partial remission); r/o 309.81 PTSD.

Axis II: 799.9 Deferred (note possible Borderline Personality Disorder traits – may be better explained by PTSD).

Axis III: Periodic Migraine Headaches; Recurring pneumonia (currently clear); herniated disk.

Axis IV: Stressors: dual income career couple with two young children; multiple unresolved grief issues (death of four children in childbirth or premature labor; father burned in fire), job stresses (husband's involvement in pornography and his request to wife to seduce another man for him came out later, as did Bonnie's multiple sexual encounters with mentor figures including a rape by the father of a girlfriend whose family she lived with in college at age 19).

Axis V: CGAF: 50 HGAFPY tentatively 60.

Rx: Prozac (changed to Paxil by the psychiatrist I referred her to following intake. Later this was changed to Serzone + Xanax + Ambiens, H.S., PRN).

Course of Therapy

Sessions 1–4: Conjoint with spouse: assessment and establishing boundaries for outpatient therapy; referral to psychiatrist for Rx evaluation and management; discussion of her work responsibilities and personal limits that balance self-care and care for others.

Focus: on job stress, personal limits in terms of energy and keeping healthy boundaries, husband's "guilt" for not being able to save her from her depression, Bonnie's increasing suicidal ideation.

Sessions 5–6: Grief over deaths of four children in childbirth and/or premature labor. Bonnie feels "daddy took them." She reports she is collecting pills to take in case it "becomes too much for me. "Suicide is something I can control. That's why it's attractive." She agrees to turn the pills over to me to keep. (She refused to allow anyone else to have them.)

Religious intervention: Bonnie says she feels close to Jesus, who was "abandoned by God," but not to the Father, "who caused my children to die." I gave her an icon of Christ being taken down from the cross. (She wept as she held it in her hands.)

Focus: Discussion of God's humanity and compassion – suffering with us. Bonnie says, "For the first time since coming here I can say that I want to feel better."

Sessions 7–11: Bonnie makes the decision to resign her job. There is a fear of opening up old wounds: "I'm afraid I will hurt so bad that I want to die, and I don't want to die!" Her husband "has other things to do." Bonnie says, "You see, when I get better he abandons me!" She tells me, "You have helped me look at my relationship with God the Father, but what you don't realize is that the closer I get to this the more I want to die to be with God and be away from the hurt." I responded, "Murder is not the way to God."

Religious intervention: I reframe her pain in terms of "dying before you die," suggesting that she is holding on to her pain as if it were God – defining herself in terms of her suffering. This clicks with her. I suggest that she pray the Lord's Prayer and Psalm 23 on the way home (more than an hour's drive), asking God to help her where she cannot help herself. This begins to prepare the ground, psychologically, for her Christian faith as the primary arena of her healing, with her faith as a "transitional object."

Sessions 12–14: "Pain has been my God. I am less suicidal now, but my arms ache (as they had when she lost her children)." I placed a teddy bear on the sofa beside her. She did some grief work, and we reviewed a picture album of her children. During this time, her best friend dies suddenly, leaving two children.

Religious intervention: I gave her an article I had written on the death of our 6-year-old, entitled, "Dear Jesus Why Did our Child Have to Die?[5] It was originally delivered as a sermon, dealing with anger with God and reconciliation in a personal, autobiographical way.

Sessions 15–17: Bonnie identifies the relational pattern in her marriage: "He loves me when I'm sick, and when I'm better he eats and plays with our son and works." The focus is on Bonnie developing her own life. Suicidal thoughts reoccur after she receives a Christmas card from the man who raped her. She talks more about the rape.

Religious intervention: Self-assigned – Listening to Christian music, "praise tapes," after the session on the way home.

Sessions 18–19: Began EMDR work.[6] Bonnie relives age 9 with her father: hyperventilation, nausea, feeling rejected, arms hurting as when losing her children. Her positive cognition is "I am a worthwhile person," and she utilizes holding the bear and talking to the bear as her 9-year-old self, from her adult part. Laughter is interspersed with pain. She felt much better during the week. Focus is on her attitude: "I don't care if you don't love me; just hold me." She returns to the death of her babies: "My daddy is killing my babies."

Religious intervention: Ended EMDR with intentional awareness of Jesus present with her as a means of recontextualizing her pain and memory with her faith, as well as trusting safe relationship in therapy in the here and now.

Session 20: Bonnie had contact with her mother, who told her "You turned on your father, and I guess I'm next." She experiences binging and purging five times during the week. "I can't blame my parents so I have to blame myself." She feels abandoned by her husband. There is more dissociation, binging.

Religious intervention: I suggest, "Every sin is against the Lord and hurts all of us." "Checkmate," she replies. This interaction had to do with Bonnie assuming responsibility for herself and her actions now, even though earlier in life she had not been able to because of the power differential and developmental stages inherent to her childhood relationship with parents. She was then indeed a victim.

Introduction of the idea of a "prayer bear," keeping a log of her binges, and "eating only enough to have some pleasure but stopping in order "to protect the bear" from any further self-hatred or abuse. This draws on the executive functions of Bonnie's adult ego to help her reparent her wounded child and be responsible for providing healthy nurture and boundaries for herself.

Session 21: Bonnie tells me, "I have to be honest with you. I have counted out all my pills. I can't take it any more."

This is a reaction to perceived abandonment by her husband and not being able to control the binging, fear of therapy being cut off because of managed care pressure, and consequent anger with me as potentially another abandonment in her life. Bonnie dissociates in the room. I ask her about it. "I'm leaving you." I process her anger with her and tell her, "I can't work with you in outpatient therapy if you need inpatient care because you are unstable and actively suicidal." She agrees to bring the pills she's collected. I ask for her husband to accompany her next time to enlist his support.

Session 22: Collateral consult with spouse for support.

Sessions 23–25: More EMDR work; scene of infants' death; hyperventilation, nausea, despair. She reports that her husband is more supportive now. She visits the scene of her father's death and her anger: weeping, gritting teeth, hyperventilation.

Religious intervention: Ended session with imaging Jesus present with her in the room with her father. Theologically, she wrestled with "God the Father, who could have saved my babies," and Jesus, who suffers with her. Again, this is an attempt to draw on the ego strength associated with her faith and to recontextualize her pain.

Session 26: Bonnie reports she got an "A" in her first counseling class. She identifies the sequence of acting out: "I feel empty. I eat. I purge. I cry. I feel better." She has memories of her father spanking her so hard up and down her back that he left handprints all over her. He also shamed and bullied her into not expressing feelings.

Session 27: She reports four days without sleeping medication. There are fears of being alone, and her arms are hurting.

Religious intervention: I suggested she receive the Lord's supper daily through Easter and use psalms and prayers to replace thoughts and impulses to fill emptiness with food. Emptiness is to be filled only by the Eucharist. I give her some incense to burn and remind her that she is taking nourishment by way of her breath from God's spirit and in her mind feeding on God's word. She is to accept this as sufficient for her, no matter what, for the duration of one week. (Tears: "I want this so very much!")

Session 28: Bonnie is tearful most of the session. She reports having a panic attack in a traffic jam, preventing her from reaching school on time. Then she came home to a dark house (abandonment, uncared-for) with husband already asleep. She brought pictures of her dead child but was afraid to show me "because no one takes it seriously."

Religious intervention: She had not waited for Easter week to receive the Eucharist, as I'd instructed, but immediately began receiving it when she went home. "I was looking for magic and it didn't work." I suggested by way of a story and reframing that Bonnie was trying to do things herself rather than trust in God to help her. I called this making "sorcery" of religion, in which the self was still attempting to be in control (which is central to addiction.) This was aimed to interrupt her intense, perfectionistic, self-blaming side that punishes her for not being able to control her victimization or her father's rejection of her.

Session 29: We make a review of Bonnie's progress to date: decrease in suicidality and interpersonal manipulation while being able to bear greater emotional intensity. I affirmed my willingness to continue with her even if insurance denies further sessions.

Session 30: EMDR session targets the rape. Bonnie hyperventilates, experiences rage and resignation at penetration, which she feels as the same experience as resignation at gaining 30 pounds. She relives the sensory details. She reports that sexuality with her spouse occurs through the lenses "either of rape or of my father taking my babies out of me." There is always an undercurrent of anger and/or victimization. Bonnie's biological feeling-memory is a conflation of three images: "father spanking me for a mushroom I didn't eat and not believing me, the man who raped me not believing I was a virgin, and the man (whom her spouse asked her to seduce) not believing that my husband asked me to do it." There is intense anger, powerlessness, and grief over her father's death.

Religious intervention: I pray the Jesus prayer out loud for Bonnie during her EMDR session. (She is weeping.)

Session 31: Bonnie informs me, "When you were praying the Jesus Prayer out loud for me, it was nothing short of miraculous (tears)." She reports that she felt release of shame and a sense of God's presence. She reports growth in her prayer life and recognition of Christianity as her primary therapy. "You have been my pastor for the past eight months, and that is what I have needed."

Session 32: Four days go by without binging-purging, and then, with news of the doctor being unable to help her back pain unless she loses weight, she "knew I was going to binge when I got home."

Religious intervention: I give her material on "formation of passions" from a synthesis of the teachings of the Philokalia[7] regarding stages of linking of attention with suggestions. I suggest she is "going to vomiting as to her lover (and god), for the release of tenderness involved."

Session 33: Bonnie tells me, "I was angry with you last session over something you said that really struck home, and I haven't vomited for 17 days. ("She has gone to vomiting as to tenderness," etc.) She says she has found tenderness and trust in God the Father again, and a sense of spaciousness in her life, interrupting the drivenness of the "gospel of perfection" that had been terrorizing her.

Religious intervention: She is ready now to follow up on the suggestion that she get spiritual direction, and she will make arrangements to begin seeing Fr. B. for this.

Session 34: Still no vomiting. She is using the Jesus prayer to cut off thoughts and as prevention of "abandonment" fears.

Session 35: Bonnie's face is shining, and her affect is bright, as in the previous session. She had her first contact with Fr. B for her spiritual direction, and she reports it went well.

Religious intervention: She is reading books appropriate for her; experimenting with fasting in the context of spiritual discipline and growing in her appreciation for the "mystery" of the faith. She is viewing herself more as "defined by God" in contrast to others around her or to clinging to her past. Used EMDR to lay down positive track of a new sense of trust in God over primary traumas.

Session 36–38: Bonnie brought pictures of her dead children with her, and we went through her photograph album. She worked with EMDR. Still no vomiting.

Religious intervention: She is reading a book on fasting and the Jesus prayer. I lent her *Youth of the Apocalypse* [8] and *Beloved Sufferer.* [9]

Session 39: I asked for a collateral consult with Bonnie's spouse in order to make a referral to begin marital therapy. Bonnie's fears of abandonment resurface. Her face is visibly changed during the session to an expression I haven't seen since she first came.

Session 40: Her abandonment feelings have returned. "I'm trapped and just want out of the marriage." She has a fear of decompensation and relapse if she begins to confront the marriage problems. She is still feeling punitive toward herself for having reached out to touch me in a previous session as she was leaving. (I had brought this up to process with her the following session.) This connects with not forgiving herself for having become sexual in relationships with men she had been seeking fathering from in the past. She fears I will blame her and reject her. I offer reassurance of care and professional boundaries, etc.

We again assess the supports in place in her life now: her growing prayer life, spiritual direction relationship, church work, her successful school work and new career direction, love for her children, regular exercise. She agreed that these were true, "now that you point them out," but felt paralyzed by the thought of losing our relationship. I was going on vacation for a week, and there were no appointment vacancies the week after except at 5 P. M. I told her she could have that, or a morning in three weeks. The session was 10 minutes over already, which was unusual. She was upset and would not choose, so I said, "I will choose for you, then. I choose three weeks, because I believe in your strength and ability to care for yourself."

Session 41: Bonnie reports that she binged on the way home from the previous session, but with no vomiting. She says she hasn't dealt with her sexuality yet and is not ready to terminate. She reported other sexual relationships she hadn't talked about and said that touching my hand and her subsequent feelings had elicited a flood of memories of her father blaming her for wearing makeup, and she felt I was rejecting her for her "bad" desire for closeness and the guilt she feels for her sexualized relationships. "As long as I can count on you not abandoning me, I think biweekly sessions will work."

Sessions 42–45: Stable mood. Still no vomiting. Good developing contact with spiritual director, who is also helping her with the Eucharist and fasting in the context of God's leading gently rather than a compulsive desire for perfection. EMDR focus is on sexual encounters: self-blame vs. victimization. Her mood is more stable.

Religious intervention: Letting go of rule-conscious urgency and enjoying more freedom. I recommend *Beginning to Pray*.[10]

Session 46: Bonnie reports that one of her church mentors, the chairman of the pastor search committee that was considering her husband for a position, "kissed me on the lips after stopping by the church." Her husband saw it and said nothing. I asked about this in context of her husband's earlier asking her to seduce one of his friends "who needed comfort." She responds, "I had always blamed myself for that until you brought it up when he was here. He was angry about it."

Religious intervention: I suggest that Bonnie pray the Jesus prayer from the place in her where she "cannot love my fat 10-year-old self."

Session 47: She had a panic attack and sleep disturbance. She relates this to praying the Jesus prayer at the point of her rejection of the inner "fat" child, but she feels good that she was able to do this without falling into old self-destructive habits. We worked with EMDR around the scalding shower scene, which she connected with binging and purging.

Religious intervention: I suggested that she let all physical pain convert to emotional pain and feel it in her heart so Jesus can help her. Deep attentive breathing begins while she is saying the Jesus prayer. She wept while I prayed Psalm 23 out loud during EMDR. Bonnie inhales sweet Jerusalem incense during EMDR and laughs as she reports that "the scalding water turned into a bubble bath, and Jesus was present." We both laugh as she relates this. The session ended with her "inner little girl" feeling loved.

At the end of this session I broke off a piece of my African milk plant and suggested that it was prickly outside but full of life within, and that if given the right conditions it would grow. It would shrivel a little at first because of being in a new environment, etc. (This transitional object is alive and represents her growth and acceptance of her "prickly" parts. It is also an extension of the feeling and reality of the therapeutic relationship that Bonnie is internalizing, and carries with it the implication of her responsibility to care for her own life by drawing on her desire to care for others.)

Session 48: Bonnie reports that she stopped at church on the way home from last session, prayed, and felt Jesus healing parts of her she had not let in before. "Then I received the phone call from (spouse's) father being sexually inappropriate, as he has been in the past." She hadn't talked about this before. She reports he has touched her before inappropriately. Husband doesn't know. "What do I do to cause this kind of thing to happen?" She reports her mother lost 150 pounds after her father's death and then gained it back after a man at work came on to her. She later told Bonnie the weight was for "protection."

Sessions 49: Bonnie reports a terrible binge. She was curled up in the fetal position with the urge to vomit. She began the Jesus prayer, and it went away. "When I have sex with my husband I say the Jesus prayer, but I am somewhere else. Is this right?"

Religious intervention: I tell her I do not know the answer about her use of the Jesus prayer in the sexual context with her husband. We talk about it, and I give her Mother Alexandria's commentary on the Jesus prayer[11] to read and suggest that she discuss this with her spiritual father.

Session 50–52: Bonnie begins to work more definitely around sexuality: "I have never had a loving, nonanxious sexual encounter. My sister at 14 had sex with the youth pastor in our house. My father found out. I began to try to be in control of men (by tempting them) the way they had been in control of me. I married to avoid being alone." She reports that her husband is not present in the sexual act, and neither is she.

Religious intervention: I gave her Thomas Hopko's article on forgiveness and feelings when trauma is involved.[12]

Critical Incident

Bonnie calls in tears to report she has been sexually assaulted in her home by a former student

Session 53: Bonnie is numb: "I shut everything off." She brought a drawing with her of the man and faulted herself for letting him in the door. Later that same week, she had to see her husband's father at an event, and he sexually came on to her. She vomited (not deliberate purging but because of nausea).

She reports she left for a couple days with a bottle of pills and prayed and wept. "I took the icon of Christ you gave me. It was a spiritual battle inside between life and death. I chose life." She threw me the bottle of pills. "You can have these. I had just decided to address how messed up I am in the area of sexuality, and then this happened. Now I just want to run away and not have to deal with sex."

Sessions 54–56: Bonnie reports, "I haven't binged or purged, but now for the first time in my life I want to cut myself." We debrief the sexual assault. Her face has the flicker of a sardonic smile that hasn't been present in months. She is dissociated, removed from her pain, not sleeping well. Her arms are hurting again. Police investigation stirs up her emotions. EMDR: safety with the Jesus prayer. Husband is asking for all the details; she is disgusted, thinking of his pornography addiction. Bonnie's legs are jumping, hyperventilation, flashbacks to previous sexual assaults, suicidal darkness. Panic. I tell her, "It is not God's will for you to die." As in previous sessions when she is upset, we use guided relaxation, movement, or other techniques to help her shift her awareness from the painful places before she leaves the session.

Session 57: Collateral consultation with spouse to enlist his support. He wants to help. I tell him he can help by throwing out all his pornography to help his wife see she is not a mere object to him. He agrees.

Session 58: Bonnie is doing much better. Lots of rage emerged, but she went to a church music workshop with "two hundred people who love God," and she says she was "bathed by God's forgiveness."

Session 59: The perpetrator's mother, a member of the church, is questioning Bonnie about the assault and validating her. Her husband is not following through with his promise to discard the pornography. All the men have made excuses, like the perpetrator, who told her, "I saw the outline of your breast," and thus his attack was "her fault" for being a woman.

Session 60–61: Bonnie gives me copy of H. Nouwen's *Here*

and Now.[13] She is finding a new source of strength in her Christian faith.

Session 62: We resume EMDR, targeting the binging and the conflict between "good and bad." Bonnie experiences a sensation of nausea at men not listening to her, beginning with her father and the men who raped her or coerced sex from her. She wanted relationships, not sex. There is a sense of emptiness. "I eat to fill the emptiness created by the lack of relationships."

Sessions 63–64: Bonnie fears, "If I am truly forgiven by Christ and my faith grows, I will no longer love my husband." I respond, "Christ loves the world through us, and if you feel loved by Christ you will have more capacity for love." EMDR focus is on grief – dead babies and rapes.

Session 65: Bonnie is afraid of relapsing into major depression. "I fear if I have another major depression I won't have the strength to get out." Her panic attacks return "out of nowhere."

Religious intervention: I ask her to describe the inner territory where she deals with suggestions coming into her mind, and she has a moment of relief when she realizes that the Jesus prayer "is not like an ember, but a little flame now in my life, and that is the major difference from how I was before. I trust the love of the Father, and I couldn't before."

Session 66-69: Bonnie's spouse still hasn't kept his promise to give up the pornography. I recommend that she read *An Affair of the Mind*.[14] Bonnie struggles over the book and initial anger "that I have to be responsible for his problem!" She works through this and struggles for clarity about the difference between self-blame and self-responsibility, and setting appropriate limits in relationship with husband's pornography addiction as it parallels her relationship in the rapes. "Who is responsible?" She wants to "put my head in the sand and ignore it. Why do I have to be responsible for him?" Work on distinguishing responsibility from need to honor and protect her own boundaries.

Session 70: Her perpetrator is leaving phone messages on her phone. Her car hydroplaned into a ditch along with a truck and sank. She said she was "collecting pills again." "I hoped it would go away. I didn't want to disappoint you. I didn't want to admit I was going backwards." There is a sense of having no control in her life.

Sessions 71–75: More EMDR: working through sexual assault and related themes

Religious intervention: I remind her that Christ refused medication on the cross, suggesting that opening her eyes and being present to her pain without loss of faith in God is a metaphor for continuing grief work until she is finished.

Session 76: Bonnie is aware of her deepened capacity to experience pain and can acknowledge that as true without falling prey to binging/purging. Her weight is slowly coming off. Panic attacks are under control. Major depression is no longer in evidence. Transferential elements of borderline personality spectrum related to abandonment themes emerge briefly from time to time, and the therapeutic alliance is such that these are confronted and discussed. I tell her, "I'm the junior therapist. God is your primary therapist."

Current Diagnostic Picture

Axis I: 307.51 Bulimia Nervosa (binging in partial remission; no purging x 2 years); 300.01 Panic Disorder w/o agoraphobia (in remission); 296.22 Major Depression, moderate recurrent (in remission); 309.81 PTSD (partial remission).

Axis II: (Borderline Personality Disorder organization) – mood is more stable with increased capacity for direct experience and articulation of feeling w/o acting out.

Axis III: Hx of migraine headaches and frequent pneumonia (clear x 2 years).

Axis IV: Stressors: multiple grief issues from family of origin to current, as noted, plus sexual assault by former student 8 months ago in her own house, marital problems (husband's involvement in pornography and poor boundaries).

Axis V: CGAF: 68 HGAFPY 60

Current Rx: Zoloft and Serzone concurrently + Xanax TID.

Bonnie continues in therapy at the time of this writing and continues to improve. We have used her reading of this material as part of her therapy process, examining feelings elicited as she has read about herself, seeing everything "condensed into black and white." Because of her training as a therapist, she is able to use it both from a personal standpoint and with some professional interest in the process that helps her understand and grow. It has helped her weave together with greater understanding some of the "compartmentalized" aspects of her history. We agreed beforehand that none of the material would be used if either of us had any doubt about its usefulness to her therapeutically.

ISSUES FOR REFLECTION

I have presented this sketch of a working pastoral psychotherapy relationship as a means of stimulating dialogue about the integration of psychotherapy and Orthodox Christian faith. As I read it, several areas stand out for me as places for further discussion with regard to the larger issues of discernment, diagnosis, timing, and so forth that inform the interventions. I am only going to comment briefly on some of the themes that emerge, as these have been discussed ably and in some depth by Markos Nickolas in his response.

Physical Setting and Context of Therapy

It is not without significance that the counseling relationship occurs at the Pastoral Institute, an interdenominational counseling center and training institute that is explicitly Judeo-Christian in orientation, although we work with persons of all faiths or no faith, including Hindu, Moslem, Jewish, atheist, and Wiccan.

A large icon of Christ Pantokrator hangs on the wall of my office. St. Joseph, St. Seraphim of Sarov, the Holy Theotokos, the Stoning of St. Stephen, Sts. Cosmos and Damian, the Last Supper, and the Holy Transfiguration are some of the other icons participating in therapy silently from various points in my office. Projections are made on to them from time to time, and these are part of the discussion of the therapy. Frequently there is the smell of incense in the air from my daily morning preparation before I see my clients. As in the Divine Liturgy, the witness of the saints and the ambience of the setting are conducive to responding with attention to the presence of oneself with others in the presence of God. This same context, I believe, is the most appropriate one for psychotherapeutic healing, because it points to the larger web of relationships in which the therapeutic alliance exists. In some ways, this is even more potent for persons like Bonnie who have not grown up with such symbols, so they are a fresh and vivid witness.

Bibliotherapy

Books provide an ongoing contact in the form of a transitional object that links the client's reading of the material with the therapeutic relationship, which is gradually internalized, adding stability to the sense of self. This material offers valuable reframing and instruction beyond what is given in the session, particularly related to assisting in the client's faith journey and broadening the "cloud of witnesses" who may offer sustenance for the continuing journey.

These readings are selected specifically for the person and her circumstances in light of where she appears to be in the journey. To the degree that they are timely and are received by the person as a further extension of the care and specificity of her therapy process, they provide important follow-up to the work done in therapy as well as a means of self-soothing and additional support during post-session periods. This also encourages the person to reflect and integrate material that is surfacing in therapy through the perspectives offered in the books, which frequently point to the faith journey as the primary arena for healing.

Prayer

This occurs in many ways. The therapist prays for clients before the sessions and sometimes afterward. In addition, there may be prayer during sessions. With Bonnie, prayer sometimes occurred during her EMDR sequences. Initially, praying the Jesus prayer out loud for her was a spontaneous action; later, it was requested by Bonnie. Sometimes Psalm 23 was used. Occasionally I invite persons to pray a selected psalm out loud in a session in order to elicit feelings in the relational context with God. Tears and remembrance of injury in the presence of God and the witness of the saints who have also felt such pain is more healing than tears that are cried alone.

Sometimes prayer occurs before an EMDR session. Frequently I pray the Jesus prayer silently, and generally I use the prayer rope during therapy sessions, dividing my attention at times between the person's words and my prayer for them as well as to my own presence engaging them.

Bonnie also uses the Jesus prayer continuously following her sessions on her drive home. A "prayer bear" was used for gestalt and inner child work in the session to help Bonnie get a tangible sense of the victimized, injured part of her inner world and make her care for herself and her prayer for herself tangible emotionally and physically. It helps engage her "adult mind" to care for the dissociated wounded part of her that has been too painful to allow into experience along with the attached irrational self-representations.

Bonnie got herself a "prayer bear" for holding in bed when she feels alone at night while she prays, remembering the "inner child" who needs God's love and her good parenting. It is a tangible means of expression that allows the senses and feeling to connect with the remembrance of suffering while allowing the adult mind to care for the wounded part of the self in ways that she did not have at the time of the injury.

Eucharist

I suggested that Bonnie receive the Eucharist (Lord's Supper in her context) daily during the week of her Easter. I tried to help her frame the feelings of physical emptiness in the context of the fullness of God's gifts in the place of other food. Framing this in the context of emptiness as preparation for fullness and connection, rather than reiteration of loss and abandonment, was designed to draw on her strong faith orientation, which is heightened during the celebration of Easter week, to help her heal a dismembered part of herself and begin to recover from her bulimia. I wanted her to recontextualize the feeling of emptiness that was a trigger for self-abuse.

The cycle of the Church year – its feast and fast days and the activities of fasting, almsgiving, confession, and so forth – are extremely important means of healing. They are further vivified when entered into in conjunction with one's psychotherapy process. There is a cross-fertilization that occurs between the spiritual direction, worship, and pastoral psychotherapy journey that persons take. I believe Bonnie's journey is strong testimony of this even though she is not Orthodox, but she benefits from the Orthodox context, which still has much to offer her.

Incense

The sense of smell is powerfully connected to our feeling life and our early memories. This was utilized intentionally on one occasion during an EMDR sequence related to Bonnie's memory of taking the hot scalding shower as punishment. She said the scene "turned into a bubble bath" at the moment she smelled the incense. I subsequently gave her a piece of incense to light during a difficult time, which again served as a transitional object to help stretch therapy beyond the session as preparation for "referral to God" for ongoing care and healing. I hoped she would receive a palpable sense of the presence of God during prayer and "fill" her inner emptiness with a sense of God's presence through the tangible inhaling of the sweet incense.

Re-membering in Context of Biblical narratives

When persons are traumatized, a dismemberment occurs in the psyche. We are cut off from parts of ourselves, particularly between mind, body, and feelings, and from the community at large. This is frequently accompanied by a sense of not being loved by God, as was the case with Bonnie. Remembering is the work of therapy, and it occurs within the body in the context of a beloved relationship through encountering missing links between sensations, feelings, and thoughts that are painful and were forced into the unconscious in order to allow the person to survive. From that "wilderness place" split off from consciousness, these feelings and conflicts create moods and compulsive acting out, which in turn continue the person's victimization with increasing anger, grief, and hopelessness and a host of PTSD symptoms, including depression and compulsive addictive self-medicating to achieve psychic numbing.

In working through memories, biblical stories prove useful as narrative therapeutic interventions. Jacob wrestling with the angel and walking away a new person with a limp as evidence of his struggle; the renewal motif in Joseph's painful initial journey; the renewal experienced by the woman at the well; the woman caught in adultery; the woman with the hemorrhage – all at one point or another in our work together offered valuable healing lenses to make new meaning out of Bonnie's suffering.

Bonnie re-members her pain in the presence of a trusting relationship with a man, where the boundaries are increasingly experienced as safe for her to feel, in contrast to her previous history with her father. When this occurs explicitly in the larger context of her Christian faith (and mine) with hope in God's eternal love, it recontextualizes those past events so that the emotions can be named and discharged through her body without fear of being overwhelmed. They can be re-membered, and meaning can be extracted from them that enhances the sense of control in her life as well as confirms a sense of her belovedness.

God's presence is made more tangible via the therapist (as is the case with the priest in confession). Her faith in God is strengthened simultaneously.

Confession

Existentially (in contrast to sacramentally) this occurs within many of the sessions. Bonnie is explicit at times in asking for this. Sometimes this occurs as the therapist prays "May God forgive you" or in the Jesus prayer during an EMDR session as Bonnie "confesses" by way of her own internal memory without speaking outwardly.

This also occurs in a more formal way in the context of her relationship with the priest who is her spiritual director (for example, her responsibility as an adult for not telling her husband "no" when he invited her to have sex with his friend).

Spiritual Direction

This is a frequent and important adjunct to therapy (or vice versa). Pastoral psychotherapy and spiritual direction frequently overlap, but they are different functions. In Bonnie's case, the referral is to an older priest with experience in contemplative methods and spiritual direction. It serves to expand her support network and to prepare for our eventual termination of formal psychotherapy. She will then continue in her Christian faith as her "primary psychotherapy for the rest of her life." Ultimately, this is the task of pastoral psychotherapy as I understand it: to help others become able to enter freely with intention, responsibility, and joy into their respective faith journeys, which are in essence designed to heal the human soul and complete our development.

Spiritual Retreat

This is an area that provides needed boosts at important times. Bonnie gained a great deal from attending a short retreat on Church music. I have at times suggested that clients pray at the tombs of saints in locations they have visited, which has been very beneficial, or to go to a monastery for several days of retreat. Later, the experiences are discussed and further suggestions are offered.

Discernment

Discernment comes from the Latin word *cernere*, to "sift apart" or "select." It refers to the theological arena having to do with human responsibility in light of the presence of God, the condition of the *nous,* and the inclinations of the will toward good and evil. In the context of pastoral psychotherapy, discernment has an important role, along with diagnosis, as part of the progress of distinguishing or "sifting apart" the symptomatic characteristics of trauma and psychological illness from the effects of actively participating in the evil of continuing to choose self-destructive patterns to the extent that one becomes capable of doing otherwise. The former is a sickness, while the latter can involve sin. Frequently, as in Bonnie's case, they are woven together like the tares and wheat.

For example, fornication, despondency, and rancor are words drawn from the language of discernment and spiritual warfare. Drawing on the patristic experience regarding suggestions and the movement of the attention and will, Bonnie is offered a valuable means of beginning to train herself in self-observation of her inner world in order to discern the intent of various motivations. She begins to distinguish what she is responsible for and what she is not, what is a healthy direction and what is not.

Bonnie first developed her habit of purging after her friend's father sexualized his relationship with her while she was in college. She had dissociated when he first fondled her, feeling confused and fearing abandonment if she protested. Immediately after the experience, she vomited spontaneously. Subsequently, she developed a bulimic pattern, which became a means of acting out the dissociated split-off feelings of fear, anger, repulsion, and shame, in effect continuing the revictimization of herself at the psychological level.

This was all hidden behind the mask of "tenderness and surrender" that began to collect around the act of vomiting which soothed her by releasing a flood of endorphins and keeping the underlying feelings hidden. I used the metaphor of the serpent in Genesis offering to the soul that which is already given by God: "It seems you believe the lie that you can only have tenderness and surrender and comfort by making yourself vomit. This lie hides the ugly nature of the acting out of self-hatred, guilt, and anguish." There was also the parallel, in her eating and vomiting, of the premature births/deaths of her children. She said, "I don't deserve to have live babies. I can't finish anything. That which is given is always taken away." So she continued to punish herself inappropriately and blame God for it. Even after much previous therapy, Bonnie stopped vomiting for the first time in 19 years only after she recognized the "lie" that was involved in this. It was a major step in reclaiming responsibility for her actions as well as an act of trust and faith in God to care for her even when she felt "bad."

Intentionally letting go of old defenses that were once partially protective, but later become a burden, is an important act of responsibility, which the adult victim of trauma must eventually come to. Bonnie was not responsible for her original victimization, but at some point, she, like each of us however we may have been wounded in the past through no fault of our own, is responsible for stopping her revictimization at the psychological level. This involves identifying the moods and underlying feelings that generate the acting out or that activate the defenses that protect the psyche like an anesthesia, but do not empower the executive ego to act in ways that protect the whole person from danger.

This is the arena of spiritual warfare with the passions that tend to develop around such injuries and block access to God and the larger community. Getting at this requires both diagnosis and discernment, for the "wheat and tares" of victimization and responsibility for one's actions are mixed together. The grace of God, working in concert with human attentiveness and recognition, must heal the *nous*. It is critical not to "blame the victim," but it is equally important not to miss the task of empowering the adult survivor who gradually grows into a position to begin to reclaim her life from the powers that have held her back for so long, to become responsible for her own protection in effective ways that are now possible for her, and to trust God in the rest.

This is a very important aspect of the pastoral psychotherapy process, because beguilement (or "prelest," the term used by the early Fathers) often is part of the process that keeps persons enslaved to self-destructive actions. Bonnie's mentors sexualized their relationships with her out of their own needs. Her fear of abandonment left her vulnerable to this. Dissociation protected her from being overwhelmed at the time, but dissociation is essentially an unconscious automatic protective mechanism of trance that divides the *nous*. As she becomes aware of how this functions in her life, she sees that it leaves her vulnerable to further exploitation. Thus, she gradually becomes responsible for protecting herself in more effective ways. This means confronting her abandonment fears and identifying how dissociation works and what motivations she is conscious of that collaborate with it – such as anger with self, despair, and so forth. As her faith in God's love increases, Bonnie's fear of abandonment decreases, and assertiveness becomes possible because she begins to trust that God will not abandon her. The therapeutic alliance helps to offer a concrete here-and-now representation of this along the way until she has internalized this in a way that makes it her own.

Bonnie is able to claim for herself that she never wanted sex from the men, only their genuine interest in her as a person, but her fear of losing them and her previous history left her too afraid of abandonment to assert her needed limits strongly enough to be heard and respected. This has lessened the degree of self-hatred she has experienced. Nevertheless, the process of disentangling the symptoms of the initial victimization and her subsequent responsibility for allowing victimization to continue is a delicate one. The emotions this stirs have reoccurred over time as Bonnie has begun to identify her boundaries and has become able to actively protect them.

She blamed herself inappropriately for things she as a child was not responsible for, and she took into herself the disappointment and anger associated with her relationship with an emotionally abusive father and an unavailable mother. These conditions of her family of origin distorted her sense of her own value and responsibility for protecting that value as an adult. On the other hand, it is also the material God has allowed in her life that becomes the "Joseph journey" we all take in one way or another, and, by the grace of God, either are reborn through the process of abiding in faith along the way, or are lost to fate in the jaws of faithlessness.

For years, Bonnie had trouble allowing herself to be responsible as an adult for some actions that were self-abusive and continued her victimization, like her bulimia. In fact, she hated herself more for not being able to "control it" consciously, while unconsciously it was partly protective and partly a confirmation of her lack of value. Diagnosis and discernment around these issues, that occurs in the context of sensitive, ongoing, caring dialogue that allows her freedom to express her confusion, anger, self-doubt, rage, grief, and fear, are vitally important in midwifing the birth of a new being in Christ. This is the birth of one whose identity is defined no longer by previous victimization but by trust in the reality of her self, who is hid with Christ in God.

Finally, the question of whether in suffering Bonnie has drawn closer in faith to Christ, during the almost three years of her psychotherapy, can be answered with a most definite "Yes!" This is, I believe, the fundamental reason for the good direction of her healing journey. Christian faith has been the primary context for both Bonnie and me as we have engaged in this Emmaus walk together. We both acknowledge that whatever interventions, quality of presence, personal faith, and so forth have contributed to the process are testimony to the one thing we can be certain of: It is by the Grace of God that good has prevailed, and it is her faith that is making her well. In sharing this Emmaus journey together, we both encounter a sense of the Holy God emerging with fresh visage in the midst of hearts that burn with a new sense of the mystery of God's love for a fragile and sometimes bitter creation.

NOTES

[1] Abbess Michaela. "Hope in the Fields of Kosovo," *The Orthodox Word*, No. 205, p.57.

[2] Fromm, E. *The Art of Loving*. New York: Harper & Row Publishers, Inc., 1956.

[3] Rev. John Sanford pointed this out in a lecture given at Loyola College Pastoral Counseling Department in Maryland, October 1990.

[4] E.g. Yalom, I. *Love's Executioner: And Other Tales of Psychotherapy*, New York: HarperCollins, 1989.

[5] Muse, S. "Dear Jesus Why Did Our Child Have to Die?" *The Pastoral Forum*, 1995, Vol 13, No.2, pp.4-6.

[6] Shapiro, F. *Eye Movement Desensitization and Reprocessing*. New York: GuilfordPress, 1995. This is a powerful method of rapidly processing trauma and grief that proved very useful with Bonnie. It is highly person-centered and relatively free of interpretive overlays. The person re-experiences his or her pain and conflicts in a safe environment with a high degree of inner attention to the links between sensation, feelings, and thoughts.

[7] Kadloubovsky, E. and Palmer, G.E.H. *Writings from the Philokalia on Prayer of the Heart*, London: Faber & Faber, 1975.

[8] Marler, J. and Wermuth, A. *Youth of the Apocalypse*, Alaska: St. Herman of Alaska Brotherhood, 1995, pp. 168-188.

[9] Durasov, G. *Beloved Sufferer: The Life and Mystical Revelations of a Russian Eldress: Schemanun Macaria*, Alaska: St. Herman Brotherhood Press, 1997.

[10] Bloom, A. *Beginning to Pray*, New York: Paulist Press, 1970.

[11] Alexandra, M. "Conference of Mother Alexandra" in Bolshakoff, S. & Pennington, B. *In Search of True Wisdom*, New York: Alba House, 1991, pp.164-169.

[12] Hopko, T. "Living in Communion: An interview with Father Thomas Hopko." In *Parabola,* Vol (1987)11.3, pp. 50-59.

[13] Nouwen, J. M. *Here and Now: Living in the Spirit,* New York: Crossroad Publishing Company, 1997.

[14] Hall, L. *An Affair of the Mind: One Woman's Courageous Battle to Salvage her Family From the Devastation of Pornography,* New York: Tyndale House Publishers, 1996.

A Response to Muse

Markos Achilles Nickolas

> Now all things are of God, who has reconciled us to Himself through Jesus Christ, and has given us the ministry of reconciliation. (2 Corinthians 5:18)

As one expression of the ministry of reconciliation in Christ, pastoral[1] psychotherapy is a specialized form of caregiving that involves entering into the emotional depths of people who are in distress. Pastoral psychotherapists may practice one particular form of psychotherapy, or, as Dr. Muse has done in his commendable work with Bonnie, they may eclectically employ techniques gleaned from a variety of psychotherapeutic approaches – psychodynamic, cognitive-behavioral, person-centered, existential, family systemic, etc. Regardless of which psychotherapeutic techniques and methods of treatment are used, in order for psychotherapy to be considered "Orthodox Christian" it must be employed by a therapist who is a practicing Orthodox Christian, and it must involve Orthodox Christianity as an orienting therapeutic resource.

There are countless ways of drawing on the Orthodox spiritual tradition for therapeutic ends. Using Dr. Muse's work with Bonnie for purposes of illustration, I would like to suggest seven[2] features that I think ought to characterize an Orthodox Christian approach to pastoral psychotherapy. The seven things therapists who are Orthodox Christian should consider when doing pastoral psychotherapy – that is, when attempting to integrate[3] Orthodox Christian spirituality into psychotherapy – are (1) Orthodox worldview, (2) spiritual awareness, (3) acceptance,

123

empathy, and compassion, (4) clear-mindedness, (5) respect for freedom, (6) ecclesial belonging, (7) prayer.

Orthodox Christian Worldview

A worldview implies a vision of life that is incarnated in a way of life.[4] Every person lives according to a worldview, whether it has been consciously and thoroughly articulated or not. Implicit in every approach to therapy is a worldview containing certain values, ethical norms, theological presuppositions, and assumptions about human nature. With an Orthodox Christian worldview solidly in place, the integrator avoids reducing Orthodoxy to mere "window dressing" for a fundamentally incompatible perspective.[5] Or, to borrow Dr. Rediger's tastier metaphor, it locates Orthodoxy in the place of the underlying, all-encompassing "pie crust" rather than restricting it to a single "slice." Doing psychotherapy from an Orthodox Christian perspective, as Dr. Muse does, means that an Orthodox theocentric worldview informs and guides the therapist's own spiritual life, ethical commitments, understanding of personhood, theory of development, conception of psychopathology, and soteriological, teleological vision.[6]

Whereas materialists are inclined to assert that all problems of living have their origin in a person's biology (biological reductionism[7]), and spiritualists suggest that all problems issue from the spiritual realm (spiritual reductionism[8]), Orthodox Christian anthropology envisions the human person as an integrated, embodied whole – that is, as a biopsychospiritual, interrelational being, the source and sustainer of which is God, the Holy Trinity.[9] God and humanity, in the biblical, patristic, Orthodox Christian perspective,[10] are intimately related in a relationship that becomes a complete union in the incarnation of the divine-human Christ. Christ's abiding presence in the world is made evident in His Church. According to the Orthodox claim, it is in God, and specifically in Jesus Christ through the Holy Spirit, that human beings may fulfill their restless quest for meaning and find ultimate answers to the fundamental questions: "Who am I?" "Why am I?" "Whose am I?"[11]

The Orthodox Christian worldview, in other words, offers ultimate answers to the human being's deepest existential questions of meaning and identity. It accomplishes this by facilitating human contact with God. Existential questions can be answered only existentially as one comes to know God in the intimacy of personal relationship through faith within the community of faith. Faith, then, in the life-giving mystery of the Trinity – which is reflected in the cosmotheanthropic ecclesial communion of love – marks the Orthodox Christian worldview.

Spiritual Awareness

Orthodox Christian pastoral psychotherapy seeks to nurture, heal, and liberate the human spirit. It is important in our work with suffering people to discern and remain ever aware of the vital part of them: the "true self" (to use Horney's term, which Dr. Chirban cited earlier), the spirit of life that is in them, the image of God, which they bear, however distorted and obscured it may be. They may have forgotten that they have a spirit, or perhaps we should say *are* a spirit.[12] They may know nothing of their spirit's ultimate ground in the divine life. We, however, must keep this reality in our awareness and, in subtle ways that people can grasp, share this with them.

Together with this spiritual awareness of the other as an icon and gift of God, the pastoral psychotherapist cultivates an awareness of the other person's spirituality and worldview. Obviously, the relationships people have with God are as unique and varied as those they have with one another. Even people who share a common religious tradition and worldview appropriate that tradition in unique ways as unique persons with particular experiences, interpretations, and perceptions. The pastoral therapist makes a point of learning from the client what his or her religious beliefs, behaviors, and commitments are and how they came to be. A religious or spiritual assessment may be conducted in order to guide an effective treatment plan that is sensitive to this aspect of the client. The pastorally minded therapist may help a client expand one's awareness of one's own beliefs by asking whether the client belongs to a spiritual community, whether faith is something important to him or her, what one's image of God is, what one's relationship with God is like, what it would be like for one to surrender one's emotional burdens to God, what kind of doubts one experiences, what gives one hope and meaning and direction, what one perceive God's call to be in one's present life circumstances, what it is like to hold such beliefs in this culture, etc. With clarified religious values, a client will be better able to make positive decisions for himself or herself.

Dr. Muse seems to have tuned in to Bonnie's spirituality. In ways that speak to her, he reminds her of her spirit and its relation to the Holy Spirit. He does this through the use of psalms, prayers, readings, icons, incense, metaphors, and, perhaps most vividly, through the symbol of an African milk plant. He breaks off a piece of the plant and gives it to her with the suggestion that it, though prickly on the outside, like her, is full of inner life which will flourish in the proper environment.[13] It is in light, then, of spiritual awareness – awareness of the particular human spirit in the presence of the Holy Spirit – that pastoral psychotherapists ought to consider the problems at hand: the physical symptoms, the maladaptive cognitions, the disturbing affect, the family systems issues, and the interpersonal and intrapersonal conflicts.

Acceptance, Empathy and Compassion

Pastoral psychotherapy starts with the person right where he or she is in the life journey.[14] The pastoral psychotherapist tries to be with people in the way that God is with them: as one who accepts yet challenges them. The messages conveyed are "you are accepted"[15] and "there is hope for you." While a person's maladaptive beliefs or interpretations of reality may need to be challenged, such as by cognitive reframing, it is important to convey that the person himself or herself is accepted and that his or her perceptions and feelings are welcomed.

The therapist is empowered to accept others with all their imperfections through the same divine love with which the therapist is accepted in all his or her imperfection.[16] Dr. Muse's humble, loving acceptance of Bonnie seems evident throughout their work together. He accepts her even when she cannot accept herself. It is clear that she feels his compassionate acceptance when she reveals her pain to him, when she weeps in his presence, when she confides to him her secrets fears and fantasies, when she tells him in session 32 that she felt anger toward him and in session 41 that she feels rejected by him, and when, in session 53, she trusts him enough to let him hold on to her suicide pills. Gradually, perhaps in part because of his compassion for her, Bonnie slowly develops greater compassion for herself.[17]

The therapist's compassionate attitude of acceptance, then, may enable the client to accept parts of the self that he or she had once rejected in distress. These may include passions, desires, fears, sins, mistakes, imperfections, talents, interests, and painful and other emotions. The safe emotional base that the two together establish allows the client to tolerate without undue guilt or shame what was previously intolerable or threatening. Gently and noncoercively, the therapist may guide the client into his or her anxiety, helping the person bring to conscious reflection what was previously denied or repressed from awareness.[18]

While Dr. Muse cannot undo the events of the past that have left Bonnie wounded, by developing an empathic connection with her he gives her the opportunity to revisit her trauma now in a changed context. This time she is not alone.[19] There is someone with her who cares, who understands, who accepts her, who believes in her and sees the good in her. Their relationship becomes a lifeline for her. In session 40 she confides that she feels paralyzed at the thought of losing him. Faithfully, he remains available to her. He does not abandon her the way others have. Yet he, too, is limited, and there will come a time to say goodbye. Aware of this, he is concerned to help foster her bond with the One who "will never leave us nor forsake us" (Deuteronomy 31:6, Hebrews 13:5), from whom "nothing can separate us" (Romans 8:35–39). Slowly, Bonnie heals.

Clear-Mindedness

Like Bonnie, every person who comes to see a therapist has a story, a particular history, which shapes one's way of seeing the world and one's sense of place in the world. It is important, as we have stressed, to be respectful of each person's story and perceptions of reality, which undoubtedly make perfect sense given that person's experience. Some people do, of course, perceive reality in oppressive ways. For example, some believe there is no God, while others consider God to be a threatening, hostile authority. Given their life experience, these conclusions seem rational to them.[20] Furthermore, such beliefs may operate at an unconscious level in spite of the person claiming to believe in a good and loving God.

The pastoral therapist, like Christ, meets a person where he or she is. The objective is neither to affirm a person's false beliefs nor to impose a theological interpretation on the person. The pastoral task, rather, from an Orthodox Christian perspective, is to enter incarnationally into the person's world and tease out the implicit theological meanings discovered there. As with all interpretations a therapist might make, these should be offered speculatively and provisionally for the client to confirm, reject, or modify until they ring true for the client. The therapist does not try to rescue or change the person in a coercive way. Instead, he tries to understand, and help the person to understand, how it has made sense and been important for the person to be as he or she is and to see things as he or she does, however dysfunctional that may be.[21] In this way, the therapist helps the person to look at what he or she is enacting or repeating from the past.

Of course, the therapist may decide to gently challenge the client's (mis)construal of reality, helping him or her to reframe any beliefs, conceptions, or perceptions (e.g. of oneself, of God, of others, of the world) that seem to be hurting rather than helping the person.[22] Cognitive-behavioral techniques can prove effective in altering invalid assumptions and erroneous beliefs. By the same token, the therapist does well to support and affirm the client's healthy beliefs. Again, it is important to realize that not all beliefs which are operative in the client's life are consciously held. The therapist must be attuned, then, to what lies below the surface of awareness, which may be revealed through a person's actions and in other, perhaps subtler, ways.[23]

Respect for Freedom

A pastoral therapist working from an Orthodox Christian orientation will deeply respect a person's free will and self-determination. He or she will also encourage in clients the recognition and appreciation of their own freedom, and their own sense of self-efficacy as well as responsibility. As a therapist with an Orthodox Christian sensibility, Dr. Muse wants to free his client from every false and oppressive force.[24] Thus, in sessions 42–45, he helps her let go of her perfectionist, rule-conscious sense of urgency, encouraging her to embrace and enjoy her freedom.

Orthodoxy deeply respects the human will. Psychotherapy that is guided by an Orthodox Christian perspective, then, is not about the therapist attempting to change the client or even to persuade the client to change. That can be an aim of preaching, which certainly has its place in the ministry of the Church. Pastoral psychotherapy, however, is about being with a person and listening with her to the story she is telling herself, thereby helping her raise her own self-awareness and self-knowledge, which in turn can empower her to freely act to change herself.[25] The therapist does not push the client; the client sets the pace.

Yet, the client is coming to the therapist for guidance, so there is a collaborative quality to their work. Furthermore, the Holy Spirit may be invited as a third party in this collaboration. The role of the Comforter may be great or small, depending on the openness of the other two.[26]

The spirit of mutuality and collaboration may be particularly important with certain clients, such as Bonnie, whose freedom and boundaries have been violated and whose voices have gone unheard in the past. Clients who are survivors of trauma ought to be allowed a substantial degree of control over their therapy, particularly in terms of the timing and manner in which painful material is raised and addressed.[27] We see with Bonnie, for example, a powerful though often frustrated need to assert control over her life, which is quite understandable given her history of powerlessness and abuse. Her need for control is expressed, at times, in dysfunctional ways. See, for example, session 5–6, in which Bonnie states that "suicide is something I can control; that's why it's attractive." See also sessions 50–52, in which she acknowledges using seduction to establish control over men, just as men had found ways to assert dominance over her. Bonnie turns to such measures because she feels desperately powerless and out of control, as in session 70.

Working with a client like Bonnie, the therapist must be acutely sensitive to power dynamics within the therapy, as well as to gender dynamics if, as in this case, the therapist is a man and the client a woman, or vice versa.[28] A sensitive male therapist like Dr. Muse will certainly wish to avoid replicating the kind of experience with male mentors that has already caused a client like Bonnie so much pain. Yet, transference[29] and countertransference[30] are inevitable and provide important clues to the nature of the client's suffering. It should not be too surprising, for example, to find Bonnie making a slight sexual overture toward Dr. Muse at the end of one session. He is an attractive man with authority, and she longs for intimacy. But there is more going on. Perhaps the therapy is becoming too intense for her, and she unconsciously wishes to derail it. Perhaps she is asking him, by her flirtation, if he is different from the other men she has known who were all too willing to violate proper boundaries and take advantage of her. Perhaps she is testing him to see whether she can trust him with yet unrevealed, deeper levels of spiritual vulnerability.

Freedom, in the Orthodox Christian vision, is a powerful gift, which carries an enormous risk and responsibility. To choose wrongly is to distort oneself.[31] Dr. Muse wisely chooses not to pursue Bonnie's misguided lead. He is secure with his boundaries. Furthermore, he does not hesitate to raise the issue in the following session for them to process together in a way that does not feel pathologizing or shaming for her, or at least that mitigates her shame. The aim is to understand the deeper motivations, which in this instance appear to involve Bonnie's conflicted yet ceaseless longing for the love of the father. Nevertheless, she does feel ashamed and unforgiving toward herself, not simply for flirtatiously touching her therapist but for her past inappropriate sexual acts and illicit affairs. Now she is terrified he will reject and abandon her for her "badness." This disclosure conceals another temptation, which is for Dr. Muse to assume the chivalric role of the knight who rescues the distressed maiden from such unpleasant feelings. By observing all of this with her while remaining faithful to the therapeutic "covenant" they made when they agreed to begin psychotherapy, Dr. Muse helps Bonnie grow in self-awareness, self-knowledge, and self-acceptance.

Though we are influenced and shaped by many factors and experiences, human beings, according to the Orthodox Christian understanding, are never totally conditioned and determined by our past, our environment, our circumstances, our biology, or any other force. As people who bear the image of God, we make choices. Psychotherapy can help us become more conscious of the choices we have made and continue to make, so that we can make them more consciously. In this way, psychotherapy can contribute toward the human pursuit of spiritual freedom with which the Orthodox Church is so deeply concerned.

Ecclesial Belonging

As a representative of the community of faith, the pastoral psychotherapist can also serve as a bridge for people to the ecclesial community. The therapist may refer clients to priests and spiritual directors,[32] as Dr. Muse does, and encourage involvement in the healing and transformative ecclesial activities of worship, fellowship, sacrament, and service.[33] It may be appropriate and helpful to share with certain clients selected spiritual resources from the therapist's own spiritual tradition of which the client might make use. Hence, we see Dr. Muse offering Bonnie icons, books, the Jesus prayer, etc., all of which seem to be helpful to her. The therapist's task, of course, is not that of the missionary, catechist, confessor, or spiritual director. Nevertheless, it seems fitting and acceptable to Bonnie when Dr. Muse recommends in session 27 that she receive the Eucharist daily during Lent, allowing Holy Communion to fill the spiritual emptiness that motivates her binge eating. In session 58 we learn that Bonnie's participation in a music workshop with "two hundred people who love God" leaves her feeling "bathed by God's forgiveness."

To actively participate and share in the life of the ecclesial community – in the rituals of worship and sacrament, in the fellowship and friendships, in the prayer and song, in the moving symbols, in the rhythm of fasts and feasts, in the scriptural and devotional readings, in the celebrations, in the pilgrimages and retreats, in the meetings and decision making, in the social service and missionary outreach – is to enter into a very old and very healing tradition. Here, one can bring one's own story into a larger family, which has a sacred memory and story of its own. Here, one can become part of something larger than the self, larger even than the present earthly society. The pastoral caregiver can be a bridge to this vast and vital communion.[34]

Prayer

The pastoral psychotherapist may pray with a client during a therapy session. To begin a session with the mutual invocation of the Holy Spirit may be a wonderful way of inviting God's presence and assistance into the work, if that is in accordance with the client's worldview and wishes.[35] The decision to include prayer in a session belongs, of course, to the client and the therapist. Every therapeutic relationship – like every relationship – is unique. If a client asks for prayer, or the situation indicates that prayer would be appropriate, as when, for example, a client is undergoing an acutely stressful event, then the therapist might offer to pray with the client.[36] In such cases, it may be best for the client to articulate the prayer, or at least to choose whether to do so. It also seems advisable that prayers during therapy be brief. Finally, it might be helpful occasionally to explore with the client his or her experience of the prayer.[37]

Prayer is a powerful, healing art, which the therapist can also recommend to the client as a spiritual aid for use at all times and in all places.[38] In session 27, Dr. Muse advises Bonnie to use prayer and the reading of psalms (which are also prayers) whenever she feels the urge to binge. In session 34 he advises her to use the Jesus Prayer[39] to counter disturbing thoughts and fears of abandonment. By session 65 the practice of this prayer has become for Bonnie "not like an ember, but a little flame now in my life," empowering her to trust in the divine mercy in a way that she previously could not.[40]

Finally, the therapist who wants to draw upon the Orthodox Christian faith may wish to pray on a regular basis for his or her clients. Intercessory prayer on behalf of others, of course, is a standard part of Christian devotional practices. But the urge to remember another in prayer becomes even more compelling when one has received intimate access to the psyche of the other. It is an extreme privilege to be allowed into the inner struggle of a fellow human being. Psychotherapy ought always to be done with reverence for the mystery involved. Praying for divine intervention in the life of one's clients honors this mystery.

The greater the therapist's awareness, in general, of God and of God's presence in the world, in one's own life, and in the life of one's clients, the more he or she will be able to convey to clients that God is with them and for them where they are, in the midst of their suffering and struggle, working in it for good. While the pastoral psychotherapist may not fully know how God has intervened or will intervene in the client's life, he or she bears witness in subtle and direct ways to the faith that God does intervene in the lives of those who turn to Him in faith.

CONCLUSION

"The glory of God is a human being fully alive!" declared one of the saints.[41] This is the aim of all the healing mysteries and ministries of the Orthodox Christian Church. Any successful endeavor to heal or rejuvenate others must begin with the healing and rejuvenation of one's own spirit. If one's own spirit is neglected, it becomes impossible to nurture others. "First remove the plank from your own eye," says Christ, "and then you will see clearly to remove the speck from your brother's eye" (Matthew 7:5). Part of the success of Dr. Muse's work with Bonnie is undoubtedly due to the strength and purity of his spirit, which she can perceive and draw strength from.

All of us who wish to bring hope and healing to others must give attention to our own inner lives, to the purification of our own passions, and to the deepening of our own intimate bond with the Holy Spirit. "Acquire the spirit of peace," says St. Seraphim of Sarov, "and thousands around you will find their salvation in Christ." Ultimately, our hope lies in God, Who holds all (Pantocrator). We trust in the Father (literally, "source"), in the divine-human, crucified, and risen Christ ("the anointed"), and in the life-creating Spirit. One sees traces of this divine triune mystery throughout Dr. Muse's exemplary work with Bonnie.

NOTES

[1] Although, strictly speaking, the word "pastoral" connotes the shepherding ministry of an ordained priest, the word is applied here in a loose sense to connote a "pastor-like" quality of caregiving that is inspired, guided, or informed by religious faith.

[2] I settled on this biblically symbolic number because it suggests that there are many more features as well.

[3] The word "integration" is used here in a loose sense. Instead of integration or synthesis, we might speak of interrelation, correlation, configuration, cooperation, etc. The idea of allowing the Orthodox spiritual tradition to inform therapy in helpful ways is what is intended.

[4] Among the many helpful books now available in English that describe the Orthodox worldview, the following are particularly recommended: *The Orthodox Way* by Kallistos Ware (Crestwood, NY: St. Vladimir's Seminary Press, 1995), *For the Life of the World: Sacraments and Orthodoxy* by Alexander Schmemann (Crestwood, NY: St. Vladimir's Seminary Press, 1988), *Elements of Faith* by Christos Yannaras (Tr. by Keith Schram; Edinburgh, Scotland: T&T Clark, 1991), *The Roots of Christian Mysticism* by Olivier Clement (Tr. by Theodore Berkeley and Jeremy Hummerstone; New York: New City Press, 1995), *The Spiritual Wisdom and Practices of Early Christianity* by Alphonse and Rachel Goettmann (Tr. by Theodore J. Nottingham; Greenwood, IN: Inner Life Publications, 1994), *The Sacred in Life and Art* (1990) and *Human Image: World Image* (1992) by Philip Sherrard (Ipswich, UK: Golgonooza Press). See also a pamphlet by Seraphim Rose, *The Orthodox World-View* (Platina, CA: St. Herman of Alaska Brotherhood, 1982).

[5] The richness of the Orthodox Christian tradition is such that creative dialogists throughout the ages have been able to discern points of contact with widely differing philosophies, religions, and ideologies. This is not surprising, given the universal nature of truth and its accessibility, though to varying degrees, to all people created according to the image and likeness of God. Nevertheless, when attempting dialogue with the "other," it is important not to minimize differences. We are called to "test the spirits" (1 John 4:1). Hence, every baptism begins with exorcism.

[6] For an excellent brief introduction to the convergences and divergences between Orthodox Christian theology and the psychological theories of Freud, Jung, and Adler, see Dr. Jamie Moran's essay "Orthodoxy and Modern Depth Psychology" in *Living Orthodoxy in the Modern World*, Ed. by Andrew Walker and Costa Carras (London: Society for the Promotion of Christian Knowledge, 1996 and New York: Saint Vladimir's Seminary, 2000). This highly recommended book is soon to be reissued in the United States. For a fuller presentation of Orthodox mystical psychology, see Robin Amis's *A Different*

Christianity: Early Christian Esotericism and Modern Thought (Albany, NY: State University of New York, 1995) and Hierotheos Vlachos's *Orthodox Psychotherapy: The Science of the Fathers* (Tr. by Esther Williams, Levadia, Greece: Birth of the Theotokos Monastery, 1994). See also volume 3 – *Pastoral Counsel* – of the Classical Pastoral Care Series by Thomas C. Oden (New York: The Crossroad Publishing Company, 1982, esp. pp. 226–293).

[7] Nobel laureate physiologist and co-discoverer of DNA, Francis Crick, for example, considers "mind" to be nothing more than a biological phenomenon: "The Astonishing Hypothesis is that 'you,' your joys and your sorrows, your memories and your ambitions, your sense of personal identity and free will, are in fact no more than the behavior of a vast assembly of nerve cells and their associated molecules." *The Astonishing Hypothesis: The Scientific Search for the Soul* (New York, NY: Charles Scribner's Sons, 1994, 3).

[8] Referred to in philosophy as idealism, this concept seems evident today in much "new age" thinking.

[9] Body, soul, and spirit, then, are not to be regarded as discrete, separate, structural entities, but rather as different aspects or dimensions of personal identity. For analytic, heuristic, and pragmatic purposes, of course, it may be helpful to focus at any given time on a particular aspect or dimension of a person. Nevertheless, when doing so, it is important to not lose sight of the other dimensions nor of the theotic context.

[10] While there are certainly a diversity of voices and perspectives expressed within and among the scriptures, the patristic corpus, and the writings of Orthodox Christian thinkers, there is nevertheless a striking degree of concord and continuity on many points. In philosophical terms, we might refer to the consensual position on anthropology as ontological and soteriological wholism. In other words, there is a fundamental unity connecting God, the human being (soul and body), the Body of Christ, and the cosmos. One fulfills one's personhood as a bearer of the divine image in relation to God and within the community of the people of God, which is a microcosm of the cosmos of God. Human beings cannot be understood in their individuality, nor can parts of them be understood in isolation from the whole. For further reflections from an Orthodox Christian perspective on the relational nature of personhood and on Orthodox ecclesiology see the seminal work *Being as Communion* (Crestwood, NY: St. Vladimir's Seminary, 1993) by John D. Zizioulas, Metropolitan of Pergamon. See also *The Person in the Orthodox Tradition* by the Metropolitan of Nafpaktos, Hierotheos Vlahos, Tr. by Esther Williams, Levadia, Hellas/Greece: Birth of the Theotokos Monastery, 1998).

[11] In the words of the Epistle to the Colossians: "He is the image of the invisible God, the firstborn over all creation. For by him all things were created...And he is before all things and in him all things consist" (1:15–17).

It is a Christian belief that in Jesus Christ, all things hold together and in him human nature is revealed in its original and potential wholeness and oneness with God. From the Christian perspective, then, Christ is the source, norm, and standard of human health and wholeness. Through the mysteries of Christ, the Holy Spirit liberates the human spirit from subjection to the ego, enabling persons to love as God loves. It is precisely love that defines the reign of God and characterizes the new, abundant, eternal life that Christians call the life "in Christ," or *salvation*. The life in Christ is marked by "agape love, joy, peace, patience, kindness, goodness, faithfulness, gentleness, and self-control" (Galatians 5:22). To actualize such fullness of life is the aim or telos of all Christian mysteries and ministries, including pastoral psychotherapy. The precise way in which salvation is realized, of course, is unique to each person. Pastoral psychotherapy is one way of attending to, and entering into the uniqueness of each person's story.

[12] Orthodox commonly use the word "spirit" (or *nous* or "heart") to refer to the heart of the soul, which is the seat of consciousness and freedom. This aspect of a person is the contact point with God. Through the spirit the soul relates to the Holy Spirit and to the spiritual world, and through the body the soul relates to the material world. The soul, then, is mediated by the body (of which the brain is a part). The body is the instrument of the soul. The soul, meanwhile, is directed by the spirit, which in turn may be guided and directed either by the spirit of the world or by the Holy Spirit (1 Corinthians 2:12). For an extended discussion on this, see Hierotheos Vlachos, *Orthodox Psychotherapy: The Science of the Fathers* (Tr. by Esther Williams, Levadia, Greece: Birth of the Theotokos Monastery, 1994).

One implication of attending to the human spirit is the validation of the client's sacred worth. Specifically, the psychotherapist deliberately identifies and supports the client's strengths as well as noticing weaknesses, with the emphasis upon the person's capabilities, positive qualities, and spiritual potential.

[13] Session 47. For a perceptive conceptualization of human potential in light of the Orthodox hesychastic teachings articulated by St. Gregory Palamas and brought into conversation with contemporary theories, see Daniel M. Rogich's *Becoming Uncreated: The Journey to Human Authenticity* (Minneapolis: Light & Life Publishing, 1997).

[14] In this respect, pastoral psychotherapy resembles the way Jesus deals with people by meeting, accepting, loving, and challenging them as they are. Like Jesus, the pastoral psychotherapist takes seriously one's personal life story. For a practical resource helpful for understanding and reauthoring one's personal story, see Merle Jordan's *Reclaiming Your Story: Family History and Spiritual Growth* (Louisville, KY: Westminster John Knox Press, 1999).

[15] This is the title of a well-known sermon by the late twentieth-century Lutheran philosopher Paul Tillich (*The Shaking of the Foundations*, New

York: Charles Scribner's Sons, 1948). One of Tillich's sources of inspiration, Carl Jung, has written: "But if the doctor wishes to help a human being he must be able to accept him as he is. And he can do this in reality only when he has already seen and accepted himself as he is" (Carl G. Jung, *Modern Man in Search of a Soul*, Trs. W.S. Dell and Cary F. Baynes. New York: Harcourt, Brace and Co., 1939, p. 235). For a blunt critique of the "ontology of deficiency" inherent to Augustinian, Calvinist, and Freudian ideas, see Seth Farber's *Eternal Day: The Christian Alternative to Secularism and Modern Psychology* (Salisbury, MA: Regina Orthodox Press, 1998).

[16] Implicit here is the connection much emphasized in Orthodox spirituality between humility and love. Without humility, it is claimed, there can be no love. Likewise, humility – the honest awareness and acceptance of one's own imperfection and fundamental vulnerability – is made possible by the acceptance of God's gracious love for sinners. The acceptance of one's own sinfulness and vulnerability as well as of the awesome tenderness and love of God, which is so characteristic of Orthodox spirituality, contrasts markedly with the "gospel of perfection" by which Bonnie was attempting to live (see session 33).

[17] Session 47 ends, for example, with Bonnie's "little girl" – her "fat 10-year-old self" – feeling loved.

[18] This Dr. Muse does through the technique of EMDR. It is critical when using powerful techniques, such as this one designed to facilitate the uncovering of painful emotions, that precaution be taken to prevent overstimulation and retraumatization, which can occur from emotional flooding. The client must first develop sufficient "ego strength" to tolerate uncovery work. For this reason, therapy with trauma survivors is often stage specific, with symptom stabilization preceding uncovery. See note 27 below.

[19] For a thought-provoking exploration of the meanings and subtleties of pastoral counseling with an emphasis on the primacy of empathy and fidelity in the therapeutic relationship, see Chris R. Schlauch's *Faithful Companioning: How Pastoral Counseling Heals* (Minneapolis: Fortress Press, 1995).

[20] Having been raised by a harsh, critical, and controlling father whom she perceived did not want her and who tragically died just as she was getting to know him, having been blamed by her mother for "turning" on her father, having been raped as a teenager by her girlfriend's father with whom she was living as a college student, having been repeatedly exploited sexually by mentor figures (and later by a former student) and continuing to be the target of her own father-in-law's lust, having lost four children in pregnancy and childbirth, having a husband who indulges in pornography, which presents women as mere objects of lust, and who himself tries to involve her in extramarital sexual relations for his own gratification, and who seemingly ignores her whenever her symptoms decrease, is it any wonder that Bonnie

begins therapy with a dim view of God the Father, the ultimate "father-figure"? What Dr. Muse gradually helps her to see is that God the Father is not, first of all, a man, and second, not like the men who have mistreated her. To the contrary, He is against all that oppresses her and causes her pain; rather, He is the source of all that is good, true, and beautiful in her life, and He works with her to bring liberation and healing.

[21] Dr. Merle Jordan, Emeritus Professor of Pastoral Psychology at Boston University, advocates appreciating the logic and "emotional truth" of symptoms. "There is a meaningfulness and purposefulness to every symptom," he said in a recent conversation. "I don't try to get people to change. Rather, I try to help them become aware of why they need to have the symptom… As terrible as a symptom may be, the person often unconsciously believes it would be even worse not to have the symptom" (Conversation on March 17, 1999 at the Danielsen Institute, Boston, MA). So, for example, Bonnie is able to say by session 20: "I can't blame my parents, so I have to blame myself." (See also session 48.) Implicit in Dr. Jordan's "constructivist" approach, of course, is a strong belief in the person's freedom to choose otherwise. Before the choice to change can be made, however, people typically need to look clearly at what they are doing and, in the context of feeling accepted by the therapist, feel the painful emptiness that lies behind their self-defeating actions. Bonnie, for example, is able to experience and name with Dr. Muse the painful loneliness and inner emptiness that drives her binging and purging (see sessions 32 and 62). By sessions 71–75, her grief work progresses in a way that allows her to hold both her pain and her faith in God.

[22] As for religious concepts, rules, and practices, they are desirable insofar as they bring out the best in people. Obviously, they can be important aids in the spiritual growth process of purification, illumination, and deification. However, they may also be used to ill effect. Thus, Christ taught that "the Sabbath was made for man, and not man for the Sabbath" (Mark 2:27).

[23] In a book that seems consistent with Orthodox Christianity, *Taking on the Gods: The Task of the Pastoral Counselor* (Nashville, TN: Abingdon Press, 1986), Merle Jordan describes the unconscious process whereby people replicate, in their own parenting of their inner child, the way they were parented. To put it theologically, as Jordan does, a child perceives ultimate reality in the image of human (e.g., parental) authority, which then functions in the psyche as an idol or "household god." In order to survive in the world, the child feels the need to appease this psychic idol by crucifying elements of oneself. This attempt at self-atonement invariably proves self-defeating. Healing occurs as the person accepts the good news of Christ's redemptive power and surrenders one's life ever more fully into the hands of the true, loving, and gracious God. In worshipping the true God, one is thereby freed to know, love, and respect one's true self.

[24] Orthodoxy, by definition, is concerned about truth, knowing that truth is liberating. As Jesus said to those who believed, "If you abide in my word, you are my disciples indeed. And you shall know the truth, and the truth shall make you free" (John 8:31–32). It is ironic that Orthodox Christianity – an ancient tradition of Christian humanism – is sometimes assumed to be restrictive of human vitality by people who are existentially unaquainted with it. For them, the word "orthodoxy" invariably connotes narrowness and rigidity, perhaps based on their experience of other orthodoxies. Of course, for an increasing number of people, "truth" also has a negative connotation. Perhaps one day "freedom" will have a negative connotation, too. Nevertheless, for a passionate articulation of the role of freedom in Orthodoxy, see Christos Yannaras' *The Freedom of Morality* (Crestwood, NY: St. Vladimir's Seminary Press, 1984, reprinted 1996).

[25] This, at least, describes one nondirective approach to pastoral psychotherapy, which I have learned at Boston University, particularly from Dr. Chris Schlauch.

[26] I find helpful Dr. Muse's view of psychotherapeutic treatment as temporary and ancillary to participation in the community of faith in God which may be the primary and ongoing therapeutic modality for people of faith. Thus, in session 76, he tells Bonnie: "I'm the junior therapist. God is your primary therapist."

[27] For an excellent guide to understanding this population, see Judith Lewis Herman's *Trauma and Recovery* (Basic Books, 1992). Also see *Treating Sexual Shame: A New Map for Overcoming Dysfunction, Abuse and Addiction* (Northvale, NJ: Jason Aronson, Inc., 1998) by Anne Stirling Hastings, for an approah to sexuality which resonates well on many points with Orthodox Christian teachings.

[28] In addition to individual psychotherapy, a referral to adjunctive women's group therapy designed for sexual trauma survivors would be appropriate if such a group is available in the client's area.

[29] A psychoanalytic term referring to the unconscious projection by the client of feelings he or she has (or wishes to have) toward others, on to the therapist.

[30] Unresolved conflicts of the therapist that are projected on to the client.

[31] Professor Yannaras writes, "For freedom carries with it the ultimate possibility of taking precisely this risk: that man should deny his own existential truth and authenticity, and alienate and distort his existence, his being" *The Freedom of Morality*, (Crestwood, NY: 1984, 1996, p. 15).

[32] It has become customary in our culture for priests, rabbis, and ministers to refer people with complex psychological problems to therapists. This is appropriate. What seems equally appropriate but much less common is for psychologists and psychiatrists to refer religious clients to pastors. Perhaps this will change as the mounting empirical evidence substantiating the

efficacy of certain forms of religious intervention becomes more widely known. For a helpful meditation on the ministry, history, theology, and psychological methodology of spiritual direction in the Orthodox tradition, see Joseph J. Allen's *Inner Way: Toward a Rebirth of Eastern Christian Spiritual Direction* (Holy Cross Press, Brookline, MA). See also the forthcoming book by John Chrissavgis *Soul Mending: The Art of Spiritual Direction* (Holy Cross Orthodox Press, 2000). For a fascinating glimpse at one of Orthodoxy's most influential contemporary spiritual elders, see *Elder Paisios of the Holy Mountain* by Priestmonk Christodoulos Ageloglou, 1998 (available through Holy Cross Bookstore [1-800-245-0599]). See also, on the web, Cyberdesert.com. Incidentally, Fr. Paisios has this to say on p. 31: "Concerning the spiritual progress of a disciple monk, it is more important for him to develop good thoughts than to be guided by a spirtual father who is considered a living saint."

[33] Empirical studies show that clerical and congregational support in stressful times positively affects one's mental health. Similarly, "greater social involvement in the church has been tied to lower levels of loneliness and greater life satisfaction" (Kenneth Pargament and C.C. Brant, "Religion and Coping" in *Handbook of Religion and Mental Health*, edited by Harold G. Koenig. New York, NY: Academic Press, 1998). Unfortunately, not all congregations are supportive communities. For a critical appraisal of the current state of Orthodox ecclesial life and recommendations for communal renewal, see Philotheos Faros's *Functional and Dysfunctional Christianity* (Brookline, MA: Holy Cross Orthodox Press, 1998). For a useful discussion of religious community and the healing arts, see *Cultivating Wholeness: A Guide to Care and Counseling in Faith Communities* by Margaret Zipse Kornfeld (New York: Continuum, 1998). Helping to build genuine Christian communities is certainly one of the most important tasks before all members of the Church.

[34] The better informed the therapist is about the various congregations and resources of faith in the local area, the better able he or she will be to make an appropriate and effective referral.

[35] "Heavenly King, Comforter, Spirit of truth, present everywhere, filling all things, Treasury of blessings and Giver of life, come and dwell in us, cleanse us from every stain, and, O Good One, save our souls." Note the paradox: although we believe that the Spirit is everywhere, still we ask the Spirit to come be with us. Sung with particular beauty on the feast of Pentecost, this prayer to the Holy Spirit inaugurates virtually every service of Orthodox worship.

[36] Harold G. Koenig and John Prichett offer the following as a way of posing the question: "Some of my patients find comfort in prayer, others do not. Would my praying with you over this situation be helpful to you, or do you feel that it would not be particularly helpful?" In "Religion and Psycho-

therapy," *Handbook of Religion and Mental Health* (Boston: Academic Press, 1998, p. 333).

[37] These suggestions are adapted from Harold G. Koenig and John Prichett, "Religion and Psychotherapy," *Handbook of Religion and Mental Health* (Boston: Academic Press, 1998, p. 333). When using prayer or any other religious intervention in therapy, such as validation and reinforcement of effective religious coping, religious reframing of maladaptive cognitions, scriptural affirmation, use of biblical stories and religious metaphors, forgiveness intervention, or meditation, it is important that the therapist be alert to cues and inquire about the ways in which a person experiences, interprets, and uses religious concepts or practices. Does the person use religion to justify or rationalize intolerance, to disavow responsibility, to excuse excessive dependency, to mask aggression, to avoid grieving, or for some other purpose? This is not to suggest analyzing sacred moments in an immediate or reductive way. One of the purposes of invoking God is to consciously open the work up to the graceful mystery of a power greater than that of the human minds of the client and therapist. To reductively analyze such an invocation would be to miss the point and possibly to foreclose some of the beneficial effects. On the other hand, it should not be automatically assumed that the client's experience of such interventions is what the therapist imagines or hopes it is. There are ways of reflecting on sacred moments that honor their sacredness.

[38] On the subject of prayer, see the relevant books by Metropolitan Anthony Bloom as well as the enlightening testimony of Archimandrite Sophrony Sakharov entitled *On Prayer* (Tolleshunt Knights by Maldon, Essex, UK: Patriarchal Stavropegic Monastery of St. John the Baptist, 1996). A disciple of St. Silouan, Archimandrite Sophrony (1896–1993) was one of the great spiritual fathers of the contemporary Orthodox Church. For a profound and edifying meditation on his own spiritual journey see his autobiographical work from the same publisher, *We Shall See Him As He Is* (1988).

[39] "Lord Jesus Christ, Son of God, have mercy on me" (or, "...on me the sinner"). The prayer can be prayed repeatedly, verbally or inaudibly, in solitude or in the midst of activity. A couple or a group can practice the prayer together by alternating, among the members, series of "Lord Jesus Christ, Son of God, have mercy on us." Certain Orthodox monasteries and congregations practice this prayer communally.

[40] See *Prayer of Jesus, Prayer of the Heart* by Alphonse and Rachel Goettmann (Greenwood, IN: Inner Life Publications, 1996), *A Night in the Desert of the Holy Mountain: Discussions with a Hermit on the Jesus Prayer* by Hierotheos Vlachos, Tr. by Effie Mavromichali (Levadia, Greece: Birth of the Theotokos Monastery, 1991) and *The Way of a Pilgrim*, Tr. by Helen Bacovcin (New York: Doubleday Image, 1978).

[41] St. Irenaeus, Bishop of Lyons (2nd c. A. D.)

Sickness or Sin?

Philotheos Faros

Although we very often hear triumphant reports about the impressive successes of modern Western medicine, reports about the impasses that modern Western medicine is facing are also constantly increasing.

Modern Western medicine's understanding of health and disease has been based on Descartes' mechanistic view of the world and of the human organism. According to Descartes' theory, the human is a machine with different parts, which sometimes break down and have to be replaced, or they do not function well and have to fixed, and the human body is totally separated from the rest of human existence. Descartes' theory profoundly affected Western medicine and biology and may have contributed to some success, but because of that, Western medicine has not been able to understand the real nature of the great contemporary diseases. It cannot say why a certain disease attacks this individual and not another and at this time of his life and not at another. Unavoidably, it deals with human pathology on the level of symptoms. It brags about being able to remove symptoms, and this is exactly what it promises to do, but the removal of symptoms without discovering and dealing with their cause may be useless to extremely dangerous because the symptoms, as warnings that can prevent disasters, are a blessing in disguise. The symptoms tell us that there is something about our way of life that we must change if we want to save our life. Modern Western medicine is proud of being scientific and having freed medicine from the superstitious belief that it is the demons that cause diseases – in other words, that diseases are caused by external mysterious powers over which man has no control. But modern medicine operates on the exact same understanding. It has only changed the names of those mysterious powers; instead of calling them demons, it calls them viruses, bacteria, or neoplasia. Their names are different, but their essence and the way they operate are exactly the same as those of the demons. Modern medicine may not be trying to exorcise them with magic spells, but it is trying to exorcise them with all those wonderful drugs, like antibiotics, without finding the reason why those mysterious entities attack and tantalize human beings. I believe that any serious physician would unquestionably consider it quackery to treat an individual who suffers acute stomach pains, which are caused most likely by an ulcer, with painkillers so that the patient does not feel the pain. Not only to a physician but to the simplest man, it would be obvious that just stopping the pain is not merely a therapeutic medical intervention but may be disastrous, not only to the well-being but even for to life of the patient. And if it is unscientific to just stop the pain of an ulcer without doing anything for the ulcer itself, why is it not unscientific to merely remove the ulcerous part of the stomach without doing anything about the repressed anger that caused the ulcer and that may do something worse to the patient after the operation. For anybody who is not under the bondage of the mechanistic Cartesian view about human nature and the world as well, it is obvious that the cause of every pathological symptom not only involves the whole existence of the individual who has it, but also involves the whole universe. What does medicine really do when its wonderful medical technology is used for bypass and open heart surgery to restore the heart function of a man who suffered a heart attack because he violated his human limits and his human nature by being covetous or hungry for power? It has not consciously exploited and deceived him, but it has definitely deprived him of the precious opportunity to do something for his spiritual maturity and avoid what is worse: not only his biological but even his spiritual death (although the latter is not really the concern of modern man).

Of course, the immediate results of the removal of symptoms, which may be very impressive although temporary, on one hand become consciously or unconsciously a temptation for the physician because they bring him easy wealth and enable him to exercise tremendous and often satanic power over others; on the other hand, they are very attractive to modern people who want immediate satisfaction at any cost and who want to get rid of the unpleasant symptoms without changing the way of life that violates human nature and caused the symptoms.

In addition, the removal of symptoms does not require personal cost, which is absolutely indispensable for genuine healing. For the accomplishment of genuine healing, the healer has to give a piece of his own soul, and this is always the case: that nothing genuine and worthwhile can be done without personal cost.

When the woman who was sick for twelve years touched Christ's clothes to get well, and she did, Christ, "aware that power had gone out of Him, turned round in the crowd and asked 'who touched my clothes?'" (Mark 5: 30). If it was necessary for Christ to lose some of His strength to heal, it cannot be otherwise for anybody else. This is one of the main reasons why the way of healing of modern Western medicine is preferable to almost all other ways of healing. This is why the relations between physicians and patients are constantly deteriorating. This is why the healing touch of the physician's hands has been replaced by the application of machines. The cost of modern Western medicine's healing, by definition, is not personal but monetary. This is why medical expenses are constantly increasing so that they threaten to lead the economies of Western states to bankruptcy. The increase in medical expenses and the deterioration of the relations between physicians and patients are two of the major impasses of modern Western medicine, but they are not the only ones.

Reports on iatrogenic diseases and on the side effects of drugs and surgical treatments are horror stories. There are three kinds of iatrogenic diseases: socioiatrogenic, psychoiatrogenic and physioiatrogenic. The two kinds are impossible to estimate. The physioatrogenic diseases in the hospitals are almost 15%. "A study authorized by the U.S. Congress in 1976 revealed that 2.4 million unnecessary operations were performed in 1974 and that 11,900 lives were lost from these procedures."[1] These are only a few examples indicative of the seriousness of the situation, but what is happening with antibiotics should suffice to make us realize that the Cartesian mechanistic understanding of the human organism, and of health and disease as result, is leading to disaster. We all know that not only the antibiotics will very soon be totally impotent to protect us from infectious diseases, but they are contributing to the development of some super bacteria, real monsters, against which we will be entirely helpless.

Since 1900, there has been a major shift in advanced industrialized countries in the pattern of illness from acute infectious diseases to chronic stress-related illnesses, which are clearly the result of our modern way of life and which cannot be effectively treated with medications and medical technology.

These are only a very few examples of the increasing evidence that the Cartesian understanding of disease is not adequate and that the human being and the universe as well are unities that cannot be compartmentalized and that have an internal equilibrium. Man's whole existence is a perfect unity, and whatever happens to him happens to his whole existence. He is also a member of another greater unity, the family; and families are members of an even greater unity, the community; and finally, all those successive unities are incorporated in the unity of the universe. Whatever happens to the universe affects even the smallest cell. The nature of the world as well as that of man is ecclesial. Whenever man violates his ecclesial nature – that is, instead of turning toward the other to be united with the other, he turns to himself and cuts himself off from the greater unities instead of relating and uniting with the other – he tries to rule and manipulate the other. Instead of sharing whatever he is and has with the other, he keeps everything for himself, and his whole existence suffers.

Diseases are not external enemies but internal needs. They are efforts of man's nature to restore its equilibrium, which has been disturbed by man's attempt to violate his nature. The symptoms are protests against the violation of man's nature, and they call for the restoration of its equilibrium.

This wholistic understanding of human nature and of the whole world, as well, was and is prevalent in all other medical traditions except modern Western medicine.

Ancient Greek medicine is a good example. For the Greeks, health was not the absence of unpleasant symptoms but fullness of life. A man's way of life is a decisive factor for his health. Hippocrates believed that the man who lives appropriately does not get sick, that man's health depends very much on physical and social environmental conditions, and that there is a direct connection between his psychological and physical condition, since he believed in man's psychosomatic unity.

This unity of man is presented in a memorable way by Plato in his dialogue *Charmides*. In this dialogue, Socrates having returned from the war, he meets his friends and, after telling them the news from the war, has a conversation with Charmides, a very interesting young Athenian man. Charmides had been complaining of a headache when he rose in the morning, and they told him that Socrates knew the cure for his headache. When Socrates met him, he told him that he did know the cure: a kind of a leaf, which nevertheless required to be accompanied by a charm. If a person repeated the charm at the same time that he used the cure, he would be made whole. But without the charm, the leaf would be of no avail. Then Socrates asked

Charmides, "Are you quite sure you know my name?" When Charmides replied, "I ought to know you, for there is a great deal said about you among my companions; and I remember I was a child seeing you in company with my uncle Critas," Socrates said, "I am glad to find that you remember me, for I shall now be more at home with you, and shall be better able to explain the nature of the charm about which I felt a difficulty before. For the charm will do more, Charmides, than only cure the headache. I daresay that you have heard eminent physicians say to a patient who comes to them with bad eyes that they cannot cure his eyes by themselves, but that if his eyes are to be cured, his head must be treated; and then again they say that to think of curing the head alone, and not the rest of the body also, is the height of folly. And arguing in this way, they apply their methods to the whole body and try to treat and heal the whole and the part together...Such, Charmides, is the nature of the charm which I learned when serving with the army from one of the physicians of the Thracian King Zamolxis, who are said to be so skillful that they can even give immortality. This Thracian told me that in these notions of theirs which I was just now mentioning, the Greek physicians are quite right as far as they go; but Zamolxis, he added, our king, who is also a god, says further 'that as you ought not to attempt to cure the eyes without the head, or the head without the body, so neither ought you attempt to cure the body without the soul; and this,' he said, 'is the reason why the cure of many diseases is unknown to the physicians of Hellas because they are ignorant of the whole which ought to be studied also; for the part can never be well unless the whole is well.' For all good and evil, whether in the body or in human nature, originates, as he declared, in the soul, and overflows from thence, as if from the head into the eyes. And, therefore, if the head and body are to be well, you must begin by curing the soul; that is the first thing. And the cure, my dear youth, has to be effected by the use of certain charms, and these charms are fair words; and by them temperance is implanted in the soul, and where temperance is, there health is speedily imparted, not only to the head but to the whole body. And he who taught me the cure and the charm at the same time added a special direction: 'Let no one,' he said, 'persuade you to cure the head, until he has first given you his soul to be cured by the charm. For this,' he said, 'is the great error of our day in the treatment of the human body, that physicians separate the soul from the body.' And, he added with emphasis, at the same time making me swear to his words, 'Let no one, however rich, or noble, or fair, persuade you to give him the cure without the charm.' Now I have sworn and I must keep my oath and, therefore, if you will allow me to apply the Thracian charm first to your soul, as the stranger directed, I will afterwards proceed to apply the cure to your head. But if not, I do not know what I am to do with you, my dear Charmides.'" The text is very explicit, but it may be useful to underline some very important points. First, Socrates considers it absolutely necessary that the healer makes a personal contact with the patient. Second, he makes clear that the medication cannot have any results without the charms: "and these charms are fair words; and by them temperance is implanted in the soul, and where temperance is, there health is speedily imparted." It is obvious that what Socrates suggests here is what today we call psychotherapy. It is interesting that English translation uses the word "temperance" for Plato's word σωφροσύνη. The word "temperance" has a puritanic nuance. "Prudence" may be a closer translation of the word σωφροσύνη, which is the main theme of the dialogue *Charmides*, and which may be what we would call today in English maturation and growth. Finally, the English translation says "physicians separate the soul from the body," and Plato's corresponding words are σωφροσύνη and υγεία, that is, prudence and health. Plato, in his letter to the relatives and friends of Dion, also makes a statement that represents a medical ethos and an understanding of the meaning of health and disease that is too far advanced for modern Western medicine, since progress in discovering medical techniques for removing symptoms is not progress in restoring health, and the goal of ancient Greek medicine was more the restoration of health than the removal of symptoms. "He who advises a sick man," says Plato, "whose manner of life is prejudicial to health is clearly bound first of all to change his patient's manner of life, and if the patient is willing to obey him, he may go on to give him other advice. But if he is not willing, I shall consider one who declines to advise such a patient to be a man and a physician, and one who gives in to him to be unmanly and unprofessional" (Plato's Seventh Letter).

I have already said that all other medical traditions besides modern Western medicine have a holistic orientation. They view man as a wholesome unity. They see the disease as a result of a violation of the universal order, and they try by their interventions to restore that order rather than remove the unpleasant symptoms.

The wisdom and the value of all those old and venerable traditions are especially important in our times because of the explosive situation that the mechanistic Cartesian view has created. Since in the tradition of the Church the wholistic understanding of man and the world reaches its fullness, it is imperative to study it extensively and utilize it appropriately.

In the Church tradition, it is very clear that man is a unity and the universe is a unity, as it is also clear that man is to a tremendous extent the master of his health, life, and death.

In the Old Testament, we see that man gets sick because he violates God's commandments. We read in Deuteronomy,

> If you do not obey the Lord your God by diligently observing all his commandments and statutes which I lay upon you this day...May the Lord cause pestilence to haunt you until he has exterminated you out of the land which you are entering to occupy. May the Lord afflict you with wasting disease and recurrent fever, ague, and eruptions; with drought, black blight and red; and may this plague you until you perish...May

the Lord strike you with Egyptian boils and with tumors, scabs and itches, for which you will find no cure...May the Lord strike you with paralysis, blindness, and madness...May the Lord strike you on knee and leg with malignant boils for which you will find no cure; they will spread from the sole of your foot to the crown of your head (Deutoronomy 28:15,21,22,27,28,35).

Leviticus completes this with the following passage:

But if you do not listen to me, if you fail to keep all these commandments of mine, if you reject my statutes, if you spurn my judgements and do not obey all my commandments, but break my covenant, then be sure that this is what I will do: I will bring upon you sudden terror, wasting disease, recurrent fever and plagues that dim the sight and cause the appetite to fall (Leviticus 26:14–16).

Eusebius, commenting on Isaiah, chapter 57, points out that as man gets sick because he sins, he can also get well by repenting.

Although for a while for sins which were committed because of human weakness, I afflicted those who sinned and I punished them as the father corrects the sons 'for the Lord disciplines those whom he loves; he lays the rod on every son whom he acknowledges' (Hebrews 12:6), since you felt my discipline and you felt the godly sorrow and you walked downcast because you repented, therefore, seeing your return and repentance and your actions and your way of life after that, I healed you and I comforted you, giving you true comfort.[2]

At this point, there is a need for some explanation. In the Old Testament, disease is a punishment given to man because of his disobedience to God's commandments. In the Old Testament, man is commanded to do or not do certain things just because God wants it that way. There is no other explanation. But in the New Testament, God's commandments are presented as revelations by God to man of what man needs to do that would be appropriate to his nature and therefore for his benefit, and what not to do because if he did it, it would be a violation of his nature and against his benefit. The directness of the approach of the Old Testament is appropriate for people who are not mature enough; we still use it with small children. It is many times more effective to tell a child that if he gets close to the stove you will punish him than to try to explain to him what will happen to him if he does. On the other hand, even many adults very often feel that they will be able to control their sinful drives only by intimidation, or that only by intimidation can they be protected from their sinful drives, and they still prefer the Old Testament approach. For those people, the fullness of time has not yet come. Nevertheless, the Old Testament calls divine punishment what for the New Testament is the consequence of man's violation of his own nature.

Ecclesiasticus, one of the most recent texts of the Old Testament, seems to constitute a transition from the approach of the Old Testament to the approach of the New Testament. Here, it is beginning to become apparent that man gets sick because he surpasses his limits and violates his physical as well as his psychological nature.

> A man of good upbringing is content with little and he is not short of breath when he goes to bed. The moderate eater enjoys healthy sleep, he rises early, feeling refreshed. But sleeplessness, indigestion and colic are the lot of the glutton. If you cannot avoid overeating at feast, leave before the fruit and you will find comfort. Listen to me, my Son, do not disregard me. Whatever you do, do it cautiously, and no illness will come your way (Ecclesiasticus 31:19–22).

> A merry heart makes a cheerful countenance but low spirits sap a man's strength (Proverbs 17:22).

> A merry heart keeps a man alive, and joy lengthens his span of days. Indulge yourself, take comfort and banish sorrow; for sorrow has been the death of many, and no advantages ever came of it. Envy and anger shorten a man's life and anxi-

ety brings premature old age (Ecclesiasticus 30:21–24).

The human body requires certain amounts and kinds of food for its sustenance and its functioning. Whenever man consumes more food or food of a different kind than the body needs, from gluttony, it gets sick as a consequence.

Also, it is in the nature of the human soul to love and not to envy, to forgive and not to get angry with other people's imperfections and mistakes. Of course, it has to be clear that anger can be present whether it is shown or hidden. Passionlessness is neither hypocrisy nor neurosis. The passions we do have are holier and, therefore, healthier not to hide. To the extent we cultivate sinful passions, we violate our nature; as a consequence, we get sick,

> Our own body which is more familiar and beloved to us than anything else it happens sometimes when we sin to fight us, defending itself, with fevers and diseases and terrible pains and the slave body whips the queen soul that sinned, not because it wants it but because it is commanded to do it. And Christ may be a witness, who says to the paralytic man 'Now that you are well again, leave your sinful ways, or you may suffer something worse' (John 5:14).[3]

Disease does not come from God. God is not the source of evil. The source of evil is man's free choice.

> No one under trial or temptation says 'I am being tempted by God' for God is untouched by evil and does not tempt anyone. Temptation arises when a man is enticed and lured away by his own lust; then, lust conceives and gives birth to sin; and sin full grown breeds death (James 1:13–15).

Whatever God has created is good as long as it is used in the spirit in which it was created, which is spirit of love and not of selfishness. Whenever man uses the goods of creation according to their nature, they become a blessing for him, and they all contribute so that he reaches fullness of life. But when he uses them selfishly, violating their nature, they bring discomfort, disease, and death.

God created the universe with an order. The world God created is not chaotic. It is dependable and predictable, and it is governed by mental, emotional, and spiritual laws of health that are as absolute as the physical laws. None of these laws can be broken without consequences, and these laws exist for the benefit of the creation and the benefit of the creatures. For real and genuine restoration of health, a restoration of the violated order of God is necessary.

Chrysostom points out that we get sick when we violate our nature not only in its physical dimension but in its psychological, emotional, and spiritual dimensions as well, and that a basic element of man's nature is his need to love God and man and be united with them.

When we become self-centered and, instead of loving the other and trying to unite with the other, we try to possess, rule, use, or manipulate him, we violate our nature, and as a consequence we get sick. Then, not medications or medical technology but the realization of our sinfulness and our repentance can restore our disturbed health.

Man has to make his contribution of faith and repentance to maintain his health or to restore it. But faith is not the self-suggestion of "faith healing," which temporarily removes symptoms. Faith is another vision with which man can see another reality from that of the fallen world: the reality of the Kingdom of God, where man can live according to his God-created nature without sickness, without decay, even without death. That reality in this life is *ecclesia*, not as an institution or a center of power and authority, but as a way of being – as a family, whose father is God and whose members are brothers and sisters who try to share whatever they are and whatever they have. Repentance is not feeling guilty for certain transgressions. It is realizing that you have been living outside of God's kingdom, and deciding to return.

Patristic Texts

Since the forefathers of our gender agreed with Satan, against the opinion of the Creator, and they were stripped of the luminous and lively garments of the splendor from above, they became themselves, alas, dead in spirit like Satan. Since then Satan is not only a dead spirit but deadens all those who get close, and those who participated in his deadness had bodies by which the deadening advice was completed in action, the dead spirits that became death producers conveyed deadness to their bodies...

You see that neither the death of the body came from God, but it also came from sin and from the soul which committed the sin and from the snake that led it with guile to sin. Therefore the illnesses of the body found also their way from sin.

Since then the first one acquired a sickly body with which he lived in constant disturbance, Cain from sin came to this weakness...

Because Cain disposed badly his bond with his brother which exists by nature, turning love to hatred which was generated from envy and ended in murder, therefore, as the languor which comes from envy contributes to unhealthiness, he is punished with a relevant incurable disease, the wounding of the nerves and of the muscles, which are the bond of the body.

You see very clearly that not only death but diseases also and illnesses of the body started from sin.

Even the imperfections of the moral nature had definitely their beginning from sin, and those who suffer the glory of God, like the blind-from-birth man who was cured by the Lord, are very rare.[4]

Because inasmuch as Adam believed the evil one he neglected the good Lord and his will was distorted and the soul los that health and wellness. Since then the body followed the same way with the soul, it adjusted and was distorted with her as an instrument in the hands of an artisan. With the tight union the soul transmits diseases to the body. The evidence for that is that when the soul is ashamed the body becomes red, and when the body is tormented by cares the body withers. But as nature went on the generation that came from that first body was extended. With everything else, wickedness was spread to the bodies that came from the first one. Because the body does not only receive the diseases from the soul but it also transmits to her its own (because the Soul sometimes is joyful and sometimes sorrowful, some people sometimes are prudent, according to the disposition of the body). This is why it was unavoidable for the soul of every man to inherit the wickedness of the first Adam, which was transmitted from his soul to the body, and from the body to the bodies which came from it, and from those bodies to the souls.[5]

Adam sinned because of his evil choice and died for his sin 'for sin pays a wage, and the wage is death' (Romans 6:23). The more he was getting away from life the nearer he was coming to death. Because God is life and deprivation of life is death. So that Adam caused his death departing from God as it is written, 'They who are far from thee are lost' (Psalm 73:27). Thus God did not create death but ourselves caused it by our evil will. But he did not prevent the dissolution that death brings for the prementioned causes, so that he does not preserve immortal the disease.[6]

Where from are diseases and the handicaps of the body? Because the disease is neither unborn nor the creation of God, but the creatures were created with the appropriate to them construction, and they were brought to life perfect and whole; they got sick because they diverted from their natural condition. Because they lose their health either for a bad way of life or for any other disease-producing cause. That is, God created the body, not the disease.[7]

Tell me: whence have diseases their evil nature? Whence is

frenzy? Whence is lethargy? Is it not from carelessness? If physical disorders have their origin in choice, much more those which are voluntary. Whence is drunkenness? Is it not from intemperance of soul? Is not frenzy from excess of fever? And is not fever from the elements too abundant in us? And is not the superabundance of elements from our carelessness? For when either from deficiency or excess we carry any of the things within us beyond the bounds of moderation, we kindle the fire. Again, if when the fire is kindled, we continue to neglect it, we make a conflagration of ourselves, which we are not able to extinguish.[8]

From the beginning could someone see that many times sins preceded the disease of the body, as in the case of Cain; because he did not do good use of his strength rightly he got paralyzed. The same thing happened also with him who was sitting next to the pool. Because the cause of his paralysis was a sin, Christ said: 'Now that you are well again, leave your sinful ways, or you may suffer something worse' (John 5:14). And Paul says, 'That is why many of you are feeble and sick, and a number have died' (1 Corinthians 11:30). Because they are sinning they were participating in the sacrament of Holy Eucharist without a clean conscience. And he delivered to the sickness of the body the man who had fornicated and asked this punishment for his sins.[9]

Wherefore then does (Paul) call the carnal mind? Because it comes to be wholly of the flesh, for when the flesh has mastery, then it goes wrong, as soon as ever it has deprived itself of reason, and of supremacy of the soul. The virtue therefore of the body consists in this, in its situation to the soul, since of itself the flesh is neither good nor evil. For what could the body ever do of itself? It is then by its connection that the body is good, good because of its subjection, but of itself is neither good nor evil, with the capacity however for both, for one and for the other, and having an equal tendency either way. The body has a natural desire, but neither for fornication nor for adultery but for union; the body has a desire for voluptuousness, but for food, not for drunkenness; mark that whenever you exceed the measure, when you go beyond the boundary lines, it cannot hold out a moment longer.[10]

When somebody is not careful and does not take care of himself concerning his health, the organism suffers a superfluity of a want, and from that the man ends up in abnormal condition.[11]

...the bodies when they are ill...with the remedies and the diet get well, and when they are cured, with progressive carelessness and gluttony they collapse again and they return to the same diseases.[12]

[Do you think that the wealthy man is superior because] he partakes of costlier meats? Truly, this is no mighty superiority. Even here, we will find you to have the advantage, for this costliness is thought by you a matter of envy because the pleasure with it is greater. Yet even this is greater in the poor man's case; not only the pleasure but the health also; and in this alone is the advantage with the rich, that he makes his constitution feebler and collects more abundant fountains of disease.[13]

When God was creating the world, He said: "Let the earth bring forth grass" (Genesis 1:2), "and instantly, with useful plants, appear noxious plants; with corn, hemlock; with other nutritious plants, hellebore, monkshood, mandrake and the juice of the poppy. What then? Shall we show no gratitude for so many beneficial gifts, and reproach the Creator for those which may be harmful to our life? And shall we not reflect that all has not been created in view of the wants of our bellies? The nourishing plants, which are destined for our use, are close at hand, and known by all the world. But in creation nothing exists without a reason...What! Sheep and goats know how to turn away from what threatens their life, discerning danger by instinct alone; and you who have reason and the art of medicine to supply what you need, and the experience of your forebears to tell you to avoid all that is dangerous, you tell me that you find it difficult to keep yourself from poisons! But not a single thing has been created without reason, not a single thing is useless. One serves as food to some animal; medicine has found in another a relief for one of our maladies.[14]

Do you love enjoyment? Then, on this very account cease being drunken. For I, too, would have you enjoy yourself but with the real enjoyment that never fades. What then is the real enjoyment ever blooming? Invite Christ to sup with you (Revelation 11:20); give him to partake of yours, or rather of his own. This brings pleasure without limit and in its prime everlastingly. But the things of sense are not such; rather, as soon as they appear they vanish away; and he that has enjoyed them will be in no better condition than he who has not, or rather in a worse. For the one is settled as it were in a harbor, but the other exposes himself to a kind of torrent, a besieging army of distempers, and has not even any power to endure the first swell of the sea. So let us follow after moderation. For thus we shall both be in a good state of body, and we shall possess our souls in security, and shall be delivered from evils both present and future.[15]

They were all adorned with order, and it was the Logos who adorned them...with order when he created the universe...when order is prevailing, the universe is an adornment and its beauty immovable, but disorder and impropriety cause on the one hand thunderbolts in the air; on the other hand on earth it causes earthquakes, in the sea floods, in the cities and in the families wars, in the bodies diseases, in souls sins. All those are not names either of order or of peace, but they are names of disturbance and disorder. And let us not think, brothers, that the very much discussed and anticipated decay is anything else but superabundance of disorder. Because on the one hand the order binds; on the other hand the disorder disbands.[16]

We will not find any healing recorded for the disciplines because he who is already a disciple of Jesus is healthy, and since he is well he does not need Jesus as a physician but with his other potentialities.[17]

[Why did Christ not first address himself] to the cure of the paralytic, but said, 'Son be of good cheer, thy sins are forgiven thee?' He did this very wisely. For it is a habit with physicians to destroy the originating cause of the malady before they remove the malady itself. Often, for example, when the eyes are distressed by some evil humor and corrupt discharge, the physician, abandoning any treatment of the disordered vision, turns his attention to the head, where the root and origin of the infirmity is. Even so did Christ act: He represses first of all the source of the evil. For the source and root and mother of all evil is the nature of sin. This it is which enervates our bodies: this it is which brings disease: therefore also on this occasion He said, 'Son! be of good cheer, thy sins are forgiven thee.' And on the other He said, 'Behold! thou are made whole, sin no more lest some worse thing happen unto thee' (John 5:14), intimating to both that these maladies were the offspring of sin. And in the beginning and outset of the world, disease as the consequence of sin attacked the body of Cain. For after the murder of his brother, after that act of wickedness, his body was subject to palsy. For trembling is the same thing as palsy. For when the strength which regulates a living creature becomes weakened, being no longer able to support all the limbs, it deprives them of their natural power of direction, and then having become unstrung they tremble and turn giddy.

Paul also demonstrated this, for when he was reproaching

the Corinthians with a certain sin, he said, 'For this cause many are weak and sickly among you'(1 Corinthians 11:30). Therefore, also Christ first removes the cause of the evil, and having said 'Son! be of good cheer, thy sins are forgiven thee' (Matthew 9:2), He uplifts the spirit and rouses the downcast soul: for the speech became an efficient cause and having entered into the conscience it laid hold of the soul itself and cast out of it all distress. For nothing creates pleasure and affords confidence so much as freedom from self-reproach. For where remission of sins is, there is sonship.[18]

Let us follow Christ: for we also have many diseases of our soul, and these especially He would fain heal. Since with this intent He corrects that other sort, that He may banish these out of our soul.

Let us therefore come unto Him, and let us ask nothing pertaining to this life, but rather remission of sins. For indeed He gives it even now, if we be in earnest... But as it is, if we have any bodily ailment, we do and contrive everything to be rid of what pains us; but when our soul is indisposed, we delay, and draw back. For which cause neither from the other sort are we delivered: since the things are indispensable; and letting alone the fountain of our ills, we would fain cleanse out the streams.

For that our bodily ills are caused by the wickedness of the soul, is shown both by him that had the palsy thirty and eight years, and by him that was let down through the roof, and by Cain also before these; and from many other things likewise one may perceive this. Let us do away then with the wellspring of our evils, and all the channels of our diseases will be stayed. For the disease is not palsy only, but also our sin; and this more than that, by how much a soul is better than a body.[19]

Nothing is so much characteristic of our nature as to be in communion the one with the other and love each other.[20]

He who does not confess to God or to a God-loving man the evils which the evil on sows in his heart will not be able to defeat him, but he who confesses them will be loved by God and his angels, and James says 'confess your sins to one another and then you will be healed' (James 5:16). The psalmist also says, 'I confessed to myself my iniquity to the Lord and you did remit the godlessness of my heart' (Psalm 31:5).[21]

Let us then contribute our share, that in this world we may enjoy a genuine health, and we may attain to the good things to come.[22]

NOTES

[1] James S. Gordon, MD. *Holistic Medicine*. Chelsea House Publisher, New York and Philadelphia, 1988. p.3.

[2] Eusebius *Commentary in Isaiah* Chap LVII.

[3] John Chrysostom *Homily on Psalm 3*, LXX.

[4] Gregory Palamas *Homily XXXI*, 13, 14, 15.

[5] Nicholas Kavasilas, *On the Life in Christ*.

[6] Basil the Great. *That God is not the Cause of Evils*.

[7] Basil the Great. *That God is not the Cause of Evils*.

[8] John Chrysostom. *Homily IX: On Thessalonians*.

[9] John Chrysostom, *In Isaiah*, Chapter 3.

[10] John Chrysostom, *Homily V: On the Ephesians*.

[11] Abbot Dorotheus, *Ascetic Works: X Teaching*.

[12] Gregory Theologian, *Oration 2: Against Julian the King*.

[13] John Chrysostom, *Homily XII: On Second Corinthians*.

[14] Basil the Great, *Homily V: On Hexaemeron*.

[15] John Chrysostom, *Homily XXVIII: On the First Corinthians*.

[16] Gregory the Theologian, *Homily XXXII: On Good Order*.

[17] Origen, *On the Gospel of St. Matthew*.

[18] John Chrysostom, *On the Paralytic Let Down Through the Roof*.

[19] John Chrysostom, *Homily XIV: On the Gospel of St. Matthew*.

[20] Basil the Great, Ὅροι Κατὰ Πλάτος.

[21] Origen, *On Proverbs, Chap XXVIII*.

[22] John Chrysostom, *Homily XIV: On the Epistle to the Romans*.

A Medical Response to Faros

John F. Schilke

In "Sickness and Sin," Fr. Philotheos Faros discusses the short-comings of modern Western medicine as stemming from the invalid assumptions of Cartesianism. That is perhaps a strained point, since it is just this approach that allows contemporary medicine to be one of the ablest of mankind's undertakings. We test all things and hold fast that which is true, as St. Paul admonishes (1 Thessalonians 5:21). The basis of Orthodox tradition itself, though apparently deductive, is experiential, based on Biblical and historical encounters between man and our Triune God. The ability – in fact the demand – to test all hypothoses against the patient himself guards us in medicine (and in the allied healing arts) from overstating our beliefs and elevating our opinions to unwarranted veracity.

Likewise, every diagnosis is tentative, awaiting further tests or the response of the patient to some therapeutic act. Often we find ourselves humbled in situations where entire plans have to be scuttled when the patient reacts in an unforeseen manner. (This is just the opposite of the commentary on Revelation.) The patient is our fellow – one who shares our sin, our mortality, and our need for care and compassion. The patient is indeed a mystery but also to a large extent is knowable and, to some extent, predictable. We can propose "cures" and (more often) palliation for his illnesses, but only, as Faros points out, if we look at the diagnosis and not the symptom.

In the Orthodox view, sin is the original fracture of the world, but to be broken is not to be without hope. Even when broken, our bodies still attempt (sometimes with expert medical help)

163

to restore homeostasis (balance) by many very marvelous mechanisms. Blood clotting, for example, is such a wonder, though there are certainly pathologic states in which it can go awry and actually kill, as in pulmonary embolism or stroke.

Yet, medicine does not heal—God does. In confession, the priest tries to encourage repentance and the reconciliation of the breaches between man and God. Likewise, the physician, also a finite creature to subject to sin, endeavors to arrange the conditions that will allow and promote the natural processes of healing to take place readily, all of them as much a gift from God as life itself.

Although, to do so is immensely human, ought we to impugn to God, who cares about His world, the horror of congenital anomaly, of accidents to innocents, or of natural "acts of God" in which many lose their lives? It is a profound mystery why these occur: why stinging wasps, pathogenic bacteria and viruses, and worms and parasites of incredible variety plague both animals and man. Does God promote evil, sickness, sin? Or course not! He goes out of His way to reclaim, limited only by our freedom to choose to turn from Him. The Resurrection begins a constant ongoing reclamation of His children and of His world.

Do the Beatitudes speak to us of brash and arrogant conjecture and intervention? No, more important is calm, compassionate consideration of symptom and sign and plan of care. Even our Lord carefully reminds us of the need for careful discernment (diagnosis) of the cause (be it spiritual or physical or both) of ailments when He remarks that some ills respond only to prayer and to fasting (Mathew 17:21).

Sin is a part of medical diagnosis and treatment as it is of any human activity. It is inherent in the brazen, magnificent, highly technical ministrations of turn-of-the-millenium Western medicine, but also in the low-tech day-to-day activities of *sophrosyne* (prudence): seat belts, handwashing, temperance, clean air and water, sewage systems, food inspection, dietary moderation, and so on. It is present in the foolishness of the gullible as much as in the deception of the quack. But should we then abandon the compassion and love (which must come from God) of those who care for us, the ill, because they use the strengths and learning that promote healing? Serious mistakes in judgement can and do occur. These are often much more horrendous because we in the late twentieth century found an armamentarium of really potent drugs and techniques. (So, it seems, have the bacteria and other agents of disease!)

Where can one draw a line between the spiritual and the psychophysical in man? Where does one draw such a line between private or corporate prayer and the ministrations of the physician, nurse, or surgeon? Why bother to do so? The Holy Spirit urges us to do all things in love towards our fellow man. All healers are acquainted with the power of love and repentance as well as the properties of drugs and the results of surgical efforts. In some mysterious way, the very presence and compassion of the healer plays a major role in healing. Medicine, knowing this, is a long history of cries for mercy; perhaps this can always be one manifestation of a return from living outside God's kingdom.

A Psychological Response to Faros

George Morelli

"Sickness and Sin" by Fr. Philotheos Faros has strengths and weaknesses that may at first glance delight the theologian but will surely confound the medical/psychology scientists and practitioners. The author's attempt to propose a holistic view of mankind – that is, body, mind, and spirit – is, of course, consistent with the Christian perspective and the goals of the Orthodox Christian Association of Medicine, Psychology and Religion (OCAMPR). This is a strength and is a quite laudable purpose. His lapses into logical inconsistencies and fallacies, use of terms with surplus meaning, broad generalizations, truncated presentation of modern medical science, and lack of scientific citations may actually serve as a barrier to the acceptance of a holistic approach by the general medical and psychological community, and thus quite unintentionally thwart his original worthy goal.

Surely as Orthodox Christians we know there are various disease paths that relate to the tripartite wholeness that we are (body/mind/spirit). However, Faros seems to excoriate the body etiology. He states that modern medicine has "changed the names of those mysterious powers and instead of calling them demons calls them viruses, bacteria, or neoplasia... their essence and the way they operate is exactly the same with that of the demons...". Not only is this statement blatantly wrong for the reason listed above, but it is theologically unsound as well. Did not the evil one tempt Our Lord to defy the laws of nature He Himself created by throwing Himself down from the temple pinnacle? St. Matthew tells us: "Then the devil took him to the holy city, and set him on the pinnacle of the temple, and said to him, "If you are the Son of God, throw yourself down; for it is written, 'He will give his angels charge of you,' and 'On their hands they will bear you up, lest you strike your foot against a stone.'" Jesus said to him, "Again it is written, 'You shall not tempt the Lord your God'" (Matthew 4:5–7). The laws of nature, including the way viruses and bacteria work, are as much God-given as our minds and souls. Are we not tempting God to think differently? The author goes on to compare antibiotic treatment to exorcism. If his point is that there is a psychological and/ spiritual dimension along with a medical factor in a disease, that should be treated, then this should be so stated. The author's reasoning is spurious. Fr. Faros then goes on to accuse modern medicine of treating symptoms instead of an underlying disease. His example is a treatment of ulcer pain rather than the ulcer itself. If this is what is generally done, the author would be correct. But this is not general medical practice. Sound treatment would look for the etiology of the ulcer (i.e., bacteria, stress) and treat accordingly (antibiotics, etc.). Furthermore the Orthodox Christian clinician would also look for psychological and spiritual factors that may be primary and/or secondary causes of such a disease, and commence a treatment plan.

While the author's allusion to medical treatment as "satanic" is unhelpful, his view that genuine healing involves "personal cost," "a piece of his own soul" is accurate. Fr. Faros refers to Our Lord's healing of the woman with the issue of blood: "and she felt in her body that she was healed of her disease. And Jesus, perceiving in himself that power had gone forth from him, immediately turned about in the crowd, and said, "Who touched my garments?" (Mark 5:29–30). Instead of indicting what is implied in his paper as "modern Western medicine," the author would have made a stronger argument if he had indicted simply the practice of soulless/spiritless medicine. (It would not be inaccurate to also indict the practice of the priest who would eschew the healing of the body, or to indict the practice of good works without God's love. We all know the words of St. Paul: "If I speak in the tongues of men and of angels, but have not love, I am a noisy gong or a clanging cymbal" [1 Corinthians 13]).

In another proposition, the author's presentation of ancient Greek medicine in demonstration of the unity of man would have been excellent if it had been presented as a metatheory rather than a theory. Such a metatheory guides OCAMPR, for example, with its emphasis on body, mind, and spirit and the attempt to effect integration and healing on all three levels. However, each discipline must be understood and reached in the way that is proper to it: the body by scientific medical procedures (drugs, surgery, etc.), the mind by scientific psychological procedures (environmental/behavioral/cognitive management[1] and the soul by natural and supernatural spiritual factors (prayer/grace etc.). This is not to say that interaction between domains does not take place, as has been demonstrated by research findings. The well-documented research on stress and health (disease) from the subspecialty of health psychology behavioral medicine is but one example.[2] The miracles Our Lord performed during His public life and that God performs through His saints also attest to extraordinary interaction between the supernatural and natural order. It should be noted that the existence of one domain, however, does not obviate the existence or functioning of the others. It should be remembered that God created the laws of nature in which the domains of body and mind lie. Thus, the domains as they function must be understood in and of themselves, followed by any attempts to understand their interaction among themselves and with the spiritual domain.

Likewise, the author's numerous scriptural citations and references to the Church Fathers may be used to describe one path among many in the disease model, namely, the spiritual path. While we may say that Adam brought on disease and death by his break with God, this does not obviate the natural laws by which they operate. The course that disease and death follows is the natural law of the way the material universe functions, which of course was created by God. Part of the reason for the confusion among theologians and scientists is the differing way the word "nature" or "natural" is defined. For the theologian, this term means, in part, what God originally intended for mankind (mankind's original state before the fall of Adam, without sickness and death). The scientist, on the other hand, defines these terms as referring to the laws by which the universe functions, which are discernible by systematic observation and experimentation. Both definitions are correct in their domains. This is even one more reason to allow the domains to be understood in and of themselves.

Models in the future that will be applicable to the medical and behavioral (psychological) domains will probably change over time, in part as a reaction to previous approaches and new questions. This would be even be more reason that as Orthodox Christians we need a holistic guide (metatheory) to direct our path in both our theory and our practice. As I write this response the cloning of a sheep and rhesus monkeys has been reported in the media. The challenge for Orthodox Christianity is not so much the ethics of cloning, but what the response should be after it takes place. (My working hypothesis scenario is that it will take place with or without official sanction.) Will we consider such clones human? Will they have a soul? Will God give them a soul even if they were made through cloning? Can clones be baptized? If a male is born (via cloning) after several generations of cloned females, will he be, for example, eligible for ordination as a priest or bishop? Such questions tend toward the core issues or our faith. Surely they will raise the issue of sin, sickness, and healing to a new level. It is possible in the face of such issues that the author's statement "Man has to make his contribution of faith and repentance to maintain his heath or to restore it" is most helpful. It is only in the context of faith and informed and spiritualized understanding that we are going to be able to work toward healing ourselves and society in the face of this and other problems yet unanticipated. Fr. Philotheos Faros has provided a reminder to us for the direction in which we should go.

NOTES

[1] Morelli G., Cognition, Emotion, Sacred Scripture and the Church Fathers. In J. T. Chirban (Ed.), *Sickness or Sin*. Westport, Conn.: 1997.
[2] Holmes, T,H, & Rahe, R.H., The Social Readjustment Rating Scale. *Journal of Psychosomatic Research. 1967: 11, 213-218.*

An Integrative Response to Faros

Vasilios Thermos

I always welcome texts written by Fr. Philotheos Faros with respect and gratefulness. In addition to their challenging content, I will never forget the decisive impact that his presence has had in Greece since 1976 in terms of bringing the grounded psychological element into the theological enthusiasm of the time and struggling for a synthesis. It is a matter of justice to acknowledge this indirect influence on my personal dedication to the task of integration as well.

By the chapter presented here, he brings to the table of contemporary medical theory and practice two realities: the psychological component and the theological dimension. The former emerged in the European psychosomatic medicine of the middle of the century (e.g., the "medicine of the personality" of Paul Tournier) as a reaction to the materialism then prevalent, but it becomes important again today because of the unbelievable advance in medical technology, which tends to dehumanize both the process and the patient. The latter enters the discussion as an open-minded reading of Patristic writings, attributing to health and disease their own theological background. Both come at a very critical moment.

A notion has developed among faithful physicians suggesting that the highest quality of care, on their own part, would be to practice their diagnosis and treatment as carefully and assiduously they can, under the feeling that they work with a living icon of God, and through the aid of prayer. Athough this deserves appreciation, by doing so one absolutely accepts the theoretical models of medicine taught (the "why" and the "how"

171

of etiology) and limits his Christian identity up to the level of the ethos of the treatment. (It is with great sadness that we discover pious mental health professionals, as well, behaving in the same way by treating the patient only clinically, without any consideration of his psychodynamics contributing to the disorder).

Obviously, one cannot demand that every clinician act like a pioneering theoretician. The almost complete lack of any questions psychologically and theologically oriented among the medical population, though, causes us to worry about the very quality of services provided, on one hand, and the depth of understanding and living of the Christian message, on the other. The reason for neglecting both the psychodynamic and the spiritual causes of physical disorders is perspicaciously described in Fr. Filotheos' lecture: *the mechanical approach does not require personal involvement*, so that the clinician may let his own defenses alone; escape from revising his own morbid lifestyle, which also may violate human limits; and avoid reexperiencing the anxiety of helplessness and death.

Physicans are not accustomed to view diseases as signs of nature's health and dynamism and as protests agains violation of psychosomatic laws. Moreover, psychiatrists and psychologists would find this idea eccentric and absurd. Unfortunately, focusing on mere relief has become an obsession mainly in Western mentality, where physical pain arouses anxiety, psychic pain produces despair, and existential pain generates embarassment.

Only God knows how many of the physical diseases treated in hospitals (some of them chronic and perplexing) and absorbing huge amounts of money are *the "legitimate" manifestation of crying, suffocating, or lethargic souls; or how many of them function as self-designed substitutes for psychotherapy and repentance.* The systemic school of psychiatry enabled us to discern the function of disease in the family as unconsciously desired, as a "solution" to marital problems, as a form of communication, as a facilitation of decision making, and so on, but all this remarkable work remains still outside of the mainstream thought of physicians. The self-confidence generated by medical technology, and the insecurity felt in front of something new and not tangible, prevent progress from fertilizing the diagnostic process and from saving a lot of money.

Quite the same resistance is found among the clergy, who prefer to view sickness as either an "accident," which has to be faced patiently and piously, or as a mere "ordeal" from God, which must be confronted without questions. By doing so, they are unable to identify disease as a hysterical maneuver or as a sign of marital conflict or as a result of repression, and *thus they cannot elaborate the spiritual origins and facilitate a spiritual awakening.*

Christians who are guided in this way tend to misrecognize their own sinfulness and to attribute God's disapproval to the wrong or minor causes, usually ignoring their inability or reluctance to love. This attitude predisposes also to erroneous understandings of the bearing of the Cross, in a rather passive-aggressive way. (Churches are full of persons practicing narcissistic sacrifices who, when their "bill" is not welcomed by their beloved, invent other ways to be paid or to punish, one of which is physical suffering.) Questions arise here about the degree to which Old Testament punitive and legalistic approaches characterize pastors and the pastoral care exercised.

Among the remarkable points of the lecture, we should count the thesis that it is natural for the soul to love and forgive and that we pay a high price if we ignore it. The more one assimilates this truth, the more frequently and intensely he poses the question "Why does the only genuine catalyst of people's change toward love and forgiveness, namely the Church, not function? When will she start too?" *It is not a surprise that Eastern religious movements have been activated "curatively" behind their holistic mask but with all their disastrous impacts, yet it is definitely a tragedy that the Church "offers" people to them through her theoretical and practical carelessness.*

The other reason for which these awakening truths come at a critical moment is the recent enthusiasm stemming from genetic research, which *tends to attribute a biological casuality to the majority of the mental disorders.* This trend has found a strong ally (if not its basic motivation) in the plans of pharmaceutical firms and in the reluctance of the insurance companies to pay for psychotherapies. A psychodynamic diagnosis and a psychotherapeutic treatment often prevent both of them from becoming richer; and in contemporary society, scientific findings are not always reliably scientific, at least to the degree that they are interwoven with economic interests. We Christian professionals feel weak before those huge financial organizations, but we still have the privilege of the possibility that we may knowledgably act in the precious domain of human souls.

The hurricane of the biological etiology, which is now almost omnipotent in America, *relieves from anxiety indeed by insulating the subject and his disorders from his inner dynamics and, consequently, from his freedom.* (And we know that freedom arouses anxiety.) For example, attributing homosexuality and alcoholism exclusively to genes, massively overdiagnosing attention deficit–hyperactivity disorder (even in cases of normal vitality culturally rejected, or hyperactivity due to anxiety stemming from family problems), and prescribing antidepressants or anxiolytics for normal effects do not offer good service to people and *reduce them to merely adapting beings;* but if this is considered sufficient by secular circles, it cannot be accepted by Christians, who are supposed to share a higher appreciation for the ultimate creature of God. Obviously, the body participates, but this is quite different from adopting cultural stereotypes as scientific truth to be exported, or from degrading the term "psychotherapy" by bizarre techniques. By thus insisting on the psychological and theological element and pursuing integration, Orthodox professionals possess an excellent opportunity to function as the leaven of the Gospel within a dehumanizing, scholar's universe.

I would like to conclude by indicating axes of future research that in my opinion should be highlighted. They stem from Fr. Filotheos' suggestions, and they are divided into three groups corresponding to the three components OCAMPR.

THEOLOGICAL INQUIRY

1). If sin results in sickness, what is the full content of sin, not in general abstract words already known but *in concrete anthropological terms?* Which are the structural threads connecting sin and disease? A reconsideration of some sins could emerge, or probably a modification of the widely accepted hierarchy of sins toward a more ecclesiological direction. *Psychology here could help by lending its terms to theological anthropology,* e.g., by helping clarify the concepts of healthy love and patience vs. the narcissistic ones, or by articulating a more integrated notion of the relationship between spirituality and sexuality.

2). *Why doesn't divine forgiveness in the sacrament of confession cure physically and psychically?* What is the real meaning of repentance and the very essence of forgiveness under the challenge of health and disease? Should the Church reconsider the way in which she perceives spiritual cure and practices her pastoral care in order to correct misunderstandings? I guess that her task here will be double: to promote confession among her members (and clergy, why not?) who ignore it, and to help some faithful, who systematically confess, to recognize their own illusion that they are really repenting.

3). It seems that certain kinds of diseases enjoy miracles whereas others do not. Does this discrimination say anything about differing spiritual backgrounds to the various illnesses? Does it require any modification of human attitudes toward them?

PSYCHODYNAMIC RESEARCH

1). *What is the relationship between temperament (as the early material) or character (as the later crystallization) with physical diseases and passions?* How could early morbid traits be discerned and treated spiritually and psychologically for prevention's sake? How are passions translated into insane patterns of behavior, and which turns into which? With the exception of type A personality, the topic has been neglected in research and is almost ignored in pastoral theology. How could psychological "schools" shed light on the pastoral implications of character and of illness?

2). How is disease related to marriage and other interpersonal interactions like friendship, collaboration, and leadership? *How and why does it become a "developmental" phase in their evolution?* What is the function of illness in the psychology of the couple, the family, the group and the Church in terms of promoting behaviors impossible before, and changing radically the dynamics in an unpleasant way but toward the desired result? Systemic theory has produced valuable pages here on the family, but there is still plenty of space for fruitful work in other contexts that are too common both in secular life and in the Church.

3). *To what degree does culture intervene and modify or distort the meaning of sin or of mental disorder or of personality?* How and to what extent does it reveal to scholars certain aspects of the truth, or prevent them from having access to others? What, then, are the implications if the truth is a divine one? Can "spirituality" be misunderstood and practiced in dangerous and non-Orthodox ways by Christian mental health professionals with good intentions, and how can that be avoided?

Medical Work

1). What are the psychological factors in physical diseases other than those already known to be psychosomatic? Which of them predispose to accidents, and which interfere and alter the patient's response to medication? Emphasis on psychophysiology, psychooncology, psychoimmunology, and psychoendicronology should be given here. Also, once new scientific paths are discovered and established, how might research expenses be compensated by the savings in reducing needless diagnoses and treatments.

2). How should medical training change? This is a key question. There is a lot of already known material waiting to be included in the curriculum once resistances are overcome, like the psychology of the patient, the psychology of the medical relationship, the psychosomatic syndromes, the psychological aspects of habits such as smoking, overdrinking, and dangerous driving, the physical consequences of which absorb remarkable amounts of money and human potential. Mental health professionals, adept in the inner processes, should be invited to help in the formation of physicians in medical schools.

3). How must professional associations protect patients by defining more clearly their own borders in order to distinguish ourselves from charlatans or dangerous practitioners who act in the name of spirituality? What are the essential criteria and what are the legal aspects of this separation? What useful challenges do these phenomena offer to Christian physicians in terms of criticizing and reevaluating their own way of treatment and its psychotheological background? Which of our gaps and defects do they try to fill?

Concluding, I would like to thank Fr. Philotheos once again for sharing his vision with us and OCAMPR for both inviting him and providing me with the opportunity of this comment. *Integration is a worthwhile and promising topic because it follows the tracks of human nature, which was simple and united before the Fall and is meant to be so again in the Kingdom to come.*

A Dialogue

Dimitrios Oreopoulos, J. Stephen Muse, and Philotheos Faros

Medical Reflections – Dimitrios Oreopoulos

One thing I had difficulty with in Fr. Faros's presentation is his statement that "physicians and psychologists should get involved with curing the symptoms and not with healing." If I remember rightly, he actually said that if a physician or psychologist attempts healing, it would be "unethical" or "criminal," or something to that effect.

When a psychologist asked Fr. Faros what we should do with a person who is suffering, he suggested that we should tell this person to go to an *ekklesia*. He subsequently defined an *ekklesia* as a gathering of people who are eager to serve each other, who should leave the Sunday service knowing two or three of the other people.

My position, which may be wrong, is that we (both lay and priests) are involved in a continuous healing of ourselves and others. I believe that the Holy Spirit, Who is the ultimate healer, acts through us, and that any encounter between two human beings, either by chance or in a therapeutic relationship (patient-physician or patient-psychologist) is therefore a holy one. There is a potential for healing if through that encounter we both submit and allow the Holy Spirit to work through us. Fr. Faros very rightly indicated in his talk that if one goes to church without knowing who the man or woman on each side of him is, his blessings will not have any effect, no matter how many he gives. The *ekklesia* he described is a thing of the past, however.

We should try to create something like it, but until that happens, there will be no healing in the manner he described.

On the contrary, I believe that each of us can create our own "*ekklesia*" in our personal environment, where we have an opportunity to provide the service Fr. Faros described. For each person, this *ekklesia* consists of those around him or her, starting with the spouse – with whom there is often a lot of animosity – the rebelling children (another relationship that needs healing), colleagues who attack or criticize him or her, or even outright enemies. I believe that we can achieve healing if we join this "*ekklesia*" and make sure to accept, forgive, avoid judging, and – the ultimate thing, as Christ said – love our enemies.

I believe that psychologists or physicians as well as nonpsychologists and nonphysicians – anybody – can help the individual sufferer achieve this type of healing. I can attest from personal experience, and from the experience of many people I know, that a good physician or psychologist can help individuals not only avoid disasters (like suicide) but also grow and become much better people, which I consider a kind of healing.

To avoid any misunderstanding, I would say that the most important contribution for each individual is to heal him- or herself. In a strange way, however, this can only be done through our brothers and sisters, and especially those whom the Holy Spirit leads us to encounter in our journey.

PSYCHOLOGICAL REFLECTIONS – J. STEPHEN MUSE

I heard Fr. Faros cleanly lifting up the community of faith, which restores the *nous* to its true existential form that cannot occur apart from the Body of Christ. Outside of community – even community with our physician and counselor as Dr. Oreopoulos points out, accurately I believe – we are not totally healed, i.e., "saved." This distinction is even in the gospels, depending on how you read the Greek: Three words for healing, and all are employed to describe Jesus' healing ministry in dis-

tinct ways: θεραπεύω, ίομαι, and σώζω. The latter alone pertains to salvation, soul-healing, while the former two concern
healing of body and body parts without salvation. If medicine
and psychology heal a hand or normalize an emotion, they have
not necessarily helped one reconnect with the marriage of the
soul and Christ's Body, His church, which is the aorta for the
medicine of the Holy Spirit coming through the sacraments
and life of the church, the *ekklesia*.

Of course, when the *ekklesia*, as Dr. Oreopoulos points out,
is little more than an ethnic social club, without prayer and
genuine search and service, one wonders if the Holy Spirit's
ability to heal is hampered. Hierotheos Vlachos, in his writings
on the Church as hospital and the priests as psychotherapists,
makes a distinction between priests who can "heal" because they
are alive spiritually and priests who cannot, although there is
still the action of the Holy Spirit, which can render the poorest
vessel a healing agent or even, as in the case of Cornelius, bring
healing even before a human agent is available! I believe one
reason psychotherapy has emerged is that in the West, the
Church lost its healing power; confession was not taken seriously, worship was diluted, and Christianity was not a way of
life but a superficial justification for a worldly status quo. Even
so, the liturgy is instructive, and God's presence is real enough.

I hope there is more of a seamlessness between the *ekklesia*
and the "world" as far as God's grace is concerned. I hope the
Lord is still crying out in the highways and byways for the
marginalized and forgotten and alienated to come into His feast.
I'm not sure what our distinctions between *ekklesia* and the Lord's
larger Body means in light of this. There is the ontological dimension of God's presence in all places and filling all things;
"the fountain of every blessing," and there is the existential or
actual everyday experience of human life in community that
seems as ordinary in the Church as anywhere else at times –
even more so, perhaps. In other words, "We Orthodox know
where Christ is, but we cannot say where He is not." All that is

good in the world is of Christ. Can it be otherwise? That would make no sense. So clearly, physicians and therapists and all human beings may be agents of healing, and those who are not against Him are for Him. It is not, as Dr. Oreopoulos points out, sufficient to tell the man with heart blockage, or the woman who is suicidal, or even the persons yearning to find depth in Christ to simply go to church. Plenty go with burning hearts, and *baklava* (a pastry) is not enough to satisfy, nor is incomprehension of the language enough to instruct. Or the priest's counsel is insipid. Many years ago, when I was searching for depth as a Protestant minister, I went to a Greek priest of a local community for help. He quoted General MacArthur and Billy Graham to me. I went away crestfallen and sought out a Roman Catholic priest, who helped me pray the rosary. Some years later I tried again. This time the new priest heard my yearning and put me in contact with Fr. Ephraim. In him I found a healer, who then directed me back to the *ekklesia* just as Fr. Faros has done, quick to avoid guruism. The sacraments are alive and well in the sickest church body that appears most superficial, just as in the lowest most marginalized apparently un-Christian person in the world, if God gives us the eyes to see whom He has wonderfully and fearfully made. So it is a full circle. Seeking the mystical, we find the mystical in that which we turned away from in search of something more. Yet, not to seek is perhaps never to find the Kingdom that is right at hand.

I don't yet know where exactly Fr. Faros and I disagree on particulars, because I am sure I am confronting my own impression of his words, more so than an accurate understanding of his full perspective. But I think he makes more of a distinction between Orthodoxy and psychology than I do. I think there is a good deal of overlap in terms of there being in every healing methodology an implicit cosmology and anthropology. Orthodoxy certainly has a view of the human person – a teleology (theosis) and a view of the universe. How healing proceeds in this context is different than in a Freudian universe, which cannot move beyond "empiricism" to affirm a transcendent God and action of the Holy Spirit, for example. Sexuality is not sacramental but more of a physical or vital drive when seen through the mechanical metaphors of the Industrial Revolution, like "drives and instinct," which Freud utilized. This is simplistic and perhaps overstated, but you get my point. Fr. Faros says, "It makes no more sense to me to talk about an Orthodox psychotherapy than it does an Orthodox plumbing, beyond the fact that such practitioners may be Orthodox Christians and thus bring a special kindness and integrity, etc. to their work." I certainly agree that the latter is true, but more than that I believe that plumbing does not have a cosmology and anthropology, as do psychotherapy and medicine (pathology-based versus wellness). For this reason, I think that we need to discuss this further, lest Orthodoxy succumb to ignoring psychology altogether or worse, like the Protestants, accept it wholesale like a Trojan horse and have the house gutted from within by a subtle anti-Christian perspective inherent in some of the relativity and positivism or New Age syncretism that is part of much of the modern psychological perspectives.

A Response – Philotheos Faros

I believe that the words "health" and "healing" have not the same meaning for each of us.

I said that the cause of every symptom is itself a symptom of a deeper cause. The cause of a stomach pain may be an ulcer; the cause of an ulcer may be an interpersonal difficulty; the cause of the interpersonal difficulty may be the immaturity, selfishness, and egocentrism of the patient; egocentrism is the symptom of man's alienation from God. How is stopping the pain restoration of health? Or is restoration of physical health, or even the restoration of the disturbed interpersonal relationship, the ultimate cure, the fullest healing?

What I say is that none of this is ultimately healing, although it may be caring and curing. Healing is the achievement of full-ness of life, and that is much more than a physician or even a psychotherapist can do, although they both can contribute to healing if they point out to the patient that curing the ulcer or restoring the disturbed relationship is not the end of the story of his or her health and disease.

To make my point more clear, I will quote St. Basil's relevant views as presented in his *Opoi Kata*:

> We should cultivate and use medicine, when it is necessary, so that we don't attribute to it every cause of health and dis-ease.... when we are deprived of the help of medicine we should not put all our hopes for the alleviation and cure of diseases on this art... to put the hope for health in the hands of physicians is bestial, which is what happens to many people who do not hesitate even to call the physicians saviours.

PART THREE

INTEGRATING SPIRITUAL DISCERNMENT
AND DIFFERENTIAL DIAGNOSIS

Restoring the Healing Effect
of the Patient/Physician Relationship

Demetrios Oreopoulos

On May 6, 1995, the lead editorial in *Lancet* under the title "Who Owns Medical Technology" described the unexpected, unpredictable, and deleterious effects of technology on medical practice and warned how bleak the future looks for doctors, ascribing this in large part to medicine's increasing dependence on technology. The editorial predicted a diminishing role for doctors and an increased one for technicians. In concluding, the editorialist said, "If doctors are to survive they should relinquish their role as the guardians and gate keepers of the technological fountain and... instead should return to their roots as healers and teachers."[1] In this chapter, I will review how, in the evolution of medicine over the last two and a half millennia, we have moved away from our initial role as healers and how I believe we can return to our roots – that is, becoming healers again, if we pay attention to the healing effect of the patient-doctor relationship.

The Hippocratic tradition with the ethical principle enshrined in the oath "With purity and holiness I will pass my life and practice my art" exhorts physicians to cultivate virtue and focus on the moral life. Adhering to this, the Hippocratic physician would attain the key virtue of *phronesis* and thereby discern the correct thing to do in each particular situation.[2]

Renaissance

Early physicians viewed the body (soma) and soul (psyche)

187

as inseparable; they believed that the soul was the ultimate source of all physiological function. Subsequently, however, Francis Bacon removed the soul and human behavior from the purview of science and thereby set the stage for the body/soul split so characteristic of modern medicine. In his classic work *Treatise of Man*, Descartes viewed the body as a machine and the soul as an entity separate from the body. Freud opened the door to the psyche and its relationship not only to psychological but to somatic disturbances, but he saw no need for "the soul," the spiritual part of man, and instead elevated "logos" to the status of "God."[3]

These philosophical systems divided the self into physical (body) cared for by the physician, mental (mind) cared for by the psychiatrist, and spirit cared for by the clergy.[4]

Since the separation of mind/body/soul, empirical science has made spectacular progress, but at a high price.[5] Physicians were enjoined to admit as valid data only verifiable perceptions of the five senses, thus barring from consideration any transpersonal phenomena. The spiritual dimensions of illness described as "subjective" were neglected because they were perceived as magic or wishful thinking.[6] However, these dimensions could not be banished from the experience the sick person. Thus it was that exclusive attention to curing the physical body did not meet the patient's need for healing of his mind or spirit, and the stage was set for conflict between physician and patient.

The practice of medicine has changed even more dramatically over the last 30 years and continues changing today.

Medicine is now being viewed as a commodity, subject to market forces.

The commerce culture, obvious in grocery stores and shopping malls, is now extending to health care. In this commercialization, the physicians, just one of the many health care providers, are no longer heroic healers but service providers suspect of their financial aspirations and their desire for status, power, and wealth.[1] Physicians have become interchangeable and have lost respect, and the patient/physician relationship is no longer sacred.

Large teaching institutions interchange the staff at all levels every 1 or 2 months, on the principle that anyone who is qualified can treat any particular patient.[6]

These changes further removed the individual physician from the individual patient, thus eroding the trust that formerly physicians earned from their patients.[7] Many began to fear that the doctors' true job of caring for sick people might soon be taken away, leaving them looking after only machines. It seems that modern medicine, while achieving enormous technological advances, has lost sight of the art, the spirit, and the intangibles such as faith, hope, and compassion for the patient, which are essential in the healing process. The close-up reassuring touch of the physician, the comfort and concern, are disappearing from the practice of medicine – a great loss to both patients and doctors.[3]

Feeling this loss, patients accuse us of being "insensitive" and "not caring" despite our conscientious efforts to do everything we can.[5] At a time when medical science has made the greatest advances in the history of mankind, the tension between doctor and patient has increased as never before.

In the meantime, while patients cry out for a closer relationship, external forces – third party payers, concerned only about costs – demand efficient "bare-bones" medicine that contains no rewards for empathy and careful listening, but instead, as we will discuss later on, provide financial incentives for doing less. The decision making power has been shifting from those who provide or those who receive care to those who pay for it.[45] Guidelines that once served as an aid to decision making will now dictate these decisions. I foresee even more profound changes in the patient-physician relationship, which already are reflected in the increasing use of such terms as "health providers," "health consumers," "cost effectiveness," and most sacrilegious of all, the word "clients" to describe our patients.

Twenty-five hundred years ago, in a remarkable passage in *The Laws*, Plato described what he called "slave medicine," where the slave physician is treating slave men. In this relationship, the slave physician "never gives the slave patient any account of his complaints, nor asks him for any; he gives him some empirical injunction with an air of finished knowledge in the brusque fashion of a dictator and then is off in hot haste to the next ailing slave."[6]

It looks as though we are heading toward the practice of "slave medicine." Our best defense against this outcome is to continuously remind ourselves that medicine, the profession we chose as our vocation, is a special kind of human activity, one that can not be pursued without the virtues of humility, honesty, intellectual integrity, compassion, and effacement of excessive self-interest.[10] We should maintain our commitment to the sanctity of the patient-physician relationship and remember why we went into medicine in the first place: to find meaning in our lives and to enjoy the spiritual dimensions of the activity of healing. In other words, as the *Lancet* editorial said, we should return to our roots as healers.

THE PATIENT

The patients' initial definition of illness, when they determine that they are ill and when the usual sense of well-being has been altered, is subjective. Thus, illness (what the patient experiences) is different from the disease (what the physician identifies).[11] By asking for the physician's help, the patient becomes dependent and therefore vulnerable, with loss of freedom and anxiety about loss of life. This sudden awareness of mortality is a distinct and dramatic departure from the sense of self that the patient enjoyed before the onset of illness. The patient experiences this loss of physical well-being as pain and suffering,[11] and it is this physical and existential uncertainty that brings the person to the physician. Despite modern advances, the patient continues to experience suffering and pain, fear of permanent invalidism, uncertainty about the type of investigations and the results of medical treatment, feelings of isolation and alienation, and, above all else, fear of death.[12]

THE PHYSICIAN

The physician, presented with a person who is vulnerable, uncertain, isolated, and anguished, responds with a promise to help and connect with the patient, an experience characterized by a particularly intense awareness of the other's feelings and a mutual closeness. The physician's sense of invulnerability and the patient's attribution to her of inappropriate powers over illness restores the patient's lost sense of immortality and has a powerful influence on the patient's response to his own illness.[11]

Physicians bring significant needs and expectations to the patient-physician relationship, including a desire to be needed by the patient and a sense of achievement and satisfaction from providing care.[13]

Physicians have the same fundamental needs as other human beings. Like our patients, we seek connection. Medicine offers us the possibility of connection with a most extraordinary range of people. We are granted the privilege of access to all manner of human experiences, which, if we are open to them, will promote our own growth.[5]

Like our patients, we also seek meaning and purpose in our lives. Our meaning as physicians is given to us by our patients. When we see that our care and attention have restored a sense of personal value to a patient who previously felt isolated and useless, we feel that our lives have value.[5]

Finally, if we watch ourselves carefully, we will often find out that we harbor particularly intense fears of death, feelings of powerlessness, or anxieties about the basic uncertainties of life. We are wounded, too. Because of this shared experience, a bond develops between the wounded healer and the patient; each is suffering, each is in need of healing, and each is capable of transforming illness into an opportunity for growth. We heal to be healed.[5] When we feel connected in this way to our patients and to our work, the long hours, the difficult decisions, and the many other stresses are sources of fulfillment.

THE PATIENT-PHYSICIAN RELATIONSHIP

I believe the patient-physician relationship is the heart and soul of primary care. It has been found to be the most important factor in most surveys of consumer satisfaction. The establishment of a healing relationship is a fundamental clinical task, coequal with the diagnosis and biotechnical treatment.

Nowadays, the term "healing" does not appear frequently in the doctor's vocabulary. It has connotations of a mystical/magical process, a spiritualism that is regarded as having roots in the unscientific and hysterical. It also implies that someone is empowered beyond scientific explanation. In this environment, we tend to concentrate on curing the disease and thus to neglect the healing of the patient.[14]

To "cure" means "to take charge" and denotes successful medical treatment. On the other hand, to "heal" means to make or become whole, to recover from sickness and get well. Healing is a process that is closely related to the word "holy": both words derive from the root term "wholeness." In our work with patients, we must aim for both curing and healing.[3]

Healing results if, in addition to curing, there is a balance of caring and compassion, blended with hope, humility, and humor.[15]

In a healing relationship, the physician must accept the patient completely, get close to the patient, listen, and try to experience his or her illness.[16] These goals cannot be achieved without becoming intimately involved. In such a relationship, both patient and physician are constantly growing, sometimes independently and at other times interdependently.

THE HEALING RELATIONSHIP

In a healing patient-physician relationship, the patient is seen as a unique and irreplaceable individual – a real and valuable person, not only as an object to be treated.[17]

To heal others, physicians must first have healed or be in the process of healing themselves. The biblical injunction "physician heal thyself" is essential in the healing of others. The most effective healers (the "wounded healers") are aware of their own wounds and know that they themselves are involved in a life-long process. In other words, one is never completely healed.

Osler believed that the physician must know herself lest she fail in her vocation of healing.

In a healing relationship the physician is warm, takes the patient's symptoms seriously, listens and asks questions about the symptoms, and treats the patient as a real person and not just "a patient." Patients always appreciate being asked about things other than symptoms, such as their family or work.

In a good relationship there is a lot of reciprocal eye contact, and the body positions face each other. Finally, touching, through a warm handshake or during the examination,[17] is an important step to break the barriers.

All of these help establish a healing relationship that will allay the patients' fears of abandonment, extinction, loss of self-esteem, and victimization. By caring in such a relationship, the physician brings hope, healing, and salvation.[4]

In a healing relationship, the physician experiences special moments of closeness and intimacy with the patient that are perceived to be both therapeutic and personally valuable.[5] These moments represent a dimension of human experience that is basic to medical care – a mutual experience of joining with a particularly intense awareness of another's feelings and mutual closeness, resulting in a sensation of wholeness, going beyond the boundaries of one's self to join with another. This moment may be followed by a feeling of love, a sense of privilege at having been allowed into the patient's life so vividly, and a humble feeling that one is part of something bigger than oneself.[5]

Such a relationship and approach are also important when we are confronted with terminally ill patients whose disease appears to be beyond treatment. Here, if we hold the narrow biomedical approach that our role is only to "cure the disease," we tend to feel helpless and pull back when "nothing can be done." In a healing relationship, we recognize that the therapeutic value of being present is an important kind of "doing," and hence we need not feel helpless or feel tempted to withdraw. We can find meaning for ourselves in helping patients maintain their connections as life ends.[5]

I will now discuss in a little more detail certain components of the healing relationship: caring, hope, trust, nonabandonment, and touch.

CARING

For healing to be achieved, the physician must care for her patients. Caring rejects impartiality, it sees individuals in relationships, it demands more rights and is sensitive not to the principles but to the person. Caring requires sympathy and asks that we recognize interdependence and attend more to the relationship.[6]

Caring is a connection between two human beings expressed by the act of accepting an individual; honoring his uniqueness, complexity, feelings, and needs; and believing that each person's life makes a difference. In an act of caring, there is a sense of oneness, fulfillment, and growth of both parties involved. Such an intimate interaction distinguishes profession from occupation.[18]

The goal of "person professions" such as theology, law, nursing, and medicine is to help individuals in life crises. Although many still assume that the modern professional still cares, physicians, patients, and others involved in health care delivery now express a growing concern over a perceived decreased level of caring. They are concerned that professionals have become de-personalized, labeling people as numbers, clients, codes, or diseases.[18]

Pellegrino describes four parts of caring that constitute what he calls "integral" caring:[19]

1). Sharing another's experience of illness and pain, or simply being affected by the experience.

2). Doing for patients what they cannot do for themselves.

3). Caring for the medical problems, i.e., understanding the patient's anxieties and need for answers.

4). Carrying out the necessary technical and personal procedures.

The care of the good Samaritan toward the unfortunate victim offers a role model for such a human fellowship.

HOPE

Hope is a vital ingredient of mental health. It is a powerful motivator, and it protects a person from the ravages of despair.

Hope begins with love from others that mobilizes what is inside and frees us to move.

Though ultimately hope is a spiritual need, and some of its dimensions can be met by God alone, we can create a milieu of hope in several ways:

1). Providing a supportive climate by loving, understanding, accepting, and caring.

2). Encouraging hopeful perceptions.

3). Helping the person make plans.

4). Assisting the person to take action.

5). Talking to them as persons and not as "cancer patients," for example.

6). Building relationships, and promoting involvement in creative projects, participation in recreation, and development of new interests.

With terminal patients, in whom complete restoration is not

realistic, goals and plans still are important because they provide focus, meaning and purpose to the continuing struggle.

Any individual who conveys hope to a patient functions as a minister because he or she educates the patient regarding the unknown and the unexpected and therefore promotes healing.[18]

TRUST

The perception that the physician will do what is best for her is the *sine qua non* of the successful patient-physician relationship.[35] Trust is not just reassuring but is also healing. Similarly, healing is impeded by even the slightest doubt about the physician's competence, sincerity, and motivation.[20]

In today's climate it is difficult to convince patients that we have their best interest at heart. This is particularly difficult in countries where the practice of medicine is considered a commercial interaction, the ultimate goal of which is the betterment of the physician. While the "client" involved in this commercial transaction may benefit from it, the main reason the provider enters into the transaction is to improve his or her own condition.[21] This attitude, implicitly felt by the patient, cannot ensure trust. A trustworthy physician is only the one who places the good of the patient as the ultimate goal of the relationship with the patient.[21] Physicians are not and must never become commercial entrepreneurs or agents of fiscal policies that run counter to their patients' interests. The patient's belief in the depth of the physician's commitment to what is best for her is essential to establish and sustain the trust in the relationship so important for optimal healing.[22]

NONABANDONMENT

The commitment never to abandon the patient is a fundamental ethical obligation of physicians once they enter into this relationship. It encompasses a large part of medical ethics, such as care of the whole person and attention to the details in the patient's life and illness.[1]

This commitment (never to abandon) makes a world of difference to the patient. It makes the difference between facing an uncertain future alone and facing it with a committed, caring, knowledgeable partner who will not shy away from difficult decisions when the path is unclear.[23]

TOUCH

As noted earlier, the close, reassuring touch of the physician and the accompanying comfort and concern seem to be disappearing from the practice of medicine. Once lost, even for one generation, it may be difficult to bring it back again. We must learn again, and teach the new generations of physicians, that holding a hand is sometimes more important than examining one.[15]

Expressive touch is beneficial as a physical, psychological and spiritual communication and meets the needs of body, mind, and spirit.[24] Such expressive touch conveys powerful healing messages such as trust, hope, empathy, reassurance, and presence.

During illness, the need for touch may increase. Under certain circumstances, touch can help overcome illness. The need for touch increases with age. Finally, touching increases the comfort of dying persons, assuring them that they are not abandoned and that their needs will continue to be met.[24]

If touch is to be therapeutic, both patient and physician must feel comfortable with the giving and receiving of it.

RISKS

The establishment of a close relationship and the sharing of personal thoughts creates a profound sense of intimacy, which can give rise to three potentially dangerous reactions[25]: (1) complementary wishes of dependency on the part of the patient and for power on the part of the clinician, (2) increased susceptibility to pain on the part of the clinician, and (3) sexual attraction.

For the physician, suppressing the sexual feeling of attraction is not possible nor valuable; however, acting on these feelings is wrong even when the patient appears to consent. Because the patient is in a vulnerable position, one cannot accept at face value a patient's apparent consent to sexual relations. Very wisely, Hippocrates forbids this in his oath.

MANAGED CARE AND THE PATIENT-PHYSICIAN RELATIONSHIP

Now I would like to address the effect that managed care, this new phenomenon, has on the patient-physician relationship.

Managed care developed in an effort to restrict costs and at the same time provide uniform, satisfactory health care to all individuals. This corporate business model of health care behaves like the supermarket chain that has no explicit or corporate responsibilities to provide food for someone who is hungry but cannot pay.[26] The focus is only on the billions of dollars to be made.

For the success of the various plans, i.e., reduction of costs or profits, the cooperation of the physicians, forced or otherwise, is mandatory.

Managed care places the physician in a terrible conflict of interest: she is expected to accept responsibility toward the plan as well as fulfill her traditional role as an advocate for the individual patients. Thus, expecting the physician is expected to be a double agent.

The most frightening aspect of managed care is the introduction of incentives to the physicians, such as year-end bonus, promotion, salary increases, renewed contracts, and increased prestige bestowed on those who limit costs by limiting care, with the inherent risk of decreasing patient advocacy and limiting the physicians' ability to respect their patients' autonomy, thus alienating the physicians and undermining the patients' trust in their physicians' motives.[27]

In this environment of managed care, the spirit of the patient-physician relationship is in particular jeopardy if both physicians and patients begin to believe that physicians are fund holders, gate closers, or clinical economists rather than physicians and healers. Physicians must never lose sight of their obligation to care for patients without regard to their ability to pay. The only reflection that the physician must engage with every patient encounter is "How can I help you?" or, even better, "How can I serve you?"[18]

Pellegrino provides a six-part prescription for collective action on the part of medical profession in a managed care environment:[28]

1). Physicians are physicians first, not managed care professionals.

2). Physicians must remain stewards of quality of care.

3). Physicians must insist on the integrity of the patient-physician relationship and on medical ethics independent of social or government pressures.

4). Physicians must oppose any financial incentives to modify their behavior in a way that can harm patients.

5). Physicians must always maintain the primacy of their patient's good.

6). Physicians must encourage support and participation in studies of therapeutic efficiency and how to improve the scientific and humane aspects of managed care.

TEACHING THE HEALING ASPECTS OF THE PATIENT-PHYSICIAN RELATIONSHIP

Can we teach a new generation of physicians the therapeutic aspects of this healing relation with their patients'? Most would agree that the present treatment of the spiritual aspects of caring in our medical education is insufficient. Although we select the best and the brightest for our medical schools, we end up with self-interested physicians who talk about money, are completely captivated by technology, and are no longer fundamentally devoted to sick persons. In many cases, the products of our medical schools are shockingly second-rate except with respect to technological competence.

Many call for improved training of physicians in interviewing and the psychosocial aspects of care. The great challenge for medical education is to create a learning experience that will teach the art of medicine. This challenge must be met if we are to train truly scientific yet fully humanistic physicians.[29]

Students who dedicate themselves to both the science of medicine and the Hippocratic oath of doing nothing that is not in the best interest of one's patients soon find out that it is not an easy way of life. But for the student who sacrifices a part of himself to achieve the essence of being a good physician, there is a special blessing that no material wealth can possibly compare.[30]

To achieve such a balanced education, we must shift our emphasis from the present biomedical model to a biopsychosocial one. We should introduce changes that emphasize relationship skills and connectional experiences, and give them the same attention and time during clinical teaching as we give physical examination skills and diagnostic reasoning. Self-awareness and personal growth would be included among the explicitly stated goals of the educational process.

Such educational efforts should begin early and extend throughout the medical school years.

We should emphasize that the therapeutic power of the patient-physician relationship lies in mutual respect and interest. For the students to learn respect for persons, they must be treated by their teachers with the utmost respect. Indeed, this is only wise self-interest, because these students are our most valuable assets and our only hope to improve our health care in the future.

Students should learn to allow the patients tell their stories without interrupting them. While taking the history they should silence any internal talk and listen to the patient's story; this will help them switch from hearing a mere description to entering the patient's life experience.[25]

If they listen what their patients are trying to say, and if they are compassionate and sensitive to their patients' needs, they will help them not only feel better but do better. Surprisingly, they will feel better, too.[15] In 1928, the famous American clinician Francis Peabody wrote that the good physician must lavishly dispense time, sympathy, and understanding in order to know his patients, but he is rewarded by a personal bond that is one of the greatest satisfactions in the practice of medicine. He wrote, "One of the essential qualities of the clinician is interest in humanity, for the secret in caring for the patient is the care of the patient."[31]

Beyond feeling understood, patients often feel the need to feel accepted, especially after personal feelings come to light.

Finally, we should emphasize to our students the need for effective clinical communication.

Effective communication between doctor and patient is a central clinical function.[1] Good communication can improve patient and physician satisfaction and has been shown to improve health outcomes. Poor communication leads to complaints, and sometimes litigation; in fact, poor communication is a major factor in litigation. Despite the documented importance of communicating well, serious communication problems are common in clinical practice.[1]

Communication skills can be taught and can be assessed with a useful degree of accuracy; current evaluation techniques can establish minimal standards of competence that each candidate should be required to demonstrate before graduation.

Such courses, which should have a relatively low student-to-teacher ratio, require development by, and participation of, outstanding clinicians who will act as role models.

They also require a major commitment on the part of all the staff to new education and study .

CONCLUSION

Like the author of the *Lancet* editorial, I am convinced that our survival depends on our scientific excellence blended with a healing patient-physician relationship. Only one word can summarize the effective healing relationship, and that word is love. But I have to specify the kind of love. I do not mean the kind of love that makes you profess that you love the whole world, but instead the kind of love that makes you love this particular person in front of you, with all his problems, who needs your time and total attention. The kind of love that will make you recognize in this particular individual your neighbor – your *plesion*– as Christ Himself. Therefore, such a love becomes essential for our survival as a profession. Many centuries ago Hippocrates said that without the love for man there is no love for medicine. Another healer two thousand years ago gave us the model of the Good Samaritan and the Golden Rule. Loren Eiseley, an evolutionist, said, "No creature in the world demands more love than man; no creature is less adapted to survive without it."[32] In this respect, I recommend M. A. Adson's excellent article, "An endangered ethic – the capacity of caring"; there Adson says, "We can understand our science, but if we have no love we are nothing to those in need. In our obligations to others, we are in an enviable position – closer to this fundamental truth than are most men and women. We can derive strength and satisfaction from our charity and at the same time help those in need. Governments and some corporations may be able to function without souls, but as healers we cannot."[33]

NUMBERED REFERENCES

[1] "Who Owns Medical Technology?" *Lancet* 1995;345:1125-6.

[2] Kenny NP. "The Ethic of Care and the Patient-Physician Relationship." *Annals* RCPSC 1994;27:356-358.

[3] Rosen DH. "Modern Medicine and the Healing Process." *Humane Medicine* 1989;5:18-23.

[4] D'Aunay D, Rodning CB. "Patient-Physician Interaction: Healing Power of a Covenant Relationship." *Humane Medicine* 1988;4:107109.

[5] Suchman AL, Matthews DA. "What Makes the Patient-Doctor Relationship Therapeutic? Exploring the Connexional Dimension of Medical Care." *Annals of Internal Medicine* 1988;108:125-130.

[6] Siegler M. "Falling off the Pedestal: What Is Happening to the Traditional Doctor-Patient Relationship?" *Mayo Clinic Proc* 1993;68:461-467.

[7] Schwartz TB. "Sinful Saints or Saintly Sinners?" (Editorial). *Southern Medicine Journal* 1995;88:596-597.

[8] Branch WT, Arky RA, Woo B, Stoeckle JD, Levy DB, Taylor WC. "Teaching Medicine as a Human Experience: A Patient-Doctor Relationship Course for Faculty and First-Year Medical Students." *Annals of Internal Medicine* 1991;114:482-489.

[9] Truant GS, Lohrenz JG. "Basic Principles of Psychotherapy I. Introduction, Basic Goals, and the Therapeutic Relationship." *American Journal of Psychotherapy* 1993;47:8-18.

[10] Cousins N. "Intangibles in Medicine: An Attempt at a Balancing Perspective." *Journal of the American Medical Association* 1988;260:1610-1612.

[11] CMA Booklet.

[12] Molendijk AD. "Balancing the Science of Medicine And the Art of Healing." *Humane Medicine* 1992;8:145=147.

[13] Schwenk TL, Romano SE. "Managing the Difficult Physician-Patient Relationship." *American Family Physician* 1992; 46:1503-1509.

[14] Longhurst MF. "Doctoring: The Healing Relationship." *Humane Medicine* 1987;3:37-41.

[15] Brandt LH. "Holding a Hand is Often as Important as Examining One." *American Journal Gastroenterology* 1993;88:1817-1821.

[16] Farmer RG. "The Doctor-Patient Relationship: Quantification of the Interaction." *Annals of the New York Acadamy of Science* 1994;729:27-35.

[17] Arborelius E, Bremberg S. "What Does a Human Relationship with the Doctor Mean?" *Scandinavian Journal of Primary Health Care* 1992; 10:163-169.

[18] Freedman A. "The Physician-Physician Relationship and the Ethic of Care." *Canadian Medical Association Journal* 1993;148:1037-1043.

[19] Pellegrino E. "The Virtuous Physician and the Ethics of Medicine." In: Beauchamp T, Walterl L (eds) *Nurse, Physician, Patient Relationships*. U Alabama Press, Birmingham, Alabama, 1985.

[20] Havre DC. "Intimacy in Medicine: Healing the Heart of the Patient-Physician Relationship." *Journal of Florida Medical Association* 1993;80:281-282.

[21] O'Rourke K. "Trust and the Patient-Physician Relationship" (Editorial). *American Journal of Kidney Disease* 1993;21:684-685.

[22] Bulger RJ. *Technology, Bureaucracy, and Healing in America.* University of Iowa Press, Iowa City, 1988.

[23] Quill TE, Cassel CK. "Nonabandonment: A Central Obligation for Physicians." *Annals of Internal Medicine* 1995;122:368-374.

[24] Simington JA. "The Power of Expressive Touch." *Humane Medicine* 1995;11:162-165.

[25] Peabody FW. *Doctor and Patients.* Cambridge, MA. Harvard University Press, 1928.

[26] Cassel CK. "The Patient-Physician Covenant: An Affirmation of Asklepios." *Annals of Internal Medicine* 1996;124:604-604.

[27] Perkel RL. "Ethics and Managed Care." *Med. Clin. N.A.* 1996;80:263-278.

[28] Pellegrino ED. "Words Can Hurt You. Some Reflections on the Metaphors of Managed Care." *J. Am. Bd. Fam. Pract.* 1994;7:505-510.

[29] Novack DH, Dube C, Goldstein MG. "Teaching Medical Interviewing: A Basic Course on Interviewing and the Physician-Patient Relationship." *Archives of Internal Medicine* 1992;152:1814-1820.

[30] Mellinkoff SM. "Are We Missing the Trees for Imagining the Forest?" *Journal of Medical Education* 1975;50:1005-1009.

[31] Peabody FW. *Doctor and Patient.* Cambridge, MA: Harvard University Press, 1928.

[32] Eiseley L. "An Evolutionist Looks at Modern Man." In: Thruelsen R, Kobler J, editors. *Adventures of the Mind.* New York: Alfred A. Knopf, 1959:3-16.

[33] Adson MA. "An endangered ethic – The Capacity of Care." *Mayo Clinic Proc.* 1995; 70:495-500.

A Response to Oreopoulos

Koula Svokos Harnett

My immediate response to Dr. Oreopoulos' chapter was that of delight. It is refreshing to see a "Western" physician so concerned about *"restoring"* the *"healing effect"* of the patient-physician *relationship*.

In the East, it seems that doctors have been having this type of relationship with their patients for years. I noticed this in my travels, especially in China. But in the West, there has been, as Dr. Oreopoulos has pointed out, a shift from the focus on the significance of the relationship between doctor and patient to that of the physician and his corporate-type managerial superiors. A recent study published in the May/June 1997 issue of *Health Affairs* reports that "More doctors are being paid a flat fee for each patient, no matter how much care is given, providing a financial incentive to give less care." The effect of HMOs on the medical healing arts has been their transition into a shrewd business venture, as doctors are being pressured to sacrifice their inituitive healing skills for grandiose institutional profits. "Show me the money!" appears to have become the chief motivator. One can almost hear the cry of that humble, earnest, and compassionate supreme healer and teacher of two thousand years ago, whose angst at this worship of mammon in the sacred temple drove him to cry out "Render to Caesar...!")

On a lighter note, there is a joke circulated by a jovial local Catholic priest about a deceased HMO executive who was greeted in heaven by the notice that he was allowed to stay there *only one month* – and when his time was up, he would have to go to the "other place." How many of us would agree that this was a befitting fate for the promotion of such a ruthless practice? I lost my father at age 87 because of a hospital's refusal to permit him to remain beyond his "covered" stay. He was sent home and had a seizure from which he never recovered. His doctor, a native of India, callously responded, "He's better off dead. You people live too long in this country." (My father's father lived to be 93 in Greece, where the laid-back lifestyle apparently was conducive to longevity.) I wish my father had had the privilege of having a compassionate doctor like Dr. Oreopoulos, who might have given him support and encouragement. (Remembering that he had asked me for a poem on "hope," I did manage to pull my father out of his coma one day by touching him gently, playing a tape of his favorite violin music, and whispering in his ear, "Κουραγιο και Δυναμη!" (courage and strength!). Though people were amazed by this "miracle," I was told to let him go.) Ironically, it was my father who in my childhood taught me about holistic healing, which was taught to him by an Egyptian physician in his youth. But he was to die in the care of an Indian physician, who was eager to send him on to his next existence without permitting him to experience the benefits of modern medical miracles. "Too old, not enough insurance" – these were the reasons I lost my father in a cold hospital setting where the staff did not really seem to care about him. Needless to say, I became cynical about the sad state of affairs and wondered what medicine had to offer to those not young and wealthy. (My father's savings were consumed by escalating health care costs.)

And I remained that way until I met the holistic physician Dr. Glen Aukerman, now at Ohio University, who was to change my life. He taught me to participate in my own healing process by doing as Hippocrates said: *use my own innate healing power.* He also served as a teacher and a guide rather than as a guru or demigod. Sometimes he would use the "modern medical miracles," other times, the ancient ones. Since then, I have begun to see that there are other physicians who are trying to integrate the two as well. Thus, my faith in the healing effect of the patient-physician relationship is becoming restored. It pleases me to see that Hippocrates' message has been reaching a new breed of doctors, humble and alert.

I appreciated Dr. Oreopoulos' enlightening paper with its reminder of "the ethical principle enshrined in the Hippocratic oath [which states that]: 'with purity and holiness I will pass my life and practice my art' [which] exhorts physicians to cultivate virtue and focus on the moral life...[that Hellenic physician/ teacher's challenge to doctors to adhere to] 'the key virtue of *phronesis* ...to discern the correct thing to do...'" And while I am gratified to see that this set of standards is still the young medical student's legacy today, I only wish that modern society might have a more permanent positive effect on them – after materialism begins to replace idealism.

According to British scholar W. H. S. Jones, in his 1928 Johns Hopkins University Press publication *Philosophy and Medicine in Ancient Greece*, "The Greek etiquette, ευσχημοσυν, was concerned not so much with the good of the profession, as with that of the patients...[for] it safeguarded their interests, not the fees and professional status of practicing doctors...[since] the Greeks felt instinctively that the good of the doctor depended upon honorable behavior towards the sick folk committed to his care...[and thus] the doctor's knowledge and skill should be duly and properly used" (p. 33). Quite a challenge indeed for today's doctors, pressured by their own financial needs and their medical institutions' expectations of them to deliver high-quality/low-cost health care. And who suffers from this scenario? Not only the patient, but the physician, the medical institution, and society.

Dr. Oreopoulos quotes from a *Lancet* (May 6, 1995) editorial that "describes the unexpected, unpredictable, and deleterious effects of technology on medical practice and warned how bleak the future looks for doctors, ascribing this in large part to medicine's increasing dependence on technology." Thus, we are further advised that "if doctors are to survive...they must return to their roots as healers and teachers [...instead of 'guardians and gatekeepers of the technological fountain']."

The former role is exactly what I observed in the Chinese hospitals and clinics, where the humble doctor examines the patient, offers her (female physicians tend to outnumber their male counterparts, possibly because of the low incomes and status attached to this profession there) diagnosis, and prescribes inexpensive traditional herbal medicine or acupuncture for the cure. Or a combination of Eastern and Western medicine may be prescribed, as was my family's experience. Had we not been American visitors, however, we might have received something more – a lesson on how to *stay well,* not just how to *get well.*

This was the case in the beginning of modern Western medicine. The doctor was the teacher: he taught the patient *how* to live in order to have good health – physical, mental, emotional, and spiritual. And that was the lesson taught by Hippocrates, who as the father of modern medicine kept the best of the ancient medicine and combined the old and new healing wisdoms in his *Corpus Hippocraticum.* In it, he advised physicians to "study not the disease but the *whole* patient, including his environment, emotions, and spiritual life...[and to] observe the nature of [his] country...the diet, customs, age of the patient, the patient's speech, manners, fashion, even his silence, his thoughts, if he sleeps or is suffering from the lack of sleep, the content and origin of his dreams" (Poole, p. 49).

This is the kind of thorough medical care that Dr. Oreopoulos seems to have in mind: something more than the superficial routine exam in which patients are lined up in rows in adjacent rooms where they must wait patiently for a chance to spend just a few moments with their physician, who barely can remember their names, let alone their stories. How can such a "relationship" possibly produce any healing? No wonder there are so many malpractice suits. There can hardly be any opportunity for either physician or patient to feel satisfied in such a scant meeting. A recent *JAMA* article on a study conducted by Dr. Wendy Levinson, University of Chicago medical professor, reports that doctors who are less likely to be sued are those who spend more time with their patients, telling them what to expect, letting them ask questions, and using humor with them. This is what Dr. Oreopoulos recommends for the "restoration of the healing effects of the patient-physician relationship."

I appreciated Dr. Oreopoulos' teaching us that modern physicians need to return to their roots: to become *healers* again in order to truly fulfill their more medical mission. In China, I saw compassionate physicians who served as teachers to their patients. (Incidentally, until recently, Chinese doctors would not get paid until and unless their patients got well!) "Dis-eases" are seen as the result of some disturbance, which needs to be corrected. Perhaps the patient is burdened by too much work and not enough time off for silent meditation, or too much of the wrong food and not enough exercise, or maybe some emotional turmoil is causing the imbalance in a person's *chi* (the life-force energy, referred to as *pneuma* by Hippocrates, called *prana* in India, or in the Catholic Church charismatic prayer in laying-on-of-hands services, referred to as the Holy Spirit based on the biblical reference to such dramatic healings). Or perhaps an addiction (defined by John Bradshaw as any "mood-altering substance or behavior with life-threatening consequences") is present, which is destroying the mind-body-soul of the patient. These may include the disease of alcoholism or other addictions, such as those to illegal narcotics, nicotine, caffeine, or even prescription drugs, or work, food, sex, or any other compulsive-obsessive or inappropriate behaviors. (Often antidepressants, yoga, meditation, or acupuncture can provide relief until therapy and 12-step recovery groups can help restrain the patient's brain to seek safer comforts rather than the old destructive ones.) The doctor has to be attentive and perspicacious.

In Eastern medical care, the doctor heals *from the inside out* —

not *from the outside in,* as in Western medicine. Otherwise, treating the symptoms without tracing the causes may result in further symptoms perhaps even more serious than the previous ones. What manifests today as a headache or an ulcer may later show up as a heart attack or cancer, for the undetected and untreated stress that may be responsible for today's minor ailment may cause tomorrow's fatal illness. The good doctor must be aware of the difference between simply "curing" an illness and truly healing the patient who happens to have this illness. Physical problems very often signal deep-rooted cries for attention – to the soul and to the emotional mental state. The wise physician learns to recognize her patient's true needs, perhaps by referral to a psychotherapist, support group, nutritionist, or spiritual mentor.

The renewed interest in Hippocrates today may be attributable to the current interest in returning to self-help holistic healing – seeing the mind-body-soul as an inseparable unit – and in the old, natural treatment methods. Recently, while in our university's medical school library researching for an abstract for a paper on Greek philosophy and medicine, I was appalled to see not one single medical journal that suggested that we humans are more than just the sum of our body parts – nothing to teach the medical students of the holistic healing that Hippocrates taught centuries ago. Until we learn that we are actually embodied spirits, we are missing the point.

It was Hippocrates who taught that "natural forces within us are the true healers of disease." And is it not a mark of true humility in a doctor to acknowledge that he alone does not possess all the magical cures to heal his patient? Notice how many doctors and patients are now starting to believe in the power of prayer. And we are reminded of Christ's words: "You too can do these things..." referring to His laying on of hands to heal, inspiring others to likewise help heal the suffering. Of course, mere mortals cannot expect to reproduce any of His divine miracles, but He does invite us to reach out and help others, as well as to assist in the healing of ourselves.

I was moved by Dr. Oreopoulos' detailed description of the five elements in his section "The Healing Relationship." These five steps, which he challenges doctors to include in their medical treatment in order to "restore the therapeutic effects of the patient-physician relationship," are (1) caring, (2) hope, (3) trust, (4) nonabandonment, and (5) touch. As any patient will agree, this form of therapy can often do more than even medicine.

The three risks, however, of forming a close bond between physician and patient, Dr. Oreopoulos lists as (1) the danger of codependence between the two individuals, (2) an overdose of empathy that might cause the doctor to take on the negative aspects of the patients whom he is trying to heal, and (3) the risks of their intimacy leading to a sexual attraction. And my response to these concerns is to learn from holistic healers, psychotherapists, and other nonmedical healers. They begin their sessions by placing psychological boundaries between themselves and the person they are healing, thereby eliminating the dangers of enmeshment or of picking up the negativity associated with the patient's problems. Thus, they do not take on the patient's pain, physical or psychological. While they do connect with those they treat, the healers do so only so they can sense what they need to do in order to facilitate (and empower the patient herself to assist) in the healing. For this, the proper frame of mind is necessary. Even the slightest words of encouragement from the healer can make a difference. As any doctor knows, the loss of will to recover is often accompanied by intense fear, and ultimately, that loss of hope may lead to the loss of life.

Today, even those in the allopathic medical community are beginning to recognize the value of complementary and preventive health care, for as the public loses its xenophobia (and its money, in today's astronomical medical costs), it demands more affordable and less invasive options. It does not have to be an either/or dilemma. At Columbia-Presbyterian Medical Center, philanthropist Richard Rotenthall founded a center for the study of these options "for those who had been told by their doctors that there was no hope for them." There, both the old and new therapies are administered simultaneously. Center director Dr. Mehmet Oz uses these nonconventional healing modalities himself, as he performs open-heart surgery on patients who receive hypnotherapy, positive affirmations, guided imagery, and laying-on-of-hands energy (*pneuma*) healing. The good news to doctors is that the benefits from such mind-body-soul healing are reciprocal, for the patient's healing energy is returned right back to the doctor, preventing the usual burnout that results from the demands of intense and lengthy medical procedures.)

As for the "three risks" of a doctor becoming too intimate with his patients, Dr. Oreopoulos mentions only the third of these risks in detail: sexual attraction. My advice to any doctor who is concerned about this risk is, once again, to emulate the behavior of any professional body worker (i.e., massage therapist, acupuncturist, Reiki practitioner, or therapeutic touch therapist): set the stage in advance for a nonromantic relationship. The healing room is not the place for auditions for sexual partners. There is, in fact, a sacred trust that is placed in the doctor's hands, and by his body language, eye contact, voice, and overall demeanor he can send the message that he is not available. (And if still not convinced of the perils of mixing business with pleasure, one should read F. Scott Fitzgerald's novel *Tender is the Night*, in which the protagonist, Dr. Dick Diver, is driven from his coveted medical career by his female patient who seduces him, marries him, and then destroys him. For further motivation to keep professional relationships purely platonic, one should also read *Sex in the Forbidden Zone*, by Peter Rutter, M.D.).

Dr. Oreopoulos' prescription for effective mind-body-soul healing is one that should be taught in all medical schools, along with regular courses that deal with the healing of the body.

Though the tone of his paper is rather pessimistic about the conditions that contribute to nonhealing relationhips between physician and patient, I am a bit encouraged, however, for I see a change occuring. There are now more compassionate physicians available. I can see this in my own back yard, for my neighbor, Dr. Melanie Fisher, just won the award for Outstanding Teacher at West Virginia University's Medical College. And last year, she was named Outstanding Physician. With her altruism, dedication, wisdom, and spirituality, she seems to be the personification of the ideal physician, as described in this paper, and she is teaching a very important message to a new generation of doctors. That lesson is that in order to succeed, a doctor must form a partnership with her patients, working *together* to increase the chances of recovery. This teamwork approach, as she likes to call it, seems to work, and it appears to be part of a national trend. Thus, I end on a note of optimism when I tell you that I believe Dr. Oreopoulos' plea for a "restored healing relationship between patient and physician" is already being answered. And for further encouragement, I recommend that you read, in the April 21 issue of the *Chronicle of Higher Education,* the guest editorial "Restoring the Proper Goals of the Healing Arts," by Daniel Callahan, director of Hastings Center in Briarcliff, New York, which focuses on both ethics *and* life sciences — a full integration of the old and the new healing modalities.

REFERENCES

Benson, Herbert, MD. *The Relaxation Response*, New York: Avon Books, 1975.

Benson, Herbert, MD. *Timeless Healing: The Power and Biology of Belief,* New York: Simon & Schuster, 1997.

Broysenko, Joan, Ph.D. *Mending the Mind, Minding the Body*, New York: Simon & Schuster, 1988.

Callahan, Daniel, Ph.D. "Restoring the Proper Goals of the Healing Arts," *The Chronicle of Higher Education*, vol XLIII, no. 33, 25 April 1997, p. A52.

Chopra, Deepak, MD. *Ageless Body, Timeless Mind.* New York: Harmony Books, 1993.

Chopra, Deepak, MD. *Quantum Healing: Exploring the Mind/Body Medicine.* New York: Bantam Books, 1989.

Cousins, Norman. *Anatomy of an Illness as Perceived by the Patient: Reflections on Healing and Regeneration.* New York: W.W. Norton Co., Inc., 1992.

Cousins, Norman. *Head First: The Biology of Hope.* New York: E.P. Dutton, 1989.

Cousins, Norman. *The Healing Heart: Antidotes to Panic and Helplessness.* New York, Avon Books, 1984.

Dacher, Elliot S., MD. *Intentional Healing: A Guide to the Mind/Body Healing System.* New York: Marlowe Publishing, 1991.

Dossey, Larry, MD. *Meaning of Medicine: Lessons from a Doctor's Tales of Breakthrough Healing.* New York: Bantam Books, 1991.

Dossey, Larry, MD. *Healing Words: the Power of Prayer and the Practice of Medicine.* New York: Harper-Collins, 1995.

Fitzgerald, F. Scott. *Tender is the Night.* New York: Scribners, 1933.

Gabel, Jon. "10 Ways HMOs Have Changed During the '90s," *Health Affairs*, vol. 16, no. 3, 134-145.

Harnett, Richard Andrew, Ed.D. & Koula Svokos Hartnett, Ed.D. "The Tao and Lagos: An Integration of Eastern and Western Philosophical and Medical Principles and Practices – Applying Ancient Wisdom to Modern Healing of the Mind-Body-Soul." Paper presented at the Ninth International Conference on Greek Philosophy: "Philosophy and Medicine: A Dialogue," Kos-Kalymnos, 20-30 August 1997.

Hippocrates. *Corpus Hippocratius.* 440-200 BC.

Jones, W.H.S. *Philosophy and Medicine in Ancient Greece.* Johns Hopkins University Press Reprints, New York: Arno Press, A New York Times Co., 1979.

Kabat-Zin, Jon. *Full Catastrophe Living: Using the Wisdom of Your Body & Mind to Face Stress, Pain and Illness.* New York: Dell Publishing, 1990.

Kinsley, David. "The Search for Meaning in Modern Medicine: The Patient Speaks." *Health, Healing and Religion: A Cross-Cultural Perspective*, Upper Saddle River, NJ: Prentice Hall, 1996, pp. 185-198.

Langone, John. "Challenging the Mainstream." *Time:* Special Issue: September 1996, pp. 40ff.

Levine, Ewin B. *Hippocrates.* New York: Twayne Publishers, 1971.

Levinson, Wendy, MD. "Physician-Patient Communication." *JAMA.* vol 277, no. 7, Feb 19, 1997, 5553-9.

Locke, Steven MD. *The Healer Within.* New York: Dutton, 1985.

McGarey, William, MD. *In Search of Healing: Whole Body Healing Through the Mind-Body-Spirit Connection.* New York: Berkley Publishing, 1996.

Moskowitz, William, MD *Your Healing Mind.* New York: Avon Books, 1992.

Moyers, Bill. *Healing and the Mind.* New York: Doubleday, 1993.

Northrup, Chris, MD. *Creating Health,* audiocassette. Boulder: Sounds True Studios, 1993.

Northrup, Chris, MD. *Women's Bodies, Women's Wisdom.* New York: Bantam, 1993.

Pelletier, Kenneth, MD. *Mind as Healer, Mind as Slayer.* New York: Dell Publishing, 1997.

Poole, William. *The Heart of Healing,* Atlanta: Turner Publishing, Inc., 1993, based on the "The Heart of Healing," TBS Television Series, Independent Communications Associates, Inc. 1993.

Rutter, Peter, MD. *Sex in the Forbidden Zone: When Men in Power – Therapists, Doctors, Clergy, Teachers – Betray Women's Trust.* New York: Fawcett, 1991.

Shealy, C. Norman, MD. *Miracles Do Happen.* Rockport, ME: Element Books, Ltd., 1995.

Siegel, Bernie, MD. *How to Live Betwee Doctor's Visits.* New York: HarperCollins, 1995.

Siegel, Bernie, MD. *Love, Medicine and Miracles.* New York: HarperCollins, 1986.

Siegel, Bernie, MD. *Peace, Love and Healing.* New York: Harper Row, 1989.

Sobel, David S., MD. *Ways of Health: Holistic Approaches to Ancient & Contemporary Medicine.* New York: Harcourt Brace & Jovanovich, 1979.

Sobel, David S., MD. *The Healthy Mind, Health Body Handbook.* New York: Patient Education Media, Inc.

Weil, Andrew, MD. *Health and Healing.* Boston/New York: Houghton Mifflin Co., 1995.

Weil, Andrew, MD. *Natural Health, Natural Medicine.* New York:

Weil, Andrew, MD. "The Art of Medicine: Healing Doctors and Patients," *Roots of Healing: The New Medicine,* audiocassette, San Francisco: New Dimensions Foundation [Registered Trademark Symbol is placed here], 1993.

Weil, Andrew, MD. *Roots of Healing.* Hay Housen, Inc., Carslbad, CA: 1997.

Weil, Andrew, MD. *Spontaneous Healing.* New York: Ballantine Books, 1995.

A Case Conference Model for Clergy Education in Counseling, Confession, and Spiritual Direction

J. Stephen Muse

Orthodox Christianity is a community of relationships knit together in Christ in which persons become humanly available with and for one another. From a practical standpoint, within this context, Orthodox clergy function as psychotherapists who help nurture and guide the lifelong formation of persons in Christ. For this cure of souls, clergy need to be well trained and informed in spiritual direction as well as familiar with the art and science of psychological diagnosis and treatment, as these frequently overlap and complement one another.

Second, priests need to be available and accountable to one another in this endeavor in the same way that those who practice psychotherapy in a secular context utilize ongoing case conferences, peer consultation, supervision, and in-service training as a means to continuing education and support. Competence in basic counseling skills, and an awareness of ethics and boundaries, along with familiarity with one's own biases and defenses, are vitally important for those priests who take their counseling ministry seriously, just as is true for psychotherapists in general.

"Opening to Personhood" is a working model presented as an example of an ongoing case conference[1] designed to foster collegiality and refine the diagnostic and discernment skills of priests for the application of traditional Orthodox psychotherapeutic intervention to persons seeking healing and growth within the context of the Orthodox faith toward the Christian developmental ideal of theosis. It is a model that facilitates a sense of safety and community among brother priests in which persons can take the interpersonal risks that are important for continuing growth.

My interest in helping to facilitate such a clergy group for Orthodox priests comes out of my experience as both pastor and mental health counselor. I have participated in a variety of groups over a period of 20 years on a weekly basis, several of which have continued for five years or more, the longest being with a group for clergy over a period of eleven years. We met weekly for about an hour and a half, many of us bringing a bag lunch to eat while we talked.

This particular group was begun by a handful of clergy who initially decided to hire a psychotherapist as a consultant to help them grow in their understanding of the counseling ministry. On a rotating basis, they each brought situations from their respective parishes dealing with counseling and pastoral concerns or staff issues. The psychotherapist facilitated the group process, offering them a chance to "not be in charge" and therefore to be able to rest and learn from one another. After several years, clergy members had come to know and care for one another to the point that when the psychotherapist left the area, the group decided to continue meeting. By this time, they felt they had learned what they wanted in the counseling area, and they decided to continue the rotation, focusing on biblical exegesis of the lectionary passage for the week, which one of the group members in turn facilitated.

This group of pastors, albeit with some changes as members moved on to other locations, lasted unbroken for more than 20 years. It functioned as a group for continuing education and as a support group for prayer, consultation, and intercession. Twice a year, day-long retreats for spiritual renewal became an annual event at the local bird sanctuary. The group became a clearing house for theology and group mentoring that nourished and refreshed us all, helping us serve our congregations more effectively. When one of the group members moved on to another parish, the group gathered for a send-off dinner. A sense of being valued and an appreciation for the call to ministry itself grew strong in our midst.

At the same time I was attending this group, over a period of nine years I was involved in psychotherapy training and participating in groups focused on helping counselors identify empathic blocks to appreciating and being present to the personhood of counselees and later of supervisees. Equal attention was paid to the person of the counselor as to the person of those being counseled, because it was understood that we cannot love or have empathy for in others what we are unwilling to see and love in ourselves. As our Lord suggests, "Remove the log from your own eye, and then you will see more clearly the splinter in your neighbor's." After 20 years of such group experiences, the value of ongoing peer consultation, confession, spiritual direction, and continuing education for parish ministry is clearly evident to me for a variety of reasons.

Isolation and Sobornost

"The great illusion of leadership is to think that humans can be led out of the spiritual desert by someone who has never been there." The priest is the spiritual father of the parish. Whoever gives direction must himself receive it. Whoever would be able to listen empathically to other's pain must have himself experienced this from others. If the priest would model humility and nondefensiveness, he must himself have experienced this among his peers. As St. John the Theologian reminds us, "It is not that we love God, but that God first loved us." That is the critical ingredient. Along with the sacramental grace of the priesthood bestowed by God, we learn how to minister to others by having first been ministered to ourselves. We learn to be trustworthy by having allowed ourselves to find others trustworthy on our behalf. We learn to be someone others will seek out for confession on a regular basis by having ourselves found a confessor worthy of our trust.

There is no substitute for this. Community is an ongoing reciprocal process. Priests who attempt to function in isolation are placing themselves and the members of their parish in jeopardy. "Cut off from me you can do nothing." Significantly, those clergy most vulnerable to falling from grace regardless of their education and experience are those who function in isolation. Orthodox clergy are among the most isolated of their brother clergy by virtue of parishes being distant from each other. When monthly diocesan meetings are focused solely on business matters, a crucial element of community is neglected without which business has little or no meaning. The church is about community and cure of the soul first, and business second. In the ecumenical group of which I was a part, clergy drove regularly from 45 miles away for this weekly hour-and-a-half bag lunch gathering. An ongoing group offers accountability to one's peers in a conciliar fashion that has been the model for the Church since the first Apostles.

Need for Competency in Two Domains

Priests need a basic knowledge of pastoral counseling. Acquaintance with standard psychological methods and diagnoses facilitates dialogue with mental health professionals and helps clergy recognize clinical syndromes requiring more specialized assessment and treatment from distinctly spiritual ones. Unfortunately in an increasingly litigious society, ignorance of basic mental health standards of care does not protect clergy and parishes from malpractice suits.

In California, a young man sought spiritual help from a clergyman. He was depressed, and the minister directed him to pray and to read his Bible for help. He killed himself. The family sued and won the case on the grounds that the minister did not recognize the clinical syndrome of major depression, for which the standard of care includes an assessment for antidepressant medication.

At the same time, clergy are in a position to notice what mental health professionals may miss. A relevant example was offered by a psychiatrist familiar with and appreciative of the art of spiritual direction. He told of a woman who had sought help from a counselor for "depression." After many weeks of standard psychological therapy, she grew worse to the point that the counselor sent her to a psychiatrist for possible antidepressant medication. The psychiatrist asked her about God and her religious faith. In one session he diagnosed her as needing spiritual direction rather than counseling because her "depression" had to do with an unrequited search for intimacy with God and was not primarily a clinical syndrome. She followed through on the referral to spiritual direction, and her "depression" vanished.

Clearly, these two situations evidence a need and an opportunity for clergy to be familiar with both worlds of psychology and the mysteriological domain of the church along with its ascetical practices. Secular psychology is a servant of the church, not its master. Nevertheless, priests benefit from having a working familiarity with major diagnostic syndromes and being conversant in the language of psychology in order to talk with mental health professionals and make referrals when appropriate. Familiarity with the language and tools of modern psychology is also useful in translating ascetical practices into the lingua franca of persons not educated in a patristic worldview, but who would nevertheless benefit from its application in their lives. This of course presumes that the priest himself is under the guidance of a spiritual father and applies such methods in his own life consistently.

CROSS-CULTURAL ASPECTS OF MINISTRY

This is becoming increasingly important as converts make their way into the Orthodox church. The group can become a clearinghouse for discussion of how best to minister in this area by addressing particular issues that may arise and drawing on group experience.

VICARIOUS TRAUMATIZATION

This is a phenomenon known to mental health counselors who, over time, have absorbed the despair and pain of clients

that stem from past trauma, known as traumatic countertransference. This accumulates over time as the priest becomes the
"container" for parishioners' unfulfilled longings, authority problems, and various other projections onto him who "represents
Christ." After sending out the 12 and the 72, Jesus received
them back, saying "Let us go away to a desert place" for debrief-
ing and restoration. This has been confirmed in the mental health
field as a necessary and important ingredient of caring for the
caregivers.

METHODOLOGY

The actual case conference can be done in one hour, although
an hour and a half is more effective by allowing increased depth
of engagement among group members.

Stage I: Encounter with Christ (5 minutes)

On a rotating basis, each group member brings a spiritual
resource to share with the group. This may be a personal anecdote in addition to a brief prayer and reading from Scripture
and/or Patristics for the day. The resource should evidence some
way in which the Holy Spirit has been active in one's life. The
purpose is not primarily devotional, but to share with the group
an "Emmaus road experience" that has been particularly meaningful for the person. It is a sharing of what most nourishes and
enlivens a person's own humanity and spirituality – what makes
the "heart burn," as on the road to Emmaus, and therefore allows members of the group to come to know the person better.
The resource is chosen without any consideration of what case
material will be presented, which is at this point unknown. To
the degree that it is freely shared in humility and without arti-
fice, the shared faith in the hearts of each person will resonate
accordingly.

Response: Encounter with Self-in-Community (5 minutes)

The purpose of this part of the group process is to elicit intuitive and feeling responses to the spiritual resource. Mere con-

ceptual associations tend to keep persons separated behind a lens of "diagnosis" rather than allowing human access to one another. In this way, group members benefit from one another's experiences as well as come to know each other more personally. There is no attempt at this point to criticize or pigeonhole any responses. All are accepted at face value as what is elicited at this moment in one another by the spiritual resource. Over time, trust is built as group members self-disclose and honor one another's experiences. Confidentiality within the group is held with the same strictness as in the confessional.

Stage II: Encounter with Other (5 minutes)

At this point, the group member who brings the case for the session is directed by the facilitator to present the person, couple, or family in novelistic form, drawing on concrete details and subjective experiences. What kinds of response do they elicit in people who know them? How do they act? What is unique about them? The presenter helps us see and feel and know this person as a unique individual. Why is he or she seeking Jesus at this particular time? What are the problems they struggle with? What are their assets? What particular feelings are generated in the priest as he works with them? A great deal depends on the encounter of the priest with the person being presented. If the person is not clear and real to the other members of the group, for example, perhaps it is because he or she is not particularly clear and unique to the presenter either. This will become evident as the group continues.

Response: Encounter with Self-in-Community (5-10 minutes)

At some point, the facilitator stops the presentation and asks group members to share their immediate responses to what their brother priest has presented. What is stirred in each one as this person is introduced? How does his/her story affect you? Notice if there are any empathic blocks – places where one recoils and does not want to touch. What feelings emerge in you? What images? At this point, as with the opening reading and anecdote, group members share personal responses to the presentation and avoid clinical and/or spiritual diagnosis, which is saved for later. The purpose is to keep the insights of the contemplative, intuitive, right-brain equally as available as those of the analytic, systematizing, left-brain, which tends to dominate more.

Stage III: Diagnosis, Discernment, and Therapeutic Interventions (25-30 minutes)

In his encounters with persons, Jesus is constantly using diagnostic abilities and criteria of various kinds to determine what is the appropriate response, which differs from persons to persons. He might ask, "How long has he had this? What are the symptoms?" as he did with the epileptic boy's father, and then specify certain kinds of healing and even asceses, like prayer and fasting, for the disciples who would attempt such. In some cases, he recognizes that persons may not want to be healed, like the man at the pool of Siloam. Still others seem to want healing but find themselves unable to make the sacrifices necessary on their part to follow through, such as the rich young ruler. Jesus recognizes that love is elicited in him by his encounter with this young man, and yet he honors his freedom to withdraw from full communion. The woman at the well responds to interpersonal relationship through an extended conversation, whereas the Gerasene demoniac requires unilateral help, such as exorcism or an antipsychotic medication.

In this section, the facilitator guides the group toward gaining a clear and distinct sense of the uniqueness of the person. Group members are free to ask questions of the presenter at this point, and they begin to think diagnostically and to utilize previous intuitive and feeling responses to discern both theological issues and psychological problems that may apply. A relationship between the initial spiritual resource and the case material may begin to emerge, but this is not something that is forced if it does not seem appropriate.

What is the relationship of the identified problem with the larger context of the person's formation in Christ? What is the relationship of the person to the faith community? What are the psychological and/or metabolic issues that may be involved? What traumatic events have contributed to the person's distress? Are there irrational perceptions and unconscious expectations of self that interfere with the person's experience of God's love? What kind of personal strengths does this person or family have to draw on? What moral issues are involved? What kind of sacramental participation or ascetic disciplines would be useful and appropriate? What is happening in the person's prayer life? Are they utilizing confession on a regular basis?

In other words, there is a full appraisal of the person's life through both psychological and spiritual lenses and by utilizing the personhood of each participant as a means of identifying openings for synergy with the Holy Spirit's work in this person's life. Full group participation is invaluable, for "Wherever two or three are gathered in my name" – He is in our midst. The exchange of questions and the offering of varying perspectives draw on the wealth of understanding and care of the whole group which is greater than the sum of the individuals.

Stage IV: Care for the Caregiver (10-15 minutes)

Group members, with the assistance of the moderator, focus on the person presenting. What are the needs of the priest bringing the case to the group at this time? What kinds of things may be stirred up in him by his encounter with this person? Why did you bring this particular situation to the group today? What questions are in you as you bring it? Is there any traumatic countertransference? Is there a parallel process between what the person is dealing with and the priest's own problems, which may interfere with his capacity to respond effectively?

Questions may be asked, such as "How have you experienced the feedback? What has been helpful to you or not?" This is respectful, and it honors the person of the priest in a context in which humility, openness, and vulnerability are highly prized as the ingredients for continuing growth toward a humanity capable of loving others as we have ourselves experienced being loved.

Stage V: Process and Theological Reflection (5 minutes)

"Holy Father, give the blessing." A previously identified person may be designated as the silent observer for the particular session. This person's task is to observe the group process and offer a concluding theological "word" by way of blessing and discernment, prophecy, etc. This is the "benediction" that ties the whole process together and ends the group by acknowledging God's presence and placing all, once again, into God's care as the group departs.

SUMMATION

This case model is presented as a means of opening to the personhood of oneself and one's brother priests in the process of focusing on the work of shepherding the souls in one's care. It presumes that those will be most effective in caring for others who feel cared for themselves, and that ongoing refinement of both counseling skills and spiritual discernment are most effectively taught in peer relationships where humility and appreciation for the presence of Christ in our midst is paramount. To be effective, the group needs to meet on a regular basis at least monthly, if not more often, in order to establish the degree of trust and safety that allows for depth of discussion to emerge.

NOTES

[1] Townsend, L. (1996) cf. "Creative Theological Imaging: A Method For Pastoral Counseling" in *Journal of Pastoral Care*, Vol 50 No. 4, pp 349-369 and Karl, J. and Ashbrook, J. (1983) "Religious Resources and Pastoral Therapy: A Model For Staff Development," *Journal Of Supervision and Training in Ministry*, Vol 6, p 8.

PART FOUR

APPLYING METHODS OF
SPIRITUAL DISCERNMENT AND DIFFERENTIAL DIAGNOSIS

Sexuality and the Church:
How Acquired Values in Child Development
Promote Healthy Sexual Expression

John T. Chirban

About ten years ago, Fr. Dean Talagan and I presented the Saints Peter and Paul Lectures, "Youth and Sexuality," to offer our thoughts about the needs of youth in view of the Church and sexuality.[1]

In my review of the literature at that time, I reported on the scant information available concerning the approach to practical aspects of sexuality from an Orthodox Christian perspective. Today, with more than ten years gone by, there are but a handful of projects that have directly addressed this subject, and no systematic program that I am aware of to guide sex education.

It makes sense that in our ongoing effort to develop an Orthodox psychology, i.e., an approach to understanding personhood, in view of our faith, which integrates appropriate information from the modern age, we confront the subject of sexuality and the church. This subject provides a vehicle for a powerful manifestation of love – the essence of our Christian identity as well as our sexual functioning, a basic motivation of human nature. In this essay I will discuss how the values acquired as one develops promote healthy sexual expression.

To provide continuity with my earlier thoughts about the role of the Church in sex education, and to relate my general perspective about sexuality and the church, I will begin this essay by reviewing an edited summary of my earlier recommendations.

Recommendations from Previous Discussion

Sexuality in the Orthodox Christian tradition is not discussed in a systematic or definitive manner. There is an abundance of theological references that express opinions concerning aspects of sexuality, but few modern questions find a *consensus patrum.* As sex education occurs in modern society through many direct and indirect influences and "answers," sexuality should be approached openly in view of Orthodox values. Therefore, the subject of sexuality, particularly given its impact in our culture, must be addressed directly. A working definition of sex education that encourages *sophrosene,* the "nurturance, guidance, development and teaching about one's wholesomeness in relationships according to Orthodox values," should be the foundation of this effort.

The topic of sexuality may be effectively approached from a developmental perspective, from infancy through physical maturity. Sexuality is inherently neither right nor wrong. There is no need to force maturity; however, there is a need to provide guidance about one's developmental sexual needs and how they are integrated with one's spiritual growth. A clear understanding of sexual matters, in view of religious principles and goals, is consistent with mature faith. Our approach to sex education must include both sensitivity to theology and insights into human growth derived from scientific studies. An Orthodox Christian program for sexuality should bring forth the liberating Christian values of faith in line with a genuinely liberated sexuality; this perspective emerges from viewing sexuality as naturally good, as an outgrowth of Christian love, reflecting a parallel in both relational and physical expressions. The developmental approach to sexuality underscores how challenges met in our developmental process affect counterparts in our sexual growth.

In specific ways, our approach to sex education should be viewed as a Church-family effort. The family is part of the program; the program is for all. Sex education should not merely impart information about physical functions but offer guidance about how our needs are integrated with the way we find meaning in life. Therefore, we need to make connections between our attitudes and values, and our sexual behaviors. The program should embrace the family and include a direct and open forum concerning personal growth that encourages understanding for all members, meeting various needs through frank discussion of the issues. By approaching sexuality in this way, we recognize and experience one's process in growth, whereby neither a person nor his or her sexuality reflects a fixed state. Language should be straightforward and according to the comprehension of the group. Discretion and moderation should temper presentations that may be provocative, yet the Church cannot renege on its responsibility to guide out of fear of "rocking the boat." Our approach should demonstrate an informative, constructive, and loving spirit.

Sex education for the Church should not be approached as a theological apology or defense. Sexuality is part of the Church's business. Silence about this matter is inconsistent with the Church's responsibility to lead people to grow in domains of their lives that are directly related to their spiritual well-being. Prudery and false modesty are in opposition to truth. Honesty and love are virtues that underlie our spiritual tradition. Sex education has depended too long on accidental information, giving the Church's helping ministry such a dysfunctional role that it generates an image of the Church as a body of "sexless angels."

Sex education begins with the clergy, who must discover themselves in view of their own sexuality. Courses, seminars, and workshops must be developed to enable churchmen first to face their particular sexual histories and needs, and second to understand how sex education results as a *process* in one's growth. In this regard, a commission on sexuality should be developed to spearhead the development of such programming by qualified persons.[2]

SEXUALITY AS A PROCESS OF DEVELOPMENT

Anxiety, discomfort, and awkwardness about discussing sexuality are not limited to Christian homes, much less Orthodox Christian homes. As parents have avoided clear discussion of sexual matters out of their own discomfort, numerous problems have evolved for children and families, resulting in the cascading avalanche of confusion about self, other, and relationships that permeates modern life.

You may remember the story of the six-year-old boy who goes to his father and says, "Dad, where did *I* come from?" The father, taken off guard, anxiously blurts out, "Oh, from Bloomingdale's! Everything that's wonderful comes from there," he adds, thinking that this will satisfy his son's questions.

The little fellow, however, is not satisfied and perseveres: "Well, where did *you* come from?" The father, recalling a childhood fable, states, "From a stork!" But the little boy, unsatisfied by his dad's answers, continues, asking, "How about *grandfather?* Where did *he* come from?"

The father, now recalling a segment of another fable, responds, "From under a cabbage patch." The little boy quietly walks away. The next day, the first-grader goes to school, and the teacher asks, "So, Johnny, did you find out how you came into being?"

With a disappointed face, the little boy answers, "No wonder I've been so confused and couldn't answer your question before. My family hasn't had normal sexual relations for three generations!"

In spite of the social revolutions that have spun us around in the past 30 or 40 years – sexual revolutions, the women's revolution, medical and ethical revolutions – our homes often fail to guide the process by which our children develop comfortable images about themselves and their sexuality, especially as they may attempt to integrate their values of faith with sexuality.

I do not propose that discussing the facts of life alone is sufficient. Isn't it strange that today's youth, much less children, watch sitcoms about adolescent pregnancy, MTV promotional videos that cross the boundaries of suggesting sexual intercourse, and explicit talk shows about child porn, incest, and sexual activity that occurs in elementary schools, thereby gaining fragments of information about sexuality, yet parents do not engage in direct communication about sexuality and how the values of their own faith relate to it?

Information about the facts of life is helpful, but intellectual information alone often falls on dead ears. Our approach to sexuality must be directed beyond such information and penetrate the very formation of one's character.

This reminds me of the story of the parents who told their son that he should never masturbate. When he asked why, they replied, "Well, if you do it, you know that you'll go blind."

After pausing a moment, he responded, "Well, can't I do it till I just need glasses?"

Rules alone do not penetrate our way of being. More problematically, they fail to convey the Spirit that may affect our lives. This is the essential point that I wish to convey in my brief comments.

Information about sexuality alone is not the answer, but knowledge, more cogently defined as "intelligence" by St. Anthony the Great, as noted earlier, "the ability to know right from wrong and do what is right,"[3] is where our efforts must be placed.

I don't think that parroting Church teachings is the answer. I am not sure that rule-oriented religious programming is what we need to cultivate as we work to develop healthy sexual behavior. Although books that outline the Church's teaching and ethical stances on issues may provide theological positions for guidance, I think that our efforts must directly relate to life. Therefore, I believe that we must consider how the experiences in one's developmental process enhance one's integration of values with actions that imbue a balanced life and concomitantly integrated sexual expression.

THE SPIRIT, LIFE, AND SEXUAL DEVELOPMENT

The Church's primary role in sexuality is to show families how to convey love in ways that nurture, advance, and strengthen the development of character. Psychological studies in the work of developmentalists like Erik Erikson[4] and John Bowlby,[5] and personality theorists like Abraham Maslow[6] and Salvatore Maddi,[7] among many others, have informed us of the process of character formation: how children develop through resolving particular life challenges, establishing relationships, incorporating motivation, and acquiring meaning. I believe that our tradition offers unique and critical insights concerning the "contents" or resources for this process. Such issues are powerfully congruent with our faith. In this way, for example, holiness and love are not moral platitudes but sustaining experiences for well-being that enhance one's character. Parents and the Church have unique opportunities to convey the values, virtues, and meaning that permit a child to establish a positive self-concept and sense of self-efficacy.

Therefore, our task is not only to *impart* information about sexuality but also to *support* one's development and moral consciousness so that one feels confident as he or she exercises his or her judgment. This role runs counter to the expression of fashionable sexual moral relativism that permeates our culture, which has established an American "religion," if you will, defining what is "politically correct." For example, such a pluralistic "faith" in sexuality says nothing or even celebrates when homosexual partners announce they are having babies through surrogates or sperm donors; when the pop singer Madonna *selects* the man with whom she will conceive, as the state of marriage is "inconvenient;" and in the face of the Internet new compulsive behavior emerges, establishing "innovative" forms of "sexual expression." The evolution of such practices (for our culture and for us individually) reflects distortion and the lack of development and integration of psychological growth and Orthodox Christian spiritual development.

To summarize, the developmental perspective that I advocate for the Church's approach to sexuality presses for direct communication of the parent with the child through their participation in critical life encounters which pre-tune sexual development. Such encounters engender concrete experiences between the child and the parent of trust, touch, care, love, the ability to relax, comfort with body image, self-esteem, management of power, sexual feelings, self-control, and the opportunity to explore and to sort out relationships with self, God, and other. The role of the Church in sexuality is to provide guidance that shows people how to integrate all aspects of their lives with reference to the process of growth. Church teachers must show the faithful how to make these connections. If sexuality is, as I believe, in part an expression of our intrapsychic state where we access our most vulnerable self and intense passions, it clearly is an opportune place for the Church to exercise counsel at the core of our being. Our work in sexuality should not be limited to providing do's and don'ts, rules and directives alone, but should more substantially involve designing opportunities whereby the faithful may acquire the experiences of the Spirit in all of life.

NOTES

[1] Chirban, John T. and Talagan, Dean. *Youth and Sexuality* (Brookline, Massachusetts: Hellenic College Press, 1985).

[2] Ibid., pp. 23-24.

[3] Kadloubovsky, E. and Palmer G. E. H. *Early Fathers From the Philokalia.* (London: Faber and Faber, 1954), p. 21.

[4] Erikson, E. H. *Childhood and Society* (New York: Norton, 1955).

[5] Bowlby, John. *Attachment and Loss. Volume 1. Attachment* (New York: Basic Books, 1969).

Bowlby, John. *Attachment and Loss. Volume 2. Separation. On Death and Anger* (New York: Basic Books, 1973).

Bowlby, John. *Attachment and Loss. Volume 3. Loss, Sadness, and Depression* (New York: Basic Books, 1980).

[6] Maslow, Abraham H. *Motivation and Personality* (New York: Harper and Row, 1970).

[7] Maddi, Salvatore R. "The Search for Meaning", *Nebraska Symposium on Motivation* (Lincoln, Nebraska: University of Nebraska Press, 1970), pp. 137-186.

A Response to Chirban

Demetra Velisarios Jacquet

Today, parents of teenagers struggle with worries about their children in an ever-expanding environment of potential perversion and violence. Most parents are dealing with their child's maturation at the same time as dealing with their exposure to smoking cigarettes and marijuana, drinking beer or hard alcohol, or doing drugs. Those who have attentively gone through teenage years with their children nod their heads vigorously when they hear another parent speak of the frustration, worry, even desperation of trying to teach and form a person whose main interest in life is suddenly to *not* be taught or formed by anyone over 20, especially you.

It is a common story. The son was an altar boy since age nine, active in Sunday School and the church youth group. Suddenly, at age 15, he does not want to go to church because it is not relevant to his life. The icons on his wall since his baptism are replaced with posters of skulls and dragons and other horrible, threatening images. He chooses to stay home less and less and is constantly testing limits. How much does one insist? Which battles are the most important so as not to lose the war? How does one encourage the youngster toward Christ when such fearsome influences are at hand?

Dr. Chirban's article proposes the sound and timeless approach of Orthodoxy for assisting each of us, even teenagers, toward full human personhood. The hallmarks of *sophrosene* that he articulates — nurturance, guidance, development, and teaching about one's wholesomeness in relationships according to Orthodox values – are keys to healthy spiritual maturation whether the application is healthy sexuality, healthy avoidance of substance abuse, healthy monitoring of behavior and pastimes, healthy psychological self-image, or healthy emotional attitudes. In keeping with the holistic approach of Orthodoxy to life and salvation, broadening the discussion to include application to these related areas of challenge during teenage years seems appropriate. At the same time, the scope of the discussion must acknowledge that the development of healthy sexual expression normally continues to mature throughout the life span.

To unfurl the growth of connections between our attitudes, values, and behaviors certainly is key and seems to call for a developmental model. Dr. Chirban, in an earlier publication, has examined several Church Fathers' teachings on spiritual growth, revealing their developmental presuppositions in explaining spiritual growth as a journey toward theosis. So, how can the Church inform us for this particular challenge: the development of sexual identity, which is usually a central task of adolescence? By teaching values; expressing them with a loving, compassionate, and healthy attitude; and behaving in accord with those values.

Dr. Chirban suggests that an Orthodox Christian program will impart information and support development and moral consciousness so the teenager feels confident as he or she gains more experience in exercising judgement and integrating psychological growth and Orthodox spiritual development. He advocates "direct communication of the parent with the child through their participation in critical life encounters." Here one might underscore that integrating psychological growth and spiritual development presupposes that the "critical life encounters" mentioned must include the everyday encounters that provide opportunities for teaching, and the ongoing modeling of those teachings by parents. The groundwork of trust, care, love, ability to relax, self-esteem, and management of power, feelings, and self-control must all be established throughout the child's life, long before adolescent issues rear their heads.

The role of the Church cannot be overemphasized in teaching and modeling how to "integrate life with the processes of growth." Life is not slow to provide challenging situations that call for spiritual wisdom. It is natural for the Church to design opportunities for prayer and education of both parents and children, in order to illumine and guide those challenges to a positive outcome.

Two critical areas during the years of adolescence seem to be community and example. Parents need encouragement and support to handle difficult times. Church members' loving presence, reassurance, and involvement with the family offer opportunities to benefit from others' experience and reinforces for both parent and child a bond of love that helps diffuse frustration, disappointment, and overreaction as each crisis occurs.

With regard to example, the vision of teenagers is remarkably clear. So often, it seems, they can spot a fake a mile away, especially the shortcomings of the generations before them, whether real or perceived. The examples of how life is lived and how persons are respected in the family system and in the Church are crucial. Are we ourselves in fact living what we preach to our children? What excesses and abuses are we perpetuating in our own lives? What consistency and discipline do we model? What *sophrosene* do our priest, our parish council, and all our church members and their actions exhibit? Are we modeling our own lives and our relationships with other adults after the Trinity, treating each respectfully as equals, all under the headship of Christ? Are we treating our children that way, too?

Acquired values in development accumulate over time, and the systemic nature of family and Church relationships requires consistency for a coherent value base to develop. Consistency is hard work, and striving to achieve it frequently results in keeping parents honest if they are willing to admit that their children's behavior is to a large extent a response to their own behavior in the first place. When a teenager sees inconsistency, or what we in the Church refer to as pharisaical behavior, they see hypocrisy, become disillusioned, and then are disenfranchised. When we as adults compromise the very values we have tried to instill, adolescents view themselves as powerless in the Church, or in the family, and so just avoid the Church.

Too often, parents and the Church try to teach when we should be listening, or we deliver our advice in dominating tones that counter whatever openness to hearing there may have been. As one mother I know put it, "Every time I get this sense of urgency and start explaining things to them, they hear it as 'the life I have for you is better than the one you are planning.'" Parenting is one of the most challenging aspects of stewardship. Our children do belong, after all, to God. Really grasping this is frequently the developmental task for parents: trust in God, and also in the spirit of your teenager.

It is a good start to agree that acquired values are important influences on developing sexual identity. But how exactly are they acquired? The discussion brings us back, once again, to that bottom line to which as Orthodox we always seem to return, no matter what the issue. Getting our own house in order is the best help to those around us. I strongly agree with Dr. Chirban's insight that those who are engaging in helping teenagers with their sexual growth must have accomplished some healthy growth themselves, in Christ. Otherwise, the efforts are futile and the results grotesque. One can say many words, but the metalearning of experience will take precedence over mere words. We do indeed learn what we live.

GENDER ISSUES AND SEXUALITY

Demetra Velissarios Jaquet

Over the last ten years, I have been very involved in a group called Orthodox People Together, a network of Orthodox Christians dedicated to united witness in North America. The objective of OPT is to promote grassroots networking and to provide a clearinghouse of information between persons doing lay ministry in the Church. During that time I have met men and women from all jurisdictions in diverse geographic locations. Two years ago, with OPT doing well, an outgrowth of that work was to start a new network called WOMEN, the Women's Orthodox Ministries and Education Network. This decision was in response to a painful need revealed over those 10 years of OPT for a similar global network dedicated to the concerns of women in the Church. As OPT's chairperson, I had heard countless stories of sorrow and frustration from dozens of women who felt ignored, harassed, or left out in their efforts to serve the Church. For those of us involved in WOMEN, the flood of grief continues. This chapter summarizes the basic themes repeated throughout their stories.

The message of God's love for us and His call to salvation through His Son has been carried forward in time for 2,000 years by the power of the Holy Spirit and is the unchanging truth in which the Orthodox Church is rooted. At every hour and in every season throughout those 2,000 years, God has lifted up pious Orthodox theologians, teachers, hierarchs, and saints to carefully articulate and clarify the ongoing Tradition of the Church.

In each generation, including our own, the prophetic, redemptive call continues – the call to be the whole Church full of the Holy Spirit. Each age seems to bring new questions never raised before. To address these questions, Orthodox Christians rely on the Spirit's ongoing presence in Church Tradition. They also rely on God's lifting up persons to seek out words adequate to further articulate the unspeakable fullness of Truth.

The subject of sexuality in general, and gender issues in particular, appears to be very popular in North America and Western Europe today. The rise in the last 25 years of Western political feminism resulted eventually in a diversity of agendas collectively labeled by the ambiguous title "feminist" in many Western Christian churches. Information from the women's spirituality movement has acted as an ecumenical gadfly among Orthodox women, spurring questions and conversations, particularly among women living in pluralistic settings. These discussions are feared by some who have hastily retreated into Orthodoxy unhealed of painful confrontations with angry radical feminists in other religious traditions. Nevertheless, the continuing process for further articulating the fullness of Truth demands and assures that authentic discernment about these subjects can result from dialogue.

Sexuality has been part of the Church as long as there have been people of God. Questions and problems about sexuality are just as old. As Orthodox Christians, we have always been blessed with an incarnational theology that seeks and finds the good in all things, including our sexuality in all its expressions. As an integral part of all persons and their behaviors, our sexuality is understood to be one of many God-given opportunities for expressing and participating in His creative energies and agape love.

Of course, we know that this opportunity can become misfortune if it is separated from goodness and isolated from God. We can use it to demean ourselves and to possess others as objects from our own satisfaction. Too often we can allow the partial truths of sexual stereotypes to masquerade as our gospel.

Then, we might proclaim this gospel by clubbing our conscience with rationalizations, clubbing others with blame, and deceiving our communities with lies. Too frequently, sexist discrimination is encoded into life practices. The psychological sustained effect on Orthodox women can work to undermine their spiritual life and their appropriate role in the family.

This chapter will only briefly lift up six areas of current discussion arising in various settings of the Church. The first and broadest is gender equality issues. Many current gender issues are in fact age-old moral and ethical questions about treating each other as persons instead of objects – questions that were addressed by Christ Himself and by many of the Church Fathers. A sexual double standard is certainly part of the issue when Christ deals with the adulterous woman and the crowd of men ready to stone her. We know from the gospels that Christ regularly interacted with all types of people. His message had a special impact on those subjected to persecution and oppression caused by racism, sexism, or social and economic sterotyping, many of whom were women. Over and over, we see Christ's healing presence lift servants, prostitutes, and even his faithful women followers from the second-class status accorded them by Hellenistic society, calling them to full human personhood alongside the men. Christ's life and message suggest that gender equality does not seem to be an issue in the Kingdom of God and that equal respect for all persons is to be our norm.

At the same time, a given in the Orthodox world has been that there is an essential distinction between male and female and an essential relationship of harmonious complementarity between them. This given has not yet undergone systematic critical reflection to determine if and/or how it truly expresses the theology of the Church historically. Much theological clarity is needed for serious future discussions about gender from Orthodox theological, ontological, and anthropological perspectives. Is the theology of the Fathers truly egalitarian, or does it in fact express that there *is* a fundamental difference between men and women? Are the characteristics attributed to males and females an essential part of their human nature? Do they describe reality or just social practice? Are they descriptive in an open-ended way, inviting spontaneity of the Spirit? Or do they prescriptively point to an authentic bottom line that may not be moved? Could they do both? What kind of human nature are we using in our typological arguments? Could we be projecting our fallen nature, the broken anthropological reality of this world, into our theological definitions? Or would the truth be better articulated as the redeemed or essential nature in which there is no slave or free, Greek or Jew, male or female? Is biological resemblance an authentic measure of the priesthood? Does the bishop who stands in for Christ in the Church do so with the same ontological reality that is expressed by the revealed names of the Trinity? Or should we be speaking on a metaphoric level as in the various scriptural descriptions, parables, and analogies of what God, His Kingdom, and the Holy Spirit are like? What would it mean to understand "the Church is the Bride of Christ" as a mystical metaphor? What would be the criteria for differentiating authentic mystical metaphors from arbitrary interpretations arising from hardness of heart? The job of winnowing out heretical sociocultural incursions from the faith requires a willingness on the part of both genders to acknowledge the sin of sexism when it occurs. Even with consistent dialogue, the Church could easily spend a century clarifying the true answers to these and many other questions – answers already present but not yet articulated in our faith.

Second, some of today's questions are in fact really new, particularly in the area of bioethics and technology, e.g., in vitro fertilization and surrogate motherhood. Some are couched in Western categories irrelevant to Orthodox thought and are non-issues in Orthodoxy at large. Contemporary pro-life and pro-choice dichotomies are not in keeping with, or adequate to express, the holistic attitude of Orthodoxy. Yes, the Church holds an absolute position of pro-life. At the same time, the Church acknowledges that in the fallen world we are sometimes forced into situations that cause us to choose the lesser evil. To understand the Orthodox view of abortion as being identical with the fundamentalist pro-life philosophy is simply inadequate. The mercy of God includes prayers in Orthodox prayer books that pray for forgiveness and healing for the loss of an unborn child, whether voluntary or involuntary. The principle of *oikonomia*, unique to Orthodoxy, reveals the faith's gentle attitude of reconciling justice toward those who truly repent. This is a far cry from the militant, condemnatory attitude of many pro-lifers.

Third, some things have long existed in the Church but have never been questioned before. The most sensational topic is ordination to the priesthood. But at several Orthodox conferences over the last 30 years, many other areas of focus have been identified. One is the presence of unnecessarily demeaning references and practices toward women in some of the prayers, hymns, and rituals within the Church. In addition, in many Orthodox countries, un-Christian social and cultural practices sometimes take precedence over the teachings of the Church with regard to women's rights to be respected, safe, and agents of choice. Battered women in some countries have sometimes been counseled by Orthodox priests to whom they have turned for help to "go home where you belong" even when the home situation is life-threatening.

Fourth, some positive things that once existed in the Church have, for various reasons, ceased to exist and left a void where there once was a vital service to the Church. I am referring, of course, to the ministry of the ancient order of deaconess in the Church. The deaconesses provided social service ministries blessed with the ecclesial authority of the Church. In this age of shrinking numbers of candidates for priesthood, it seems an obvious oversight to delay in restoring this important resource to Church and community life. This also could pertain to varieties of lay ministries according to gifts and graces as practices in the early Church. One of the most blatant failures of good stewardship in today's Church is the wasting of theologically trained resources. Orthodox women and men trained in areas of service that could be of value to the Church are working for other churches or in secular settings because of a lack of acceptance of lay ministry in Orthodox parishes.

Fifth, more education could help many married Orthodox Christians come to terms with what they often perceive to be the second-class *askesis* of marital fidelity compared to the ideal example of sexual asceticism epitomized by monastic life. A disproportionately small amount of energy in Church has been expended in teaching or praising sex education and the virtues of holy behavior between man and wife.

Finally, clergy sexual abuse is a pressing and critical reality of moral abuse and legal vulnerability for the Church. There is at this moment an unresolved case in one archdiocese in America regarding a priest who engaged in sexual activity individually with two different married women from his own parish throughout an eight-year period. The women have disclosed the details in therapy and also in confession to another priest. They refuse to testify in ecclesial or civil court for fear of their identities being revealed to their families and community. The priest has been privately confronted by the second priest to whom the women confessed, but would only discuss the matter in confession, so there is nothing concrete to take to the bishop. The offending priest has been transferred to another unsuspecting parish. The priest who will replace him is inheriting whatever has been left behind.

Although there is a community to establish policy and procedures for clergy sexual misconduct, the Orthodox Church does not at this time have any standard policy in place with regard to healing for the victims or for the community. The priest claims he is paying for his own psychiatric treatment – in his words, to protect the Church from himself in the future. Both women have undergone extensive therapy at their own expense, and both have taken their families and left the Orthodox Church forever. There is only speculation as to whether the fifteen other married and single women who silently disappeared from the parish during the course of this man's pastorate had similar reasons for leaving.

Let us never forget that there are many beautiful Christian marriages and families in the Church, just as there are many pious men, women, and clergy doing good and living in relationships of Christian love by creatively transforming and expressing their sexuality as a freedom to love many, not just one. Let us also be aware that there are instances of extremism and abuse against Orthodox men and children as well as women by persons whose lives, relationships, and actions are seriously flawed by sin.

Our first task is to celebrate and continue to support, teach, and model healthy expressions of sexuality. At the same time, as committed Christians, we cannot overlook repeated instances of abuses within the Church. It is imperative that we approach these issues with a right heart, asking to be instruments of God's peace. We must take action against abuses if we come across them, yet that action cannot be motivated by self-aggrandizing fantasies that it is up to us to purify the entire Church. God's perfect love casts out fear, and zeal for holiness – not zeal for reform – is what can and will reveal and cast out evil in our midst.

The sin of sexism is one of many sins that cause us to fall down. Nevertheless, it is unique in that it is targeted at half the population of the Church. In these truths lies the challenge for an Orthodox psychology of sexuality and the Church. But that is not the end of the challenge. The task in our generation, as never before, is not only to articulate transformed reality but to live it.

REFERENCES

Baker-Miller, Jean. *Toward a New Psychology of Women, 2nd Edition.* Boston: Beacon Press, 1986.

Behr-Sigel, Elisabeth. *The Ministry of Women in the Church.* Redondo Beach, CA: Oakwood Publications. 1991.

Balenky, Mary Field, et al. *Women's Ways of Knowing: The Development of Self, Voice and Mind.* New York: Basic Books, Inc. 1986.

Belonick, Deborah. *Feminism in Christianity: An Orthodox Response.* Syosset, NY. Dept of Religious Education, Orthodox Church in America. 1983.

Bilezikian, Gilbert. *Beyond Sex Roles: What the Bible Says About a Woman's Place in Church and Family.* Grand Rapids, MI: Baker Book House, 1986.

Bristow, John Temple. *What Paul Really Said About Women.* San Francisco: HarperCollins, 1988.

Carr, Anne E. *Transforming Grace: Christian Tradition and Women's Experience.* San Francisco: Harper & Row, 1990.

Coffey, Kathy. *Hidden Women of the Gospels.* New York: Crossroad, 1996.

Chirban, John T., Ed. *Clergy Sexual Misconduct: Orthodox Christian Perspectives.* Brookline, MA: Hellenic College Press, 1994.

Clark, Elizabeth A. *Women in the Early Church.* Wilmington, DE: Michael Glazier, Inc., 1987.

Gvosdev, Matushka Ellen. *The Female Diaconate: An Historical Perspective.* Minneapolis: Light & Life, 1991.

Hahn, Celia Allison. *Sexual Paradox: Creative Tensions in our Lives and in our Congregations.* New York: Pilgrim Press, 1991.

Horton, Anne L. and Judith A. Williamson, Eds. *Abuse and Religion: When Praying Isn't Enough.* Lexington, MA: Lexington Books, 1988.

Limouris, Gennadios, Ed. *The Place of Woman in the Orthodox Church and the Question of the Ordination of Women: Inter-Orthodox Symposium, Rhodes, Greece, Oct 30-Nov 7, 1988.* Katerini, Greece: Tertios Publications, 1992.

Osiek, Carolyn. *Beyond Anger: On Being a Feminist in the Church.* New York: Paulist Press, 1986.

Pellaur, Mary, Barbara Chester and Jane Boyajian. *Sexual Assault and Abuse: A Handbook for Clergy and Religious Professionals.* San Francisco: HarperCollins, 1987.

Schaef, Anne Wilson. *Women's Reality: An Emerging Female System in a White Male Society.* San Francisco: Harper & Row, 1985.

Thurston, Bonnie Bowman. *The Widows: A Women's Ministry in the Early Church.* Minneapolis: Fortress Press, 1989.

Topping, Eva Catafygiotu. *Holy Mothers of Orthodoxy.* Minneapolis: Light & Life, 1987.

Van Nostrand, Catherine Herr. *Gender Responsible Leadership: Detecting Bias, Implementing Interventions.* Newbury Park, CA: Sage Publications, 1993.

Walker, Lenore E. *The Battered Woman.* New York: Harper & Row, 1979.

Wilson-Kastner, Patricia, et. al. *A Lost Tradition: Women Writers of teh Early Church.* New York: University Press of America, 1981.

Witherington, Ben III. *Women and the Genesis of Christianity.* Cambridge: Cambridge University Press, 1995.

Women and Men in the Church: A Study of the Community of Women in the Church. Prepared by a Sub-Committee of the Ecumenical Task Force of the Orthodox Church in America. Syosset, NY: Dept. of Religious Education, Orthodox Church in America, 1980.

A Response to Jaquet

J. Stephen Muse

Demetra Jaquet offers a preamble to her essay indicating that her paper is to be a summary of themes revealed by "countless stories of sorrow and frustration from dozens of women who felt ignored, harassed, or left out in their efforts to serve the Church." By framing these questions under the heading of "sexuality and church," she is lifting up the ambivalence that such a conjunction reveals when we pay close attention to the psychological and political tensions within society and each individual in light of 2,000 years of Christian history. Are sexuality and church an oxymoron or a seamless embrace?

Ms. Jacquet rightly points out that Orthodox Christianity has an incarnational theology. As well, our Lord's life as remembered by the Apostles depicts someone who surprised his peers by himself living and teaching equality of value and respect for persons of all genders, races, and socioeconomic classes. In this, which is foundational for Orthodox life, there is much hope.

Why then in practice do we fall so far short of the Lord's teaching? How, for example, after 1,800 years of Christianity, could both English and American law legislate a husband's right to beat his wife with a stick "as long as it is no bigger than his thumb?"[1] Is it because the teachings of the Holy Fathers are immured in the relativity of the times they lived in and that their "patriarchal" bias needs to be critically deconstructed by advanced modern minions? Or is it simply sin?

The Protestant churches and, to a lesser extent, the Roman Catholic church have been asking questions of theology and theologians in the light of cultural relativity and historical reconstructions for the twenty to forty years now. As Orthodox, we have the benefit of hindsight in this regard as we watch the erosion of traditional Protestant theologies in favor of academic formulations that are, at best, congruent with a multiculturally informed hermeneutic and, at worst, accommodations to current intellectual fads. Does the image of a virgin mother give way to that of the goddess Sophia who "runs with the wolves" in order to avoid overtones of subservient women who remain "barefoot and pregnant" and are "saved in childbirth" exclusive of careers outside the home? Can a perpetual virgin who is married be a symbol of the God-given goodness of full-blooded sexual desire? Is a crucified son merely a representation of how an abusive patriarchal father scapegoats his child to placate his wrath and protect the appearance of his own righteousness? How can this formulation of the Gospel have saving significance for an abused child[2] who sees in it a justification for her continued subservience, victimization, and unholy sacrifice?

Such questions, which are being raised by a flood of Protestant theologians, psychotherapists, and feminist and womanist authors, challenge Orthodox Christians to articulate how traditional understandings of the faith are congruent with a universal humanitarian interest in protecting and healing these persons. The questions that Ms. Jaquet raises are the questions raised by human suffering, and we cannot ignore the challenge they present.

Having myself worked for over a decade with a substantial number of women abused beyond belief in relationships with the men they loved and/or the fathers (spiritual and biological) they depended on, I am acutely aware of the problem that the sexism, gender entitlement, and boundary confusions inherent in parental and pastoral prerogatives represents in practice. However, in light of Protestant excesses, I find myself cautious with regard to historical revisionism as an antidote, which appears to find in Christian tradition itself the roots of the historical precedents that birthed our current social malaise. There is the underlying presumption that an "enlightened" twentieth century underestimates the problem of sin, which remains a constant in every generation. The truth of Christ is such that there is no force in heaven or on earth that can separate us from the love of God in Jesus Christ, whether we are slave or free, Gentile or Jew, male or female, first century or twenty-first. If this were not true, then Christ could not save apart from political reorganization or the gradual evolution of the race à la Teilhard de Chardin. Slaves who were not free could not be saved until they were set free by their masters. Persons living in politically oppressive countries could not be saved until political change had been wrought. Theosis could not occur until the final Omega point of evolution, which I do not believe is the case. Of course, this has nothing to do with justifying continuing abuses of any kind. It is just that the etiology of abuse is not simply located in the corruption of Christianity by patriarchal bias, which has resulted in the Church's limited effectiveness as an agent of social change.

When I was in seminary twenty years ago, professors required us change our language to reflect a nonsexist gender inclusivity. The Holy Trinity was not "Father, Son, and Holy Spirit" but rather "Creator, Redeemer, Sustainer." When I offered the benediction for a presbytery meeting when I was a Presbyterian minister, a female pastor came up to me and expressed her disappointment at my antiquated sexist reference to God as "Father, Son, and Holy Spirit." She said it excluded her. I felt uncomfortable. Some twenty years later, I find myself in a quandary. Where I once heard in the Nicene Creed, "*For us men* and our salvation" as pertaining to all persons, it has become difficult for me not to hear gender exclusivity – even though I know better. As a product of modern academic revisionism, and having heard the stories of so many women who have been traumatized and dehumanized by abusive, controlling relationships, I hear ambivalent overtones in the familiar words. As an Orthodox Christian seeking to be faithful to sacred tradition, I find myself making a deliberate mental switch inwardly when I say the Nicene Creed, reminding myself what "for us men" *really* means. When I have left out the word "men" altogether and said simply "for *us* and our salvation," I have been corrected by priests who insisted on retaining the original language as a means of not allowing the Tradition of Orthodoxy to unravel as it has among the Protestant churches.

In Shakespeare's day, "nice" meant "ugly." Clearly, the meanings and nuance associated with various words and phrases in any language change over time, and we must be sensitive to that. I certainly agree with the spirit of the perspective that "Orthodoxy must change us, and not we Orthodoxy." Yet, by failing to heed the impact of language and culture on persons' understanding of Tradition, we may render Orthodoxy unnecessarily impenetrable to thirsty spiritual orphans who are not being nourished by the thin theological porridge of a shape-shifting heterodoxy that is all too accommodating to passing cultural trends. This is a difficult, thin balance beam to traverse, but then, a history of Orthodoxy shows that this is the same narrow way that it has always been necessary to walk. Fortunately, "With God all things are possible." If it had not been for Cyril and Methodius, perhaps we would not have had a Cyrillic alphabet to offer the spirit of Orthodoxy to a people who could not understand the Greek. Should we not do the same for modern ears, in some ways equally deaf to ancient language?

Finally, Jesus taught us to pray "Thy Kingdom come, Thy will be done on earth as it is in heaven." The way to new life in Christ is through the power of God, which works through humility, repentance, prayer, and love. When we lose sight of this and begin to believe that we will bring about equality and destroy sexism and abuse by changing our fundamental theologies or merely by reconstructing our language, we are gravely mistaken. On the other hand, refusing to change anything in order to accommodate changes in understanding is born of confusing the Spirit with the form that symbolizes it. Either way, sin always finds a way to wreack havoc, and faithfulness to the truth of Christ must be our first concern.

The many questions Ms. Jaquet raises must indeed be examined in a careful and sustained way. It is certainly time for Orthodox to offer a response to the current dialogue in American Christianity in these areas. But it must be more than critical in an academic sense. It must include the full spirit of Orthodoxy that breathes in places such as Mount Athos, where women are not even allowed. This in itself appears to be a strange contradiction on the surface. Yet, before we dismiss it as antiquated and unenlightened and naively set about attempting to combine what centuries of discernment have seen fit to divide, let us be very clear what it represents.

If we are to provide an antidote to the ambivalence that pervades relationships between the genders and is associated with the uneasy marriage between spirituality and sexuality as it appears in the variety of contexts summarized by Ms. Jaquet, we must always be about the task of living out Orthodox Christianity together by the grace of God. This begins not with academics but with purity and humility of heart, born of repentance. We believe and struggle to obey in order to understand. Thus, I could not agree more with the author's closing statement, which is the true challenge of our faith that is quickened by the suffering of others: "not merely to articulate transformed reality but to live it." It is not enough to be politically correct. We can change our language, but it does not guarantee a change in our behavior unless our hearts are changed as well. This has from the beginning been the mission of Christ and the hope of the world.

NOTES

[1] Muse, S. (1993) "Out From Under the Thumb: The Battered Woman Syndrome" *Pastoral Forum* Vol 11(1) p.7

[2] Cf. Imbens, A. & Jonker, I. (1992) *Christianity and Incest.* Fortress Press, Minneapolis.; Capps, D. (1995) *The Child's Song: The religious abuse of children.* Westminster/John Knox Press, Kentucky.; Miller, A. (1991) *Breaking Down the Wall of Silence.* Dutton, New York.

A Response to Muse

Demetra Velisarios Jaquet

Dr. Muse's thoughtful response invites reflection beyond the content of the specific examples I have outlined to addressing what processes and attitudes might be appropriate for Orthodox Christians who are willing to engage with these issues. This points to an encompassing, centuries-old challenge: for Orthodox Christians to articulate to their Western sisters and brothers, as well as to edify our own faithful, how traditional understandings of the faith are congruent with universal interests in not only humanitarian but also ecological, social, political, economic, psychological, emotional, and, centrally, spiritual healing in our times.

In order to understand how issues of justice, wholeness, and spiritual health are integrated throughout the warp and woof of Orthodox spiritual life, it is helpful to approach them with a hermeneutic of faith, not a hermeneutic of suspicion. In the process, most of the extreme options offered as solutions by Western feminists to the topics addressed under "sexuality and the Church" become irrelevant. "Historical reconstruction" and "cultural relativity," like "patriarchy," have a different meaning with more positive connotations for Orthodox than for our Western Christian counterparts. Ambivalence becomes creative tension. Any discussion of women in the Church is formulated out of a Trinitarian theology that never underwent the subordination of the Holy Spirit in the filioque or the parallel subordinations of "base nature" to spirit, and woman to man. Thus, the answers to the either/or questions that plague Western feminism – indeed, the questions themselves – are of little interest and usually no use to Orthodox.

While those very questions can and do serve to illumine for Orthodox the beauty of our own holistic theology, at the same time the abuses they address can be readily found in Orthodox communities, revealing our frequent shortfalls in fully living transfigured life interpersonally and sociologically. One might say they are, indeed, simply in sin. Thus, the etiology of abuse might be located in the corruption of persons by patriarchalism and other distortions of virtue, which has resulted in the limited effectiveness of imperfect social systems, created with (in)adequate good intentions by sinful persons to participate synergistically in God's grace-filled plan for liberating the world from corruption.

With regard to inclusive language, contemplation of many persons' past experiences in the Church yields several pangs of spiritual sorrow. First, theological truths can and must be expressed pastorally, not pejoratively, with careful attention to sound logic, accurate and Spirit-inspired language, and avoidance of stereotypical prescriptivism. Second, humanly implemented healing therapies must sometimes begin by spending time dealing with distorted human understandings not yet illumined by spiritual vision. My own experience for nearly a decade in counseling abused women and men suggests that understanding oneself as "having a choice" is a bedrock therapeutic issue, not the least important aspect of which is what pronouns and images one chooses in speaking personally to, or even passive-aggressively murmuring, God. Similarly, re-imaging God as female and redefining one's relationship with God as mother/daughter, in order to therapeutically catalyze freedom from spiritual arrest caused by paralyzing fears of a punishing male God, is frequently a turning point in spiritual and psychological healing, particularly for women. Both can be used by the Spirit as a starting point or milestone on one's journey toward the complete healing that only God provides. Neither precludes an ultimately reverent appreciation for and voluntary relationship with the traditional revealed identities of the Persons of the Trinity.

Last, theological reiterations and clarifications about the proper names of the Persons of the Holy Trinity, the Church as the Bride of Christ, and biblical language in general may continue for a long time, and review of prayers and practices may go on just as long. Yet, simple but profound pastoral healing is immediately available around sensitivity to inclusive language in three areas. The English language's imprecision makes it impossible to articulate the translation the careful distinctions between *anthropos* and *andros*. There is no good reason for the Church – its clergy, chanters, and choirs – not to exercise caring attention to the pain caused by using sexually exclusive language with regard to humankind, and immediately cease hurting half its people at every liturgical celebration by praying for "all humankind" instead of "all men." Additionally, avoiding the assignment of male gender to the Holy Spirit by simply repeating "the Spirit" rather than using the pronoun "He," and calling for the prayers of "our Holy Fathers and Mothers," offer no theological stumbling blocks. Such changes have been peacefully chanted in English-language parishes for some time with no outcry of any kind, much to the appreciation of their feminine members. The fullness of Orthodoxy, including its Syriac tradition of referring to the Holy Spirit as "She" and its bounteous materikon of holy women, is impoverished by anything less than such intentional good will. One delightful aside – many parishes have begun appropriately praying for those who travel by land, sea, air, and space.

EROS, ASCETICISM, AND MARRIAGE:
A SEAMLESS CONNECTION?

J. Stephen Muse

In Hebrew, God's intimate knowledge of His people is very closely related to the English word for sexual intercourse. Body and Spirit are one. Eros is intimately related to the presence of God among persons, like red-hot fire rendering iron vulnerable to the Creator's creative touch. But in contemporary Western culture, eros has been more like the Roman God Janus, who is depicted with a head facing in two opposite directions at once. Erotic desire both constitutes a deep yearning that beckons the soul toward God in repentance[1] as the author of all life and love, and simultaneously draws attention to the flesh quite apart from any awareness of its participation in the invisible dimension of Spirit and the Image of God of which personhood constitutes a unique reflection.

Our human path through the world lies between the biological demands of the flesh tinged by certain death and the longing of the heart for eternity, which is beyond what flesh and blood alone can comprehend and appropriate. The easy way to dissolve this tension is to split apart in one direction or the other, not quite realizing that it is in remaining faithful to God and persons within the seamless embrace of both flesh and spirit that the human soul matures into one capable of loving the ordinariness of ourselves and others as God passionately loves us in Christ, which is the basis of all community. This is eros fulfilled through self-emptying for the beloved, as in the case of our Lord.

As Orthodox Christian psychotherapists, how do we help

facilitate this kind of growth in ourselves and others? What are the developmental ideals for marital sanctity that include a healthy erotic component integrated with the eros of repentance and interior prayer that are traditionally part of Orthodox monastic life? What sort of theory of personal and marital growth informs our therapeutic methodologies? Are monasticism and marriage two different means to the same end? Certainly, more evidence and instruction seem to be available on how to pray and live ascetically in monastic community than about how to pray and live erotically in marital union within the marketplace.[2] To the degree that the church fails to offer constructive help and developmental norms of holy marriage in this regard, confusion will continue to reign, and secular models and methodologies will advance other norms as counselors attempt to guide and help persons shipwrecked on the rocky shoals of eros split off from the spirit. These other models may not be congruent with Orthodoxy and may in some instances lead in directions that directly oppose it..

The Confusion

One of my clinical supervisors used to counsel, "If the person begins by saying it's a sexual problem, it's spiritual. If they say it's spiritual, look for a sexual hang-up." As psychiatrist Gerald May points out, the language of Christian mysticism is full of erotic metaphors, while the language of sexual love takes up the images of spirit:

> Even a cursory reading of Western mysticism is sufficient to impress one with the prevalence of sexual symbolism in spirituality. The word *union* itself more readily brings to mind sexual intercourse than spiritual fulfillment. The writings of Christian mysticism are filled with terms such as bliss, ecstasy, rapture, burning desire, being devoured, consummation, joy, delight, holding, penetration, embracing, caressing. On the other side, popular descriptions of human ro-

mance rely just as heavily on terms that are deeply spiritual: divine, angelic, light, splendor, eternity, mystery, and so on.[3]

I was already confused about sex by the time I got into psychotherapy training. Subsequent lessons haven't totally straightened me out yet, but I continue to hold out hopes that Orthodox Christianity in its fullness will ultimately prove curative. I believe that all good things come from the Word Who is made flesh and that in Christ we are eventually rendered whole and complete through the indwelling of the Holy Spirit, which unites us with the Holy Trinity in community one with another even as we remain distinct.

This paradoxical relational model of being one yet distinct, as in the Holy Trinity, is paradigmatic for the kind of psychological differentiation that is necessary for a grace-filled, erotically passionate marriage. Yet, confusion abounds regarding what at times appear to be competing paths toward Christian life exemplified by the virginity/celibacy model in contrast to marital union: monasticism and the marketplace. Methods and instructions given in one arena do not automatically translate into helpful suggestions in the other.

What are the implications of Jesus' admonition to his interlocutors that in heaven "they neither marry nor are given in marriage but are like the angels"? Is celibacy the angelic condition and marriage a second-rate compromise until we are released from the prison of the flesh? That starts to sound like the same old mind-body split promoted by some of the gnostic teachings, which have helped denigrate sex to "something dirty you do with the one you love" because the body is hateful and the spirit good. The idea that sexuality was for procreative purposes alone, without the dimension of fulfilment of erotic desire with one's partner that strengthens the marital union, was condemned by the first and sixth Ecumenical Councils.[4] Nevertheless, that view often prevails in the Western Church, as in St. Jerome's admonition that "anyone who has too passionate a love of his wife is an adulterer" and the opinion of Gregory the Great, who counseled

> The married must realize...when they abandon themselves to immoderate intercourse, they transfer the occasion of procreation to the service of pleasure. Let them realize that though they do not then pass beyond the bounds of wedlock, yet in wedlock they exceed its rights. Therefore it is necessary that they should efface by frequent prayer what they befoul in the fair form of intercourse *by the admixture of pleasure* [my italics].[5]

This perspective appears to have continued and been confirmed by the current Pope John Paul II some 15 centuries later.[6]

In the face of this persistent confusion, what kind of ascetical methodology do we married persons employ to grow in Christ that includes erotic desire for our partners? How, to the extent that it is in my power, should I desire my spouse? I want my marriage to be the equivalent of a monastic cell in which my spouse and I remain faithful to Christ while the fires of ordinary living in light of the Gospel combine with prayer and grace to work the alchemy of transformation that is the same condition of soul toward which over a lifetime the celibate monks and hesychast on a solitary mountainside also strive. If ordinary eros in marriage is not an obstacle to theosis, how can it be an aid? How do married couples struggle with the passions that adulterate eros and split it apart from personhood rooted in the heart, in a way that frees them for the passion toward God that includes continued passion for each other? In other words, can I both lust for, sacrifice for, and befriend my spouse in an integrated way? Is this a path toward Christ? Or is it a hotbed for every sort of confusion?

SECULAR MODELS

The ideals of marriage offered up for popular consumption by Hollywood and even secular psychological models fail to inspire. Contemporary films in America portray love in terms of sexual encounters fueled purely by a sexualized-genitalized eros that is generally outside the confines of marriage, more than within the context of the deep knowingness and care that is part of God's relationship to His people. There is little if any sacrificial element. Deep, heartfelt, committed, self-giving, long-suffering love is absent. In its place is an eros shorn apart from Eucharistic communion: sex without soul, body without spirit. The sacramental context is missing. Sex has no human name. Bodies are merely meat driven by an ecstatic grasping in the face of certain death. This is soulless sexuality, a sign of the splitting of eros into "spiritual" and "physical" that God never intended. The opposite of this is equally problematic and lacking: a life together without eros – cordial and even friendly, but without passion and perhaps even developmentally stalled. How do we avoid and correct this split in us, avoiding both extremes to stay attentive to and engaged in the stuff of our human life together that is imbued with God's eros, both in couples relationships and in vital community with others?

GOD AND EROTIC LOVE BELONG TOGETHER

A woman and her husband came for therapy recently with a typical array of presenting problems: "He doesn't help around the house, doesn't manage money well," etc. "She is too demanding. Nothing would satisfy her. I don't really think there is that much of a problem."

We talked for a while of her loss of desire in the relationship, and then she said, with her face flushing, "What I really want is for him to be the spiritual leader of the family so that I will *want* to submit to him as the church does to Christ" – not out of tyranny and boredom, but out of passionate self-giving erotic love! She recognized that their sexual problems – the loss of her desire for him – and her carping at him for things he wasn't doing around the house were rooted in their spiritual problems.

We submit to Christ and yearn for union with Christ, not because he is a tyrant or because he is seductive or manipulative or is trying to sell us something, but because he is humble and vital and empathic and *interested in serving us so as to empower us to become who we truly are.* In submitting to Christ we become ourselves, which includes a maturing of our erotic potential into full manhood and womanhood.

Virtually every couple hits points in a marriage where former passionate romantic attachments cool and they begin to look around for "what is wrong. " One may conclude that someone "new" is needed to restore the feelings of the original fire. This reminds me of the situation where folks were assembled in St. Paul's day at the Areopagus with "itchy ears," always wanting to be stimulated by some new sensational religion. This condition has more in common with lack of rootedness in one's self and with addiction than with love. The purpose is not commitment to growth in truth, but rather self-stimulation, passionate feelings elicited by a sense of merger with another to avoid confrontation with one's own limits and aloneness. Analogously, it is like being in love with God not as Person but only for the consolation God brings. As Dr. Rizzuto has said, we are not likely to be less neurotic with God than we are with each other.[7] Whatever shape we are in when we fall in love, *it is precisely by intentionally and consciously remaining in the marriage when we don't have the passionate feelings that we eventually discover ourselves and each other in a new way and truly grow beyond our neurotic conflicts.* Forgiveness, mercy, acceptance, and treasuring of the ordinary otherness of another is the mark of a maturing Christian. It comes by identifying and withdrawing the projections (finding the "log in our own eye") we make onto another of the stuff of our own unacceptableness to ourselves. The cooling of passion is an inevitable midpoint through which we must pass on the way to differentiation into the fullness of our own being. One psychologist has dubbed his efforts to facilitate this process as "constructing the sexual crucible" and identified it as the primary context for doing marital therapy which presumes a seamless connection between sexuality and spirituality that is essentially hard-wired into our brains.[8]

I believe that our marriage with the Church as the Bride of Christ is similarly a "crucible" in which we grow, provided we are committed even through the "dull times" when we are confronted with our own failure to be able to attend to the here and now in such a way that we feel alive in the Divine Liturgy, in our jobs, and in our lives in general. Are we really finding Christ in the world around us? Eros again is involved, though we may not think of this, since we are not dealing with genitalia. Nevertheless, being erotically engaged with life requires a confrontation with the logs in our own eye, so to speak, as much as in a marriage, removing the film that separates us from the stuff of life and the aliveness one feels when this direct contact with the real world is made, born of simplicity of heart. The late Fr. Florovsky, of blessed memory, alluded to this fresh quality of Christian life when he wrote,

> The Church gives us not a system, but a key; not a plan of God's City, but the means of entering it. Perhaps someone will lose his way because he has no plan. But all that he will see, he will see without a mediator, he will see it directly, it will be real for him; while he who has studied only the plan risks remaining outside and not really finding anything.[9]

Without a lifelong self-confrontation with our own "love maps" and preconceptions of others, in the presence of God under the inspiration of the Holy Spirit, i.e., the "eros of continual repentance," we are subject to the dissipation and fragmentation of eros. What seems perfectly natural to the young child gazing with fresh eyes upon the world for the first time remains hidden from our view. Unless we "become as a little child." life remains just outside our grasp, hidden by the logs in our own eyes. We do not see it, as it were, directly, but once removed, as one who encounters life from outside behind the glasses of various preconceptions born of self-justification, ignorance, and attempts to protect one's separateness.

This struggle to continue in the truth until "thine eye be single and the whole body is full of light" is, of course, much easier to avoid. We avoid the confrontation with ourselves whenever we make the mistake of saying, "Oh, there must be a problem with the Liturgy. Let's add balloons or change the form of it a little to make it more stimulating," as the Protestant churches have done in endless variations. Or we say, "Since I do not have the original desire I felt when I first became a Christian, maybe Orthodoxy is not right after all, and I should become a Buddhist or something." In other words, I go "whoring after other gods" because I fail to see that the problem is with *myself*. Renewal of the heart by "first removing the log in my own eye" enables me to grow and "re-member" myself enough to rediscover my partner and my faith in ways I had not been able to see before.

HYDRAULICS THEORY OF SEXUALITY

Within the world of psychotherapy, the field of sex therapy has gone through a series of changes, which have in many ways contributed to, or at least reflected, the confusion we have about eros. In the 1960s, when the so-called sexual revolution was occurring in America, Masters and Johnson, among others, demonstrated that sex could be a clinical area of attention. They couched their work in purely amoral terms of empirical science, which ultimately led to a context of the cultural relativity of all sexual norms. Since that time, sex therapy has helped a lot of persons with orgasmic difficulties, erectile problems, and problems of arousal, but has it helped us discover ways to reintegrate sexuality and spirituality in long-term committed marriages? Has it helped us find what the wife in the above example was looking for in her marriage and within herself and her husband?

The Hebrew concept of *nephesh* implies a seamless connection between spirit and soul. Sexuality is seen as "very good" and a blessing of Sabbath. Husband and wife become "one flesh" not simply in terms of hydraulics but in terms of "knowledge, one of the other," which is rooted in being known by God. Biopsychologically, there is a neocortical involvement of self-other awareness that is an integral dimension of marital desire. It is not simply glands and groins and gyrations dictated by the lower brain processes that account for the attraction at work in copulating mammals and even of long-term mating.

A hydraulics theory of sexuality helps us understand why total strangers would want to have sex with each other on the basis of pure hormones and instinctive procreative drives to preserve the species, but not in terms of why persons married for 30 years would desire each other even more deeply than in the beginning of their relationship. A hydraulics-based theory of sexuality certainly doesn't help us understand the parallel between God *knowing* His people and a husband and wife *knowing* each other.

If sexual desire were biologically hard wired in persons as it is for animals who enter estrus, a hydraulic and purely procreative approach would perhaps make sense. But at some point in the past, women went from an estrus cycle to a menstrual cycle and became receptive to men sexually at times other than those biologically determined, thus opening the door to sexual encounters that are not procreatively based.[10] This fits with the Hebraic concept of sexuality, which celebrates it for the "sheer joy and pleasure of it, even when procreation was obviously impossible,"[11] a theme that continued in the Eastern Church to some extent, at least, as evidenced by the commentaries of St. John Chrysostom,[12] which are in contrast to those of St. Jerome and St. Gregory the Great, as quoted earlier.

Surely we can agree that the saints are those who are most alive, most fully human, most capable of love, most deeply rooted in both the earthiness of themselves as well as the Spirit of God, and thus most sensitive to the personhood of other people and the world around them in an erotic way. Gospel evidence is that both men and woman greatly loved Jesus and wept for Him and He for them. It's hard for me to believe that His eroticism (albeit expressed in celibacy) was in any way life-denying; rather, it was life-transforming in every way. Gospel evidence is that He was able to be with persons in all kinds of situations in ways that surprised, challenged, and inspired them by His aliveness, which drew sinners to Him. His love was free and pure – virginal in the sense of unadulterated by passions – and thus fully passionate, vital, and life-giving to those around him. When He spoke, "It was not as the Scribes and Pharisees, but with power."

FANTASY AND FRICTION

In the decades following the initial work by Masters and Johnson, Dr. Helen Singer Kaplan proposed and refined a model of treatment for sexual desire disorders that incorporated a focus on using sexually arousing images in combination with psychodynamic theory to help persons overcome blocks [13] that inhibit sexual desire in their marriages. Kaplan's approach enables persons to get good results by using various means of employing fantasy and friction, including at times watching pornographic movies together. What about the spiritual component? Do we compound problems for couples in the long run when we suggest entertaining sexual fantasy to excite arousal? What developmental norms for couples in terms of growth and intimacy do we indirectly advance by the methods we use to treat sexual dysfunction when we work out of this kind of clinical model of human sexuality, focused as it is on physiological functioning and/or arousal mediated by fantasy that is proscribed as potentially delusional by most of the ascetical literature on interior prayer?

St. Augustine knew this potential for beguilement so well that he feared it for the rest of his life (albeit perhaps in part because he never got totally free of the Manichaean gnostic teaching that split off flesh as bad and spirit as good). He writes in his *Confessions* that sexual relations between a husband and wife are to be for procreative purposes alone and are not to be enjoyed for pleasure – a teaching that has continued, as noted, even to the present pope. Considering that estimates are that as many as 5 percent of Roman Catholic priests are pedophiles[14] and only 40 percent of celibate priests are actually able to maintain celibacy over a lifetime,[15] something isn't working.

Moral Relativity

One problem with science giving us methods to treat "illness" that is related to the spiritual realm is that empiricism can't give us moral truth. It can't give us norms other than those based on biology and sociological samplings. Morality is the province of conviction, and revealed truth of faith and theology. This is not to say that it is merely a subjective preference, which again leads to relativism, but rather that any perspective that disavows moral claims by positing relativity based on empirical comparisons alone is itself a convictional claim and requires a theological critique. We must employ some means of identifying the relationship between moral conviction and empirical truth, particularly when we are going to be purveyors of this relationship by way of professional psychotherapeutic disciplines, which must inevitably work with persons in the convictional arena. We simply cannot fall back on the old cliche that psychotherapy is "morally neutral," because the theories we espouse and work from are laden with anthropological assumptions about the nature of humankind and developmental ideals of marriage, sexuality, and human growth and potential that may be far from consonant with those espoused and cherished by a particular faith.

For example, in Masters and Johnson's classic text *Sex and Human Loving*, widely used as a textbook in sex education in our schools, the authors review sexual mores from a descriptive cross-cultural perspective and reach this conclusion:

> What is labeled as "moral" or "right" varies from culture to culture, from century to century. Many of the moral issues pertaining to sex relate to certain religious traditions, but religion has no monopoly on morality. People who have no closely held religious creed are just as likely to be moral as those whose values are tied to a religious position. *There is no sexual value system that is right for everyone and no single moral code that is indisputably correct and universally applicable* [16] [my italics].

Just what exactly does this mean? What kind of "morality" are we talking about? Sex therapists are not likely to be moral theologians or even to ask such questions. Where, for example, in American culture and media do we learn about restraint of consumption and transformation of erotic desire toward God, other than perhaps the church? Too often sex is a subject we are either uncomfortable talking about, or we may not know how to speak of sex and spiritual growth in the same breath as an integrated whole. So our children grow up like us, perhaps not fully comfortable with their sexuality within a religious context while acting it out elsewhere in the culture on the basis of ideas learned in an academic setting, continuing the split between a nonerotic "religious" side and a nonreligious erotic side deeply immersed in the consumer culture. Significantly, one Western observer points out that there are cultural impediments to recovering from the split between sexuality and spirituality, and that the value of asceticism rightly engaged in is subversive to the economy!

> The logic of chastity is fatally opposed to the logic of consumerism. To live chastely requires that one master and control one's desires. As Thomas Aquinas points out, "Chastity takes its name from the fact that reason chastises concupiscence." The logic of chastity implies an ascetic attitude toward life. The logic of consumerism is quite opposite.

Advertising, the propaganda of consumer society, attempts to arouse desire and to convince us that a certain purchase will satisfy it....Chastity is especially threatening to a consumer society, because the one who has learned to control the desire for sexual gratification has learned that he is master of his desires and not slave to them. It is much harder to sell anything to such a person, for one must appeal not simply to one's appetites but to the reason. When gratification is no longer an end in itself, reason unmasks the propaganda of the consumer society for what most of it is:deceptive promises built on false values.[17]

The Ramsey Colloquium, an ecumenical think tank, evidenced similar concerns in a statement examining cultural trends in America and concluding that

perhaps the key presupposition of the so-called sexual revolution which has deeply influenced the ideals and methods of secular psychotherapy is that human health and flourishing require that sexual desire, understood as "need" be acted upon and satisfied. Any discipline of denial or restraint has been popularly depicted as unhealthy and dehumanizing. We insist, however, that it is dehumanizing to define ourselves or our personhood as male and female by our desires alone. Nor does it seem plausible to suggest that what millennia of human experience have taught us to regard as self-command should now be dismissed as mere repression....It is important to recognize that linkages among the component parts of the sexual revolution: permissive abortion, widespread adultery, easy divorce, radical feminism, and the gay and lesbian movement have not by accident appeared at the same historical moment. They have in common a declared desire for liberation from constraint – especially constraints associated with an allegedly oppressive culture and religious tradition. *They also have in common the presuppositions that the body is little more than an instrument for the fulfillment of desire, and that the fulfillment of desire is the essence of the self.* [My italics]. On biblical and philosophical grounds, we reject this radical dualism between the self and the body. Our bodies have their own dignity, bear their own truths, and are participant in our personhood in a fundamental way. ...This constellation of movements...rests upon an anthropological doctrine of the autonomous self.[18]

So What Do We Do?

What is transfigured sexuality and erotic desire in light of Orthodox Christianity, and how does this inform what I do as a husband and as a marriage therapist? What kind of norm does Orthodoxy invite us to in terms of marital sexuality, chastity, and celibacy, and what sorts of methodologies arise out of this to inform the practice of psychotherapy within an Orthodox context? Let me offer a few case examples by way of illustration of some possible areas of conflict.

Case 1: Using Sin to Fight Sin?

Several years ago I had a referral from the bishop of a religious body for a young man who had been convicted of sexually molesting several young girls while in the service of the church. The bishop was now seeing the man for spiritual counsel and had told him not to masturbate, which was regarded as a sin. The young man was reading Scripture and praying, but on the basis his history, I didn't think he would be able to do this. I spoke with his bishop, and we agreed that if the man did in fact masturbate he should do it with images of an adult woman to avoid reinfecting himself with images of nine-year-old girls. The young man did this, and a couple of years later he reported that he was interested in a woman his own age and was avoiding any images associated with young girls to avoid the temptation, which remained for him. He occasionally masturbated, but he did so with adult women in mind, associating the pleasure of arousal and orgasm with their image rather than images of nine-year-old girls. He had been badly abused physically and emotionally by, and there were numerous contributing factors to his problems, but this kind of manipulation of sexual imagery seemed a necessary part of the treatment, along with weekly Bible study and a confessional relationship with his bishop. He also had a relationship with a father figure who gave him the emotional support his own father had found difficult to do, and this helped lower some of the interior tension he lived with. It is of course hard to know what combination of things helped him, along with the grace of God, but he did improve.

When I raised this case up at a meeting of Orthodox clergy in light of the Church's teaching against masturbation, one father rose up vehemently and shouted: "Fathers, we can't use sin to fight sin!" Masturbation, once thought of as a grave sin and mental illness that could cause hair to grow on your hands and make you lose your mind, is now generally looked on as a standard means of treatment for a variety of disorders. Research indicates that women who masturbate have happier marriages than those who do not, as measured in terms of self-esteem, orgasms, arousal time, intensity of sexual desire, and both marital and sexual satisfaction.[19] In this study, it is interesting to note that while only 43.9 percent of the women thought masturbation was healthy, 60.9 percent felt it increased their total awareness of their sexuality, which was presumably a desirable goal.

Did I suggest sin to fight sin in this man's case? Should he have stopped fantasizing altogether? If so, what is the basis for this teaching, which contradicts much of current empirical studies and current methodologies? Is it possible to treat persons totally individually, understanding that "sin" is on a continuum and that one cannot tell merely from the outer behavior, or even the inner fantasy, the end toward which the act is intentioned? Is all "lust" a sin by virtue of the quality of the inner image and physiological arousal, or does it have to do more with the nature of one's inner consent to the particular fantasy in terms of its perceived ends; i.e, is it relationship-enhancing or self-enclosive? Can the ascetical rigor of the celibate monk simply be lifted up and applied to sexually active persons "in the world," or will we injure them by applying too strong a medicine for which they are not prepared and do not have the necessary community support and ongoing spiritual guidance? Perhaps the inner work of the celibate monastic is not entirely appropriate for those "in the world" who seek to be genitally active with their spouses. If so what adaptations are necessary, and what criteria guide their practices?

What Is the Role of Sexual Fantasy in Mature Christian Love?

Case 2: Fantasy Can Help

A couple married seven years had not had sex more than a half dozen times in several years. The woman was systematically "turning herself off" by concentrating on cleanliness and separating from her body into a kind of inner dissociated observatory "up in her head." Although she protested all her husband's attempts to interest her in sexual relations, she said she became aroused when he watched pornographic films, and she felt ashamed of herself for feeling this. She wanted to be able to desire her husband, but in bed she lost her arousal in spite of her intentions. Giving her permission to guide the man's touch where she wanted it and how she liked it and also instructing her to "put a video in her head" that she found arousing, freed her to accept her own desires. The couple felt much better, and her embarrassment was gone. This was in an overall context of affectionate love for each other and no other obvious marital conflicts.

Did I inadvertently hurt this couple by suggesting that God made sexual desire, that it was good, and that if only the woman allowed herself to accept the part of her that was aroused by the images of the video while she was with her husband, all would be well? Are these compatible as they appear to be by the couple's obvious satisfaction in subsequent weeks?

Case 3: Fantasy Can Hurt

This couple had been married for more than 20 years. After the birth of the children, the wife had begun to reject her husband's sexual attention in a similar way as in the previous example. She said that she had once cooperated with her husband's sexual fantasies and had dressed for him in lacy clothing from Victoria's Secret, which had heightened his desire. Over many years, in combination with other difficulties in the marriage and some unconscious conflicts of her own from a promiscuous life, before she was married, she felt used – "like a prostitute." When her husband approached her for sexual relations, she avoided him. When she was alone in the house, she would fantasize about his coming home and would be aroused. When he got home, she felt put upon. The only place she felt desire while actually with him was when they were sitting in church together! She was feeling a renewal of her life in God and becoming involved in leadership capacities in the church, and she deeply wanted her husband to share this part of her life with her. It was to her a validation of her personhood which was a precondition for permitting herself to experience sexual desire for him that was "pure" and untainted by the obligation she felt as his "prostitute."

What was the role of acting out sexual fantasy in ultimately damaging the relationship between this man and woman? What appeared to work, in the beginning of their relationship, eventually backfired. As in the initial example, this woman intuitively understood that the erotic dimension of her self-giving and her enjoyment of her husband was seamlessly connected with her spiritual yearnings, with her sense of self-worth and with her husband's capacity to identify it and to some extent share it with her. Sex without love was not something she was interested in. Her husband, on the other hand, felt that love without sex was something he could not endure. Not to be erotically desired by her in a demonstrative way was tantamount to not being loved and cared for emotionally – a scenario not uncommon in marital crises and an indication, perhaps, that sex and love are made for each other and that when united in this way they both contribute to the validation and valuation of personhood.

Case 4: Does It Matter What Kind of Fantasy It Is If Love Is Behind It?

This man needed to imagine sex with men in order to get an arousal with his wife. His homoerotic feelings were ego dystonic. He loved his wife and felt shame for his erotic desire attached to male genitalia, beginning with sexual abuse by an older man when he was an adolescent. He had kept this a secret for decades out of shame and fear of losing her. Consequently, they were never able to really discuss the root of many of their arguments and lack of intimacy.

During marital therapy, the husband disclosed his fantasy life to his wife. She was initially repulsed and felt humiliated and rejected by his fantasies, which she took as "replacing me." The therapist worked to normalize this and suggested (à la Kaplan) that sexual imprinting of arousing fantasies early in life is very resistant to change. Would she be repulsed if he had fantasies of a woman that looked like her or that was an image of herself, seen through his eyes, even better than she actually was? At what point did she feel that the fantasies became intolerable? Ultimately, this woman was able to allow her husband freedom to express his desire for her in the only way he was able. He used imagery of male genitalia to be with her because he loved her, and he didn't know how to change the images without losing his desire until after he was near the point of orgasm. Then he could switch channels to being with her without imagery.

In this example, homoerotic imagery was allowed by a couple

who share a deep emotional attachment, presumably for the purpose of enhancing sexual arousal, which ultimately leads to strengthening their marital bond. Multiple issues of poor emotional differentiation, childhood trauma, sexual abuse, and surviving combat complicated the picture. Nevertheless, they are two committed Christians living as best they are able and evidencing tremendous mercy and forgiveness toward each other under the circumstances. The line between diagnosis and discernment, in terms of both sin and pathology as well as spiritual and psychological health, becomes complicated. Pastoral sensitivity and good clinical judgment, applied in a personal way, are critical ingredients.

RECAPITULATION

Christian ascetical practice is frequently misunderstood by modern writers seeking to affirm sexuality and incarnate experience, depending on which writers they are familiar with. Contrasting perspectives, as noted, along with errors of extremism are plentiful and lead to further extremes by way of attempted course corrections. For example, one author, in a contemporary book of essays on sexuality and the sacred, demonstrates the typically the inadequate understanding of authentic Christian asceticism that is summarily dismissed by writers seeking to deconstruct traditional orthodoxy in order to reconstruct Christianity along the lines of modern understandings of sexuality and spirituality:

> We have attempted to separate the spiritual and the erotic, reducing the spiritual thereby to a world of flattened affect – a world of the ascetic who aspires to feel nothing. But nothing is farther from the truth. For the ascetic position is one of the highest fear, the gravest immobility. The severe abstinence of the ascetic becomes the ruling obsession. And it is one, not of self-discipline, but of self-abnegation.[20]

By contrast, the authentic aim of asceticism is to render us fully human. Its motivation is not fear but love. Its purpose, as Bishop Kallistos Ware points out, is not self-abnegation as some sort of Pyrrhic victory over the self by eliminating the body, but rather a restraint of all that enslaves by further dividing the spirit and the body and making us less than human.

> The aim of *asceses* is to secure our freedom. Ascetic rules are often expressed in a negative form – don't smoke, don't drink, don't eat meat on this day – but behind the negative rules there is the supremely positive aim. The Russian theologian and priest Serge Bulkagov used to say, "Kill the flesh in order to acquire a body." That is exactly what *asceses* is doing. Using the Pauline distinction between *sarx* and *soma*, the ascetic kills the flesh in order to acquire a body. In order to have true freedom in his body, so the aim of the asceticism is freedom.[21]

But if monasticism and marriage are equally viable paths to union with God, and asceticism serves in synergy with the action of the Holy Spirit to render persons vulnerable in body and spirit to the living God, why the confusion regarding the nature of desire when it comes to expressing sexuality in marriage? What can we learn from the wealth of patristic counsel to those seeking to find God through the path of self-renunciation and imageless prayer on how to enter into the marital relationship and relationship with God at the same time?

One author in the respected journal *Pastoral Psychology* writes eloquently of eros in a way that both inspires and confuses me, perhaps because it is far beyond my own experience. In any case, with such distillations of the patristic and monastic witness available to all who can read – and who will read, not only out of pride, but also out of a sincere desire to grow toward Orthodox ideals – it is incumbent upon Orthodox Christian psychotherapists to seek to understand the phenomenon of theosis that is described here and to strive to live this in practice as far as one is able within the context of a community of faith, sacramental participation, and ongoing guidance from a competent spiritual confessor, in order to let it begin to inform how we do marriage therapy. What is true and valuable in this perspective can, according to our understanding, be offered to those who seek out help because of similar confusions inherited from the undigested and misconstrued crumbs that have fallen from the table of the Lord's disciples over centuries into the hands of those who, starving for truth, leave nothing untried, whether understood accurately or not.

> Union with God, divinization or *theosis*, rests in the highest form of spiritual love, in *eros*, since the spiritually transformed man is not only loved by God, but, because of God's love, is motivated to love God. He turns toward God with the same force and passion that a fallen human being turns toward those most desired things of the earth and of sinful life. He feeds on God's love. He hears, smells, and touches God's love. God's love pervades him. His whole being yearns for God and is satisfied only in God Himself....

> In speaking of the association between the highest form of love and the passions, we must be very careful. There are two levels at which this association can be understood. At the psychological level, one may indeed say that erotic love...can be redirected towards God and transformed, cleansed as it were. Any human motivation, even a sinful one, paradoxically enough can be made to serve God. But, again, it must be transformed. It must be purified. Thus, sexual purity – and absolute sexual purity of the kind that our perverted times rarely know – underlies all attempts to direct human emotions or passions toward God. *The libidinal "erotic" impulses of the human being serve the purpose of finding God only when they are wholly and totally freed from human sexuality.* [my italics]. For, as we are told clearly and plainly in Scripture and as the Fathers and Saints have taught throughout the centuries, "the carnal mind is enmity against God" (Romans 8:7). "Now this I say, brethren, that flesh and blood cannot enter the kingdom of God; neither doth corruption inherit incorruption."

At the spiritual level, the highest form of love has nothing to do with the psychological life or with psychological motivations. It is above such considerations and separated from them... If the passions can be transformed to serve Christian love, they nonetheless do not vitiate it or play any role in it. This is especially true of the highest form of love.

We should also note that the experience of the highest form of Christian love, which leads to union with God and an ecstatic state of spiritual communion with Him, has no physical or material dimensions to it. It is an experience typically described by the Fathers in apophatic or negative terms: as a union which no human sense of union can express or as an indescribable or ineffable state. Any sense of time or space is lost, and the content of the experience is never revealed – if only because, as the Fathers themselves so frequently point out, there are no human words to capture it.[22]

To the extent that this is an accurate distillation of the Desert Fathers concerning eros of marital union and the ascetic monastic ideal, it points us toward a methodology for psychotherapeutic interventions in marital problems and problems of sexual desire in light of an Orthodox Christian understanding of the human person that is far more complex than prevailing secular psychological perspectives indicate. How can we begin to move in a direction that allows psychotherapy to be fully congruent with the mysteriological and ascetical components of our common faith that provide the primary context for development toward the ideal of theosis? To the extent that prayer and asceticism are parts of this larger whole, to what extent can they be lifted out of their context without losing something essential? This is a particularly important question for Orthodox in America, whose formation is deeply influenced by the often inconsistent values, worldview, and social norms of the surrounding culture. Should the faithful seek help through consultation with psychotherapists who are unfamiliar with the fullness of Orthodox Christian faith, life, and practice, important opportunities to work in concert with their faith may be missed. On the other hand, the ambiguity that appears to be within the faith itself in this area provides sufficient challenge for Orthodox Christian psychotherapists to consider regular worship, prayer, ongoing spiritual guidance, and personal therapy a *sine qua non* for doing any sort of psychotherapy ourselves.

NOTES

[1] Capsanis, Archimandrite G. (1994) *The Eros of Repentance.* Massachusetts: Praxis Institute Press.

[2] Cf. Harakas, S (1996) "Dynamic Elements of Marriage in the Orthodox Church" in Chirban, J. Ed. *Personhood: Orthodox Christianity and the Connection Between Body, Mind and Soul.* London: Bergin & Garvey pp. 121-136.

[3] May, G. (1982) *Will and Spirit.* San Francisco:Harpercollins Publishers. p. 149.

[4] Gabriel, G. S. (1995) *"You Call My Words Immodest: On sexuality and the blameless marital bed* Canada: Synaxis Press, The Canadian Orthodox Publishing House.

[5] Quoted by Chryssavgis, J. (1996) in *Love, Sexuality and the Sacrament of Marriage.* Massachusetts: Holy Cross Orthodox Press. p. 52

[6] Francoeur, R.T.(1992) "The Religious Suppression of Eros" in *The Erotic Impulse; Honoring the Sensual Self.* Ed. David Steinberg. California:Jeremy Tarcher, Inc. p. 166.

[7] Rizzuto, A-M. (1996) "Christian Worshiping and Psychoanalysis in Spiritual Truth" in Chirban, J, ed. *Personhood: Orthodox Christianity and the Connection Between Body, Mind, and Soul.* London: Bergin & Garvey. p. 59.

[8] Cf. Schnarch, D. (1991) *Constructing the Sexual Crucible: An Integration of Sexual and Marital Therapy* New York:W.W. Norton & Co.

[9] Florovsky, G. (1987) *Bible, Church, Tradition: An Eastern Orthodox View.* Vol 1 in the Collected Works. Buchervertriebsanstalt: Europa. pp. 50-51.

[10] From lecture by David Schnarch (1996) "Sexuality & Spirituality" delivered at the S. E. Regional meeting of AAPC at Kanuga Conference Center in North Carolina.

[11] Francoeur, p. 164.

[12] Cf. Gabriel, (1995).

[13] Cf. Kaplan,H. S. (1995), *The Sexual Desire Disorders: Dysfunctional Regulation of Sexual Motivation.* New York: Brunner Mazel.

[14] American Broadcasting Corporation (1988, Nov. 2) *Twenty-twenty.* New York.

[15] Sipe, A.W.R. (1990) *A Secret World: Sexuality and the Search for Celibacy.* New York: Brunner/Mazel Publishers. p. 264.

[16] Masters, W.H, Johnson, V.E. & Kolodny, R (1986) *Masters and Johnson on Sex and Human Loving.* Boston: Little Brown & Co. p. 10.

[17] Decker, C.W. (1994) "Selling Desire: Would a Return to Christian Virtue Cause a Recession?" in *Christianity Today.* April 4, p.38.

[18] "The Homosexual Movement: A Response by the Ramsey Colloquium" *First Things.* March 1994, p.17

[19] Hurlbert, DF & Whittaker, KE (1991) *Journal of Sex Education and Therapy.* Vol 17, No.4. pp 272-282.

[20] Lorde, A. (1994) "Uses of the Erotic: the Erotic as Power" in Nelson, JB & Longfellow, SP eds. *Sexuality and the Sacred: Sources for Theological Reflection.* Kentucky: Westminster/John Knox Press. p. 77.

[21] Chirban, J., ed. (1996) *Personhood: Orthodox Christianity and the Connection Between Body, Mind, and Soul.* London: Bergin & Garvey, p. 101

[22] Chrysostomos, B. (1989) "Towards a Spiritual Psychology: The Synthesis of the Desert Fathers." *Pastoral Psychology* Vol 37(4) pp. 268-271.

John T. Chirban, Ph.D., Th.D., is a clinical instructor at Harvard Medical School, serving in the Behavioral Medicine Program at The Cambridge Hospital. He is also professor of psychology at Hellenic College and Holy Cross School of Theology in Brookline, Massachusetts.

Philotheos Faros is the director of the Archdiocese Youth Center in Athens, Greece. He is also the author of numerous popular works in pastoral theology.

Koula Svokos Hartnett, Ed.D., is an author, educator, and healer in Morgantown, West Virginia.

Demetra Jacquet, M.Div., is a counselor at Regis University and Avista Hospice.

George Morelli, Ph.D., ABPN, is adjunct instructor in psychology at St. Vladimir's Seminary and Rutgers University.

J. Stephen Muse, Ph.D., is senior staff psychologist at the Pastoral Institute, Columbus, Georgia.

Markos Achilles Nickolas is a Ph.D. student in Pastoral Psychology at Boston University.

Dimitrios Oreopoulos, M.D., Ph.D., is director of the Dialysis Programme and Kidney Stone Clinic at Toronto Hospital and professor of medicine at the University of Toronto.

Jeff Rediger, M.D. is a psychiatric resident at Harvard Medical Center at Cambridge Hospital.

John F. Schilke, MD, is a physician practicing family medicine in Milwaukie, Oregon.

Theodore Stylianopoulos, Th.D. is a professor of New Testament at Holy Cross Greek Orthodox School of Theology.

Vasilios Thermos, M.D. is a child psychiatrist and academic consultant in Athens, Greece.